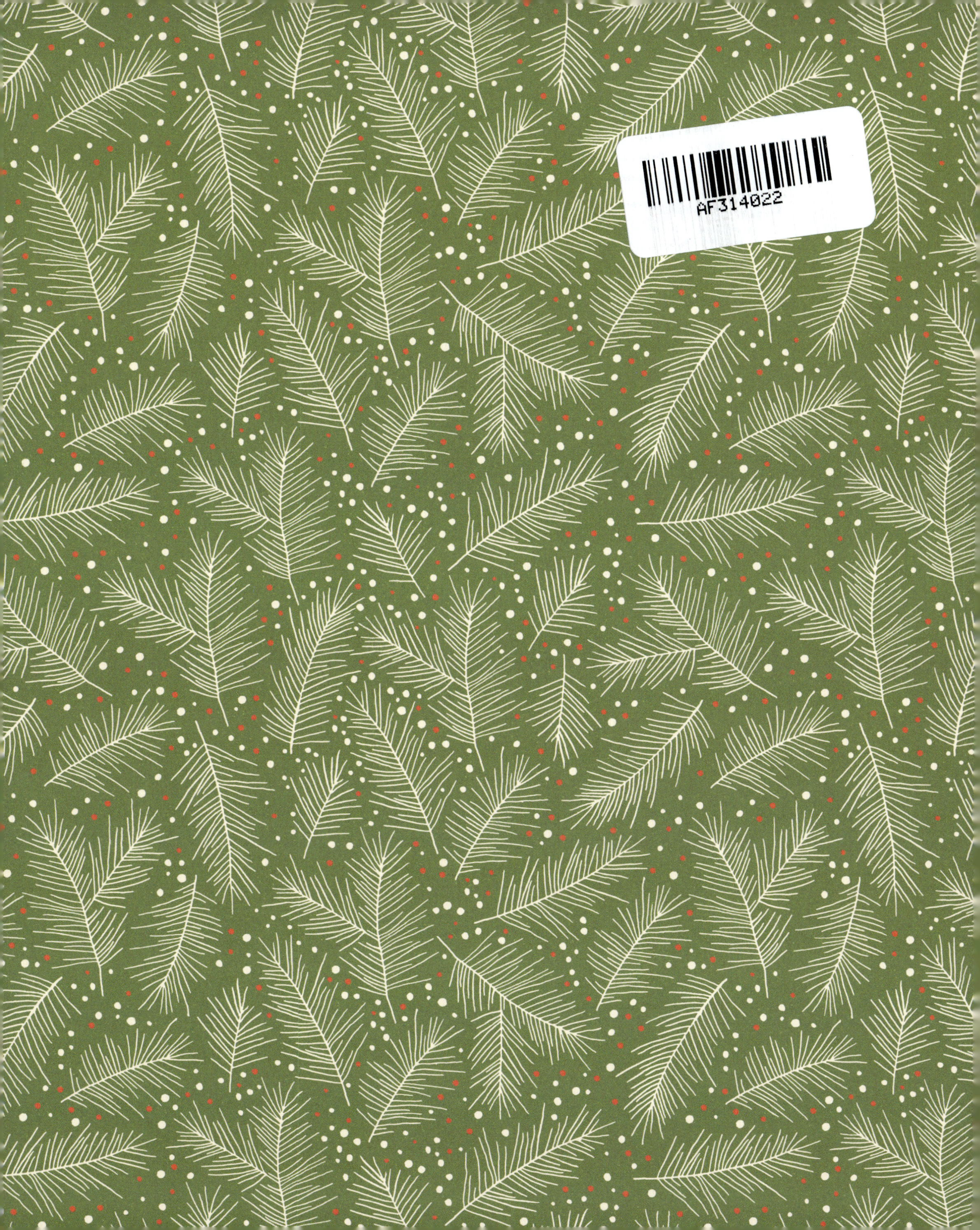
AF314022

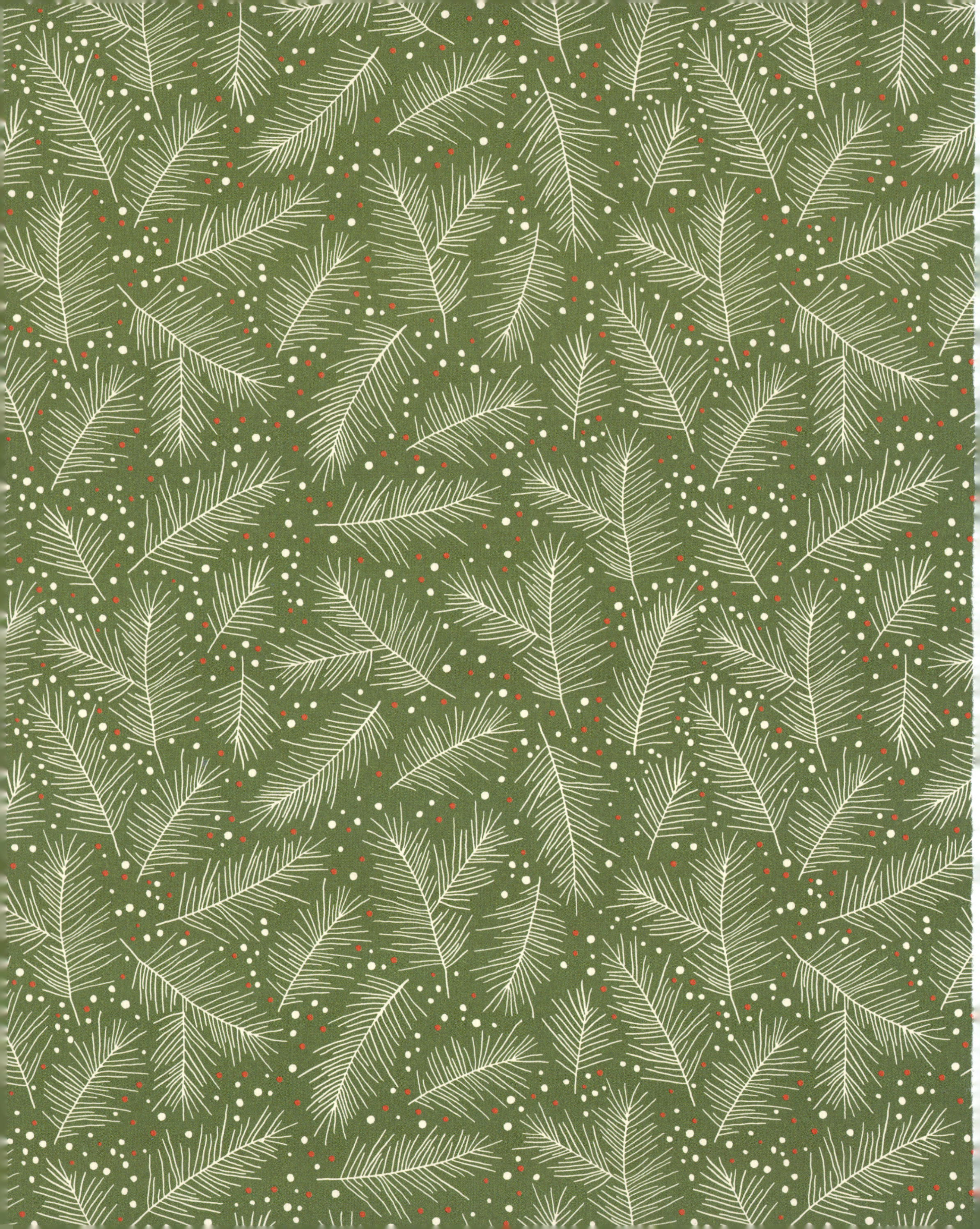

CHRISTMAS EMPORIUM

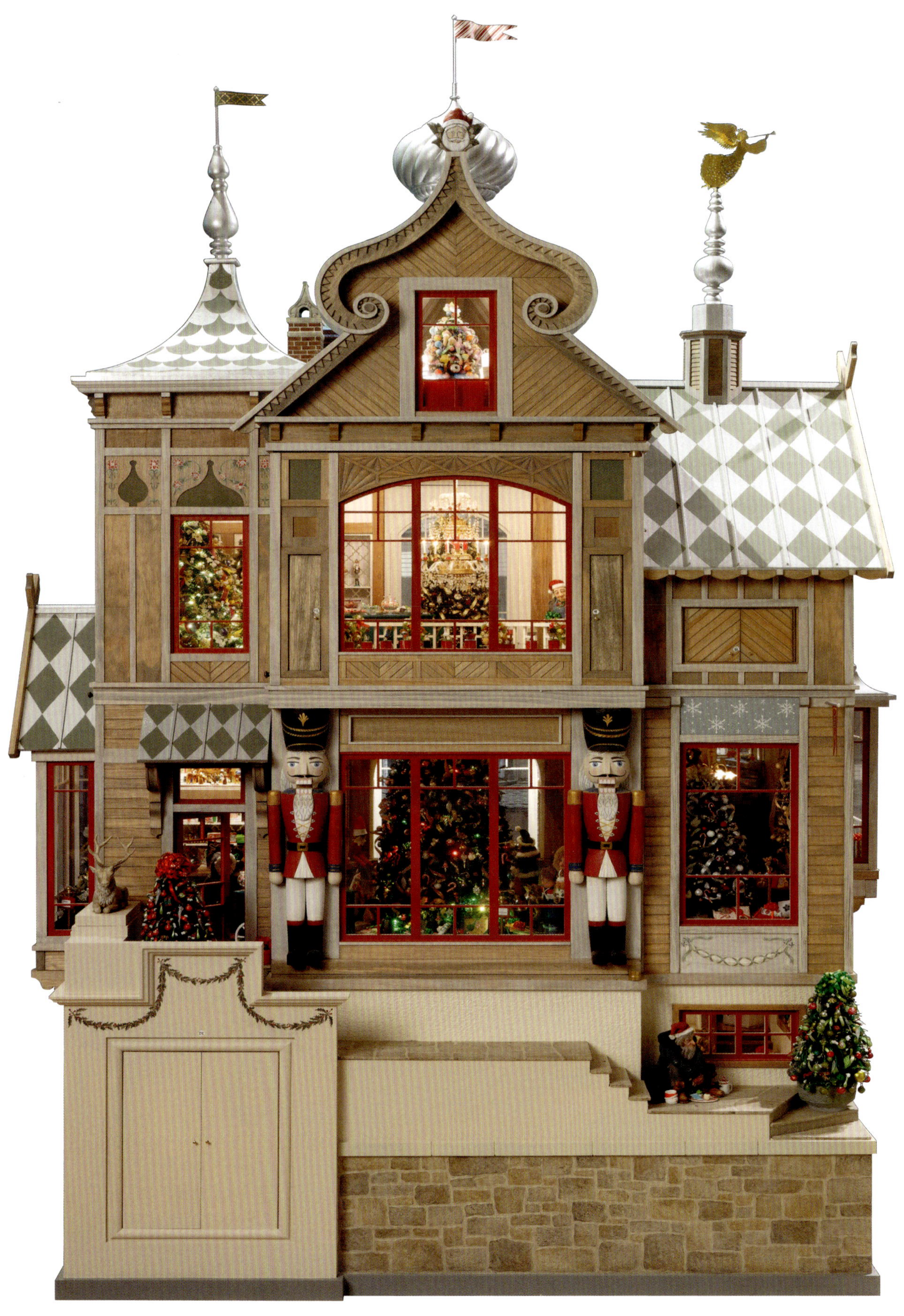

CHRISTMAS EMPORIUM

The Miniature Shop of Imagination

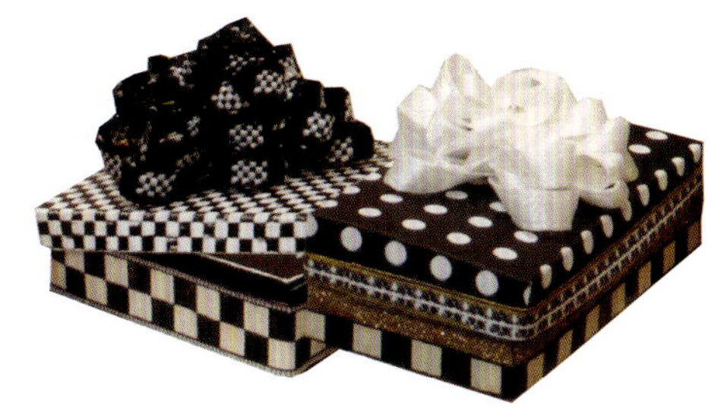

Sally Wallace

Foreword Terry E. Branstad

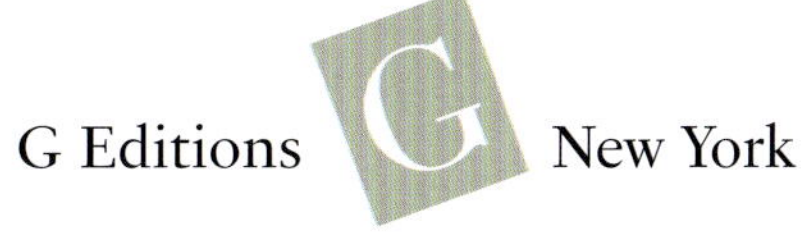

G Editions New York

Published in 2023

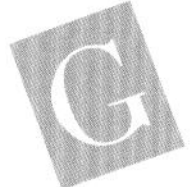

G Editions
www.geditions.com

First Printing, 2023
Library of Congress Cataloging-in-Publication Data is available
from the Publisher.

Hardcover ISBN: 978-0-9862500-2-6

Design: Liz Trovato

Printed and Bound in China

10 9 8 7 6 5 4 3 2 1

Contents

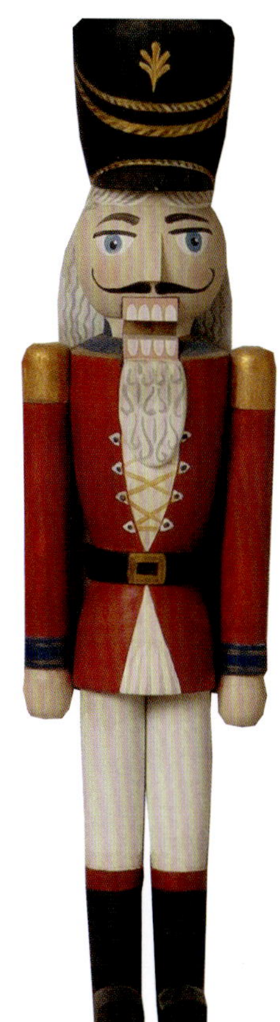

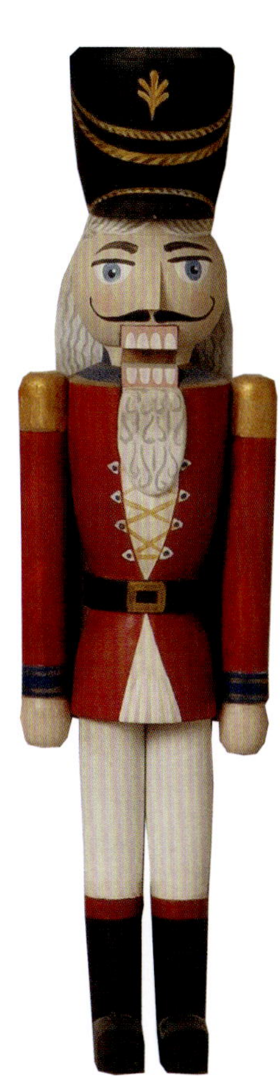

Christmas now surrounds us.
Happiness is everywhere.
Our hands are busy with many tasks
as carols fill the air.

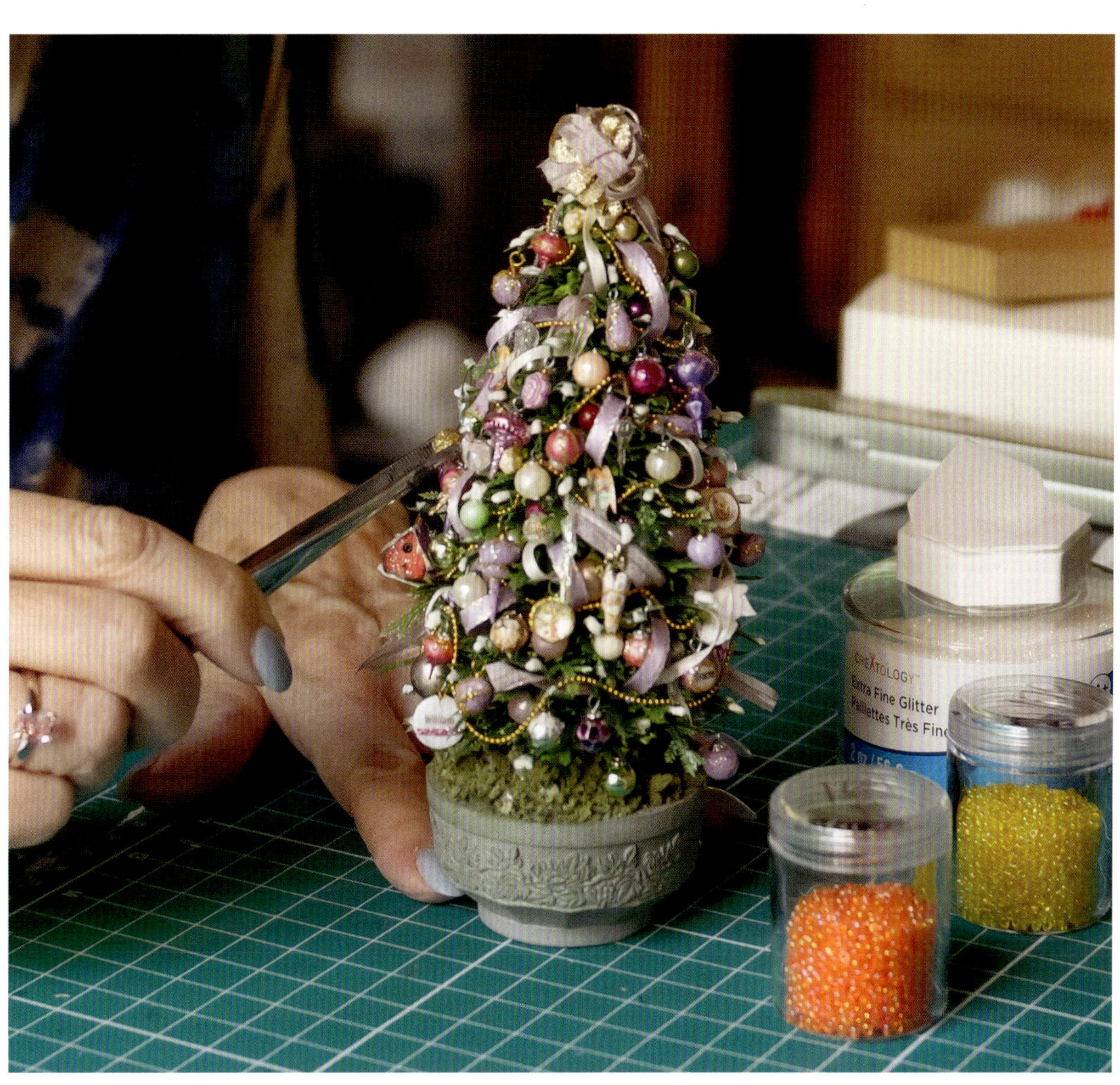

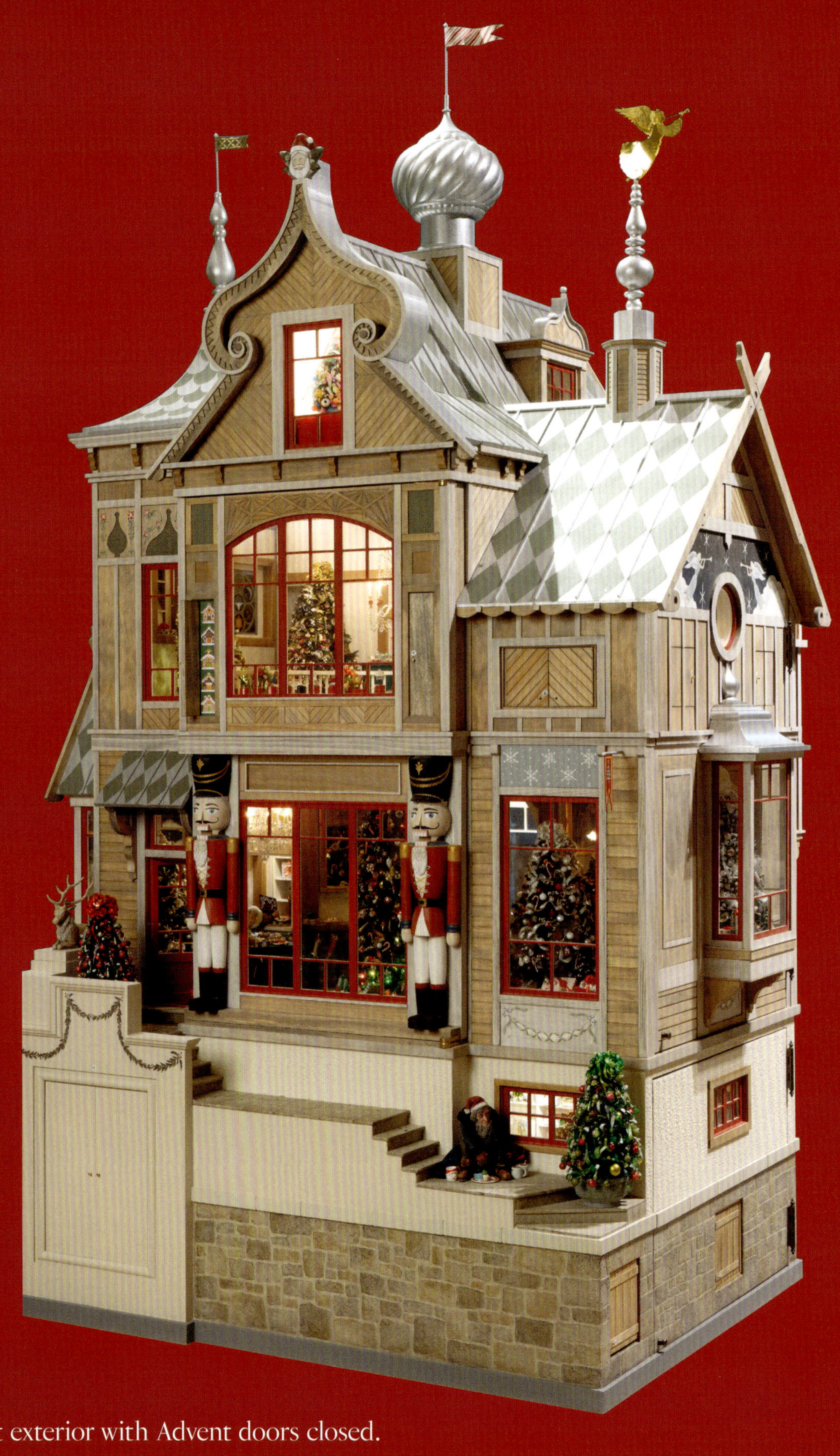

✳Front exterior with Advent doors closed.

Foreword

I have known Sally Wallace for many years.
I have had the opportunity to watch
Sally's miniature collection grow—and
change. Recently she showed me the Christmas
Emporium—with all the details, ornaments,
Advent calendar pieces, toys, and people. I was
impressed with the piece and delighted when
she asked me to write the introduction to a
book that will share this work with other people.

As governor of Iowa and the ambassador to
China, I have had the unique opportunity to
meet many different types of artists. I am
always impressed when someone can take a
concept and make it visual—either in painting,
sculpting, or in this case, a miniature piece. It
takes a unique talent and a special gift.

As I looked at the Emporium, I was struck
with the number of details—ornaments,
packages, blown glass, and light fixtures that
I would never remember when I walked away:
Almost too much detail to comprehend and
remember. That is art. Previously, when

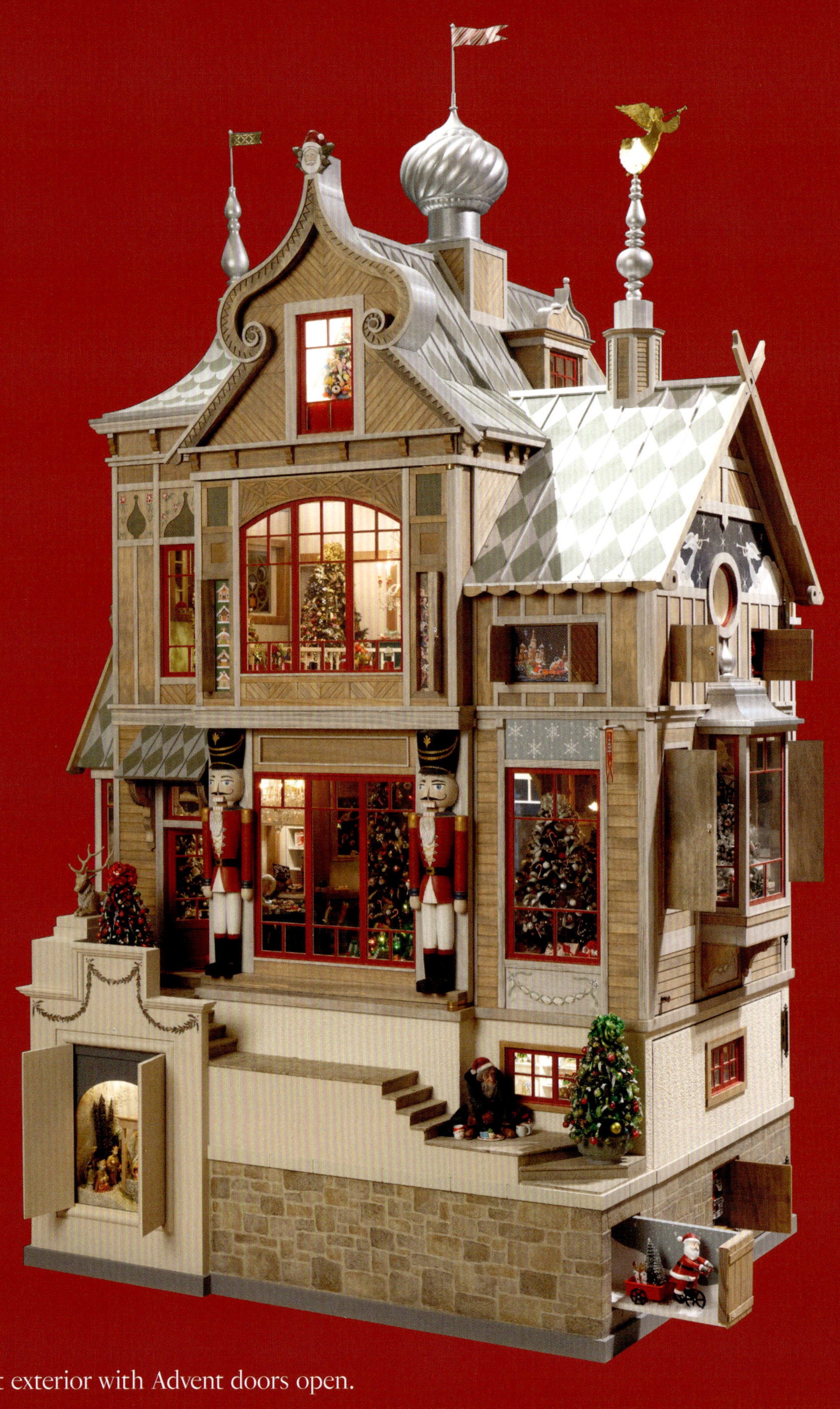

✳ Front exterior with Advent doors open.

someone talked about a dollhouse, I assumed they were talking about a children's toy. I certainly have a different idea now. It is an art form.

I have known Sally for over twenty years—she doesn't much talk about her creations, but when you see them, you don't forget them. I am pleased that she and her husband, Sam, and I have been friends for a very long time. I am honored to write the introduction to a very unique book about a very unique piece of art.

—Terry E. Branstad
Former governor of Iowa and ambassador to China

✳ The exterior of the Emporium offers bay windows with unique views of the 18 trees, two nutcrackers standing guard over the front, stained glass representing many faiths of the world a very special Santa. But equally as important to note is that there are 25 small doors on the outside of the Emporium that serve as a very special Advent calendar.

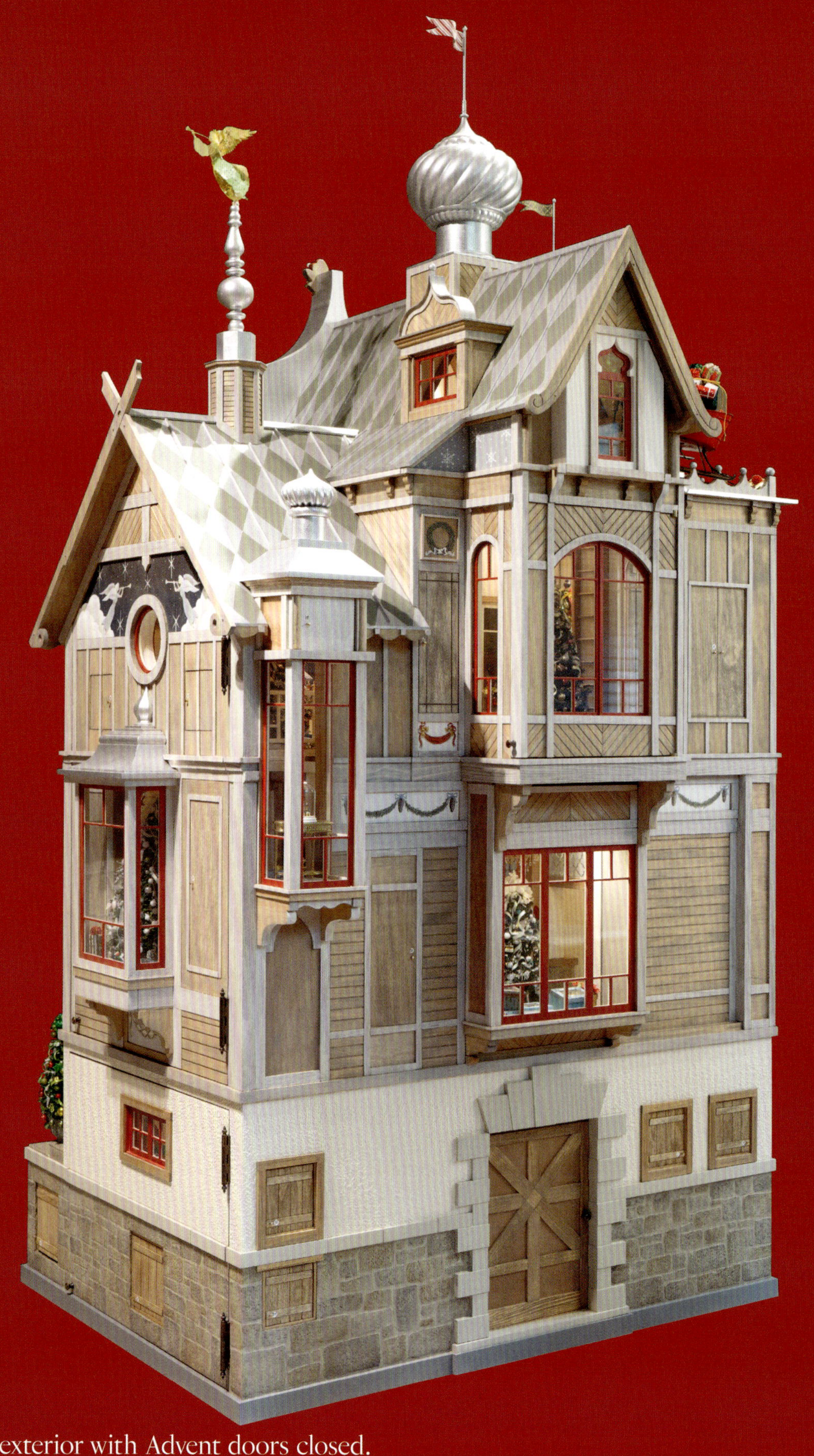

Back exterior with Advent doors closed.

Introduction

I think nearly everyone has significant holidays, family events, or traditions that they celebrate with their loved ones. My family's most cherished holiday was Christmas. As I continue to honor my family's traditions during the Christmas season (my favorite), I've realized that the most significant part of Christmas, to me, is the giving, sharing, and caring that occurs this time of year. And so, I created a miniature in dedication to the special feelings this holiday invokes. I present to you . . . the Christmas Emporium.

Every December, my family displayed an Advent calendar. We opened one window each day. Each of us was always up for the challenge of locating the correct window for the day and getting to enjoy the treat inside.

My Christmas Emporium is also an Advent calendar, with small dated doors positioned all over the outside of the miniature. So this Emporium is a twofold treasure—a delight to the eyes, with eighteen trees, gifts, and fun items throughout—and a wonderful Advent calendar, that I hope you will enjoy exploring.

—Sally Wallace

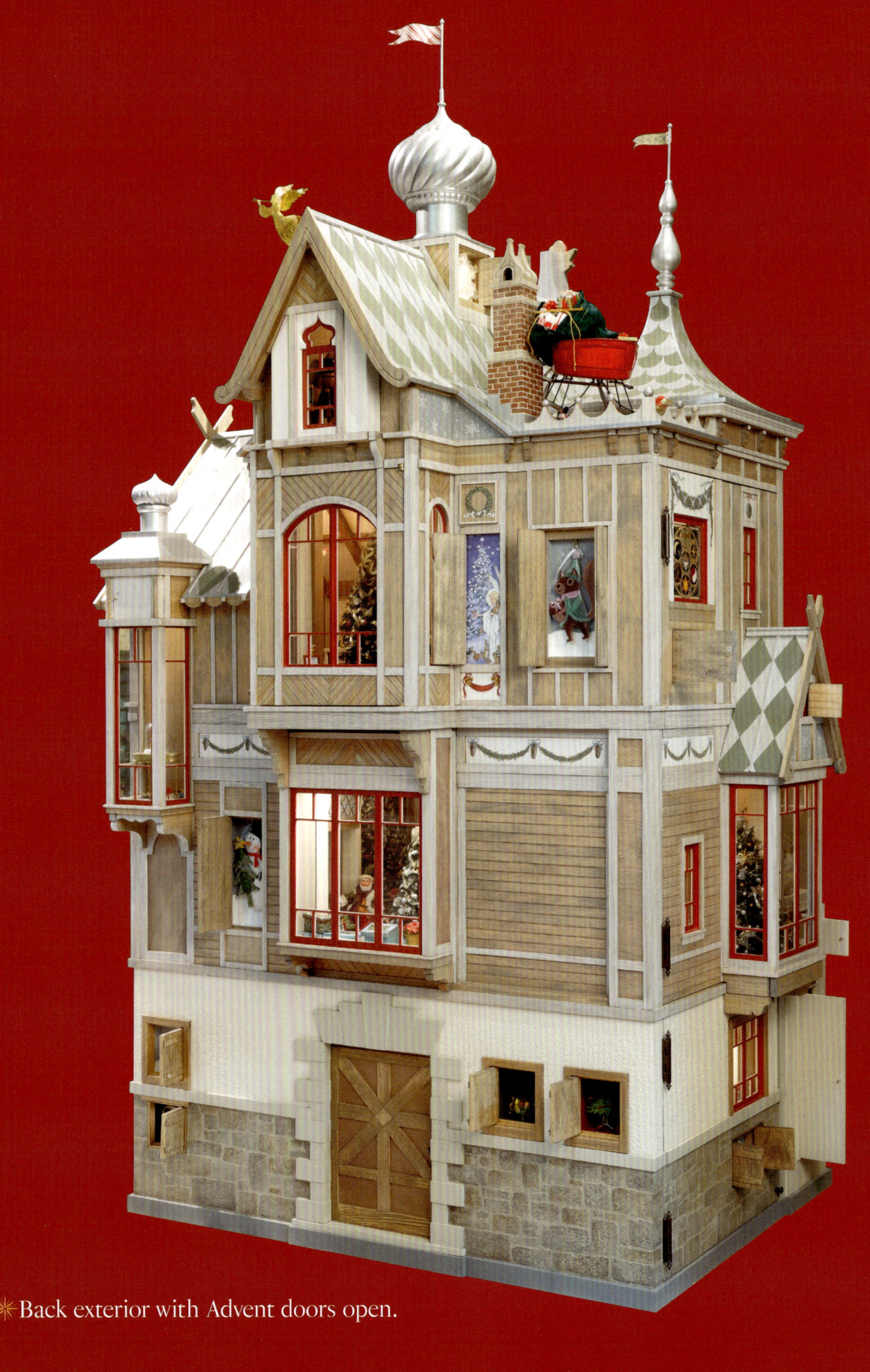

✳Back exterior with Advent doors open.

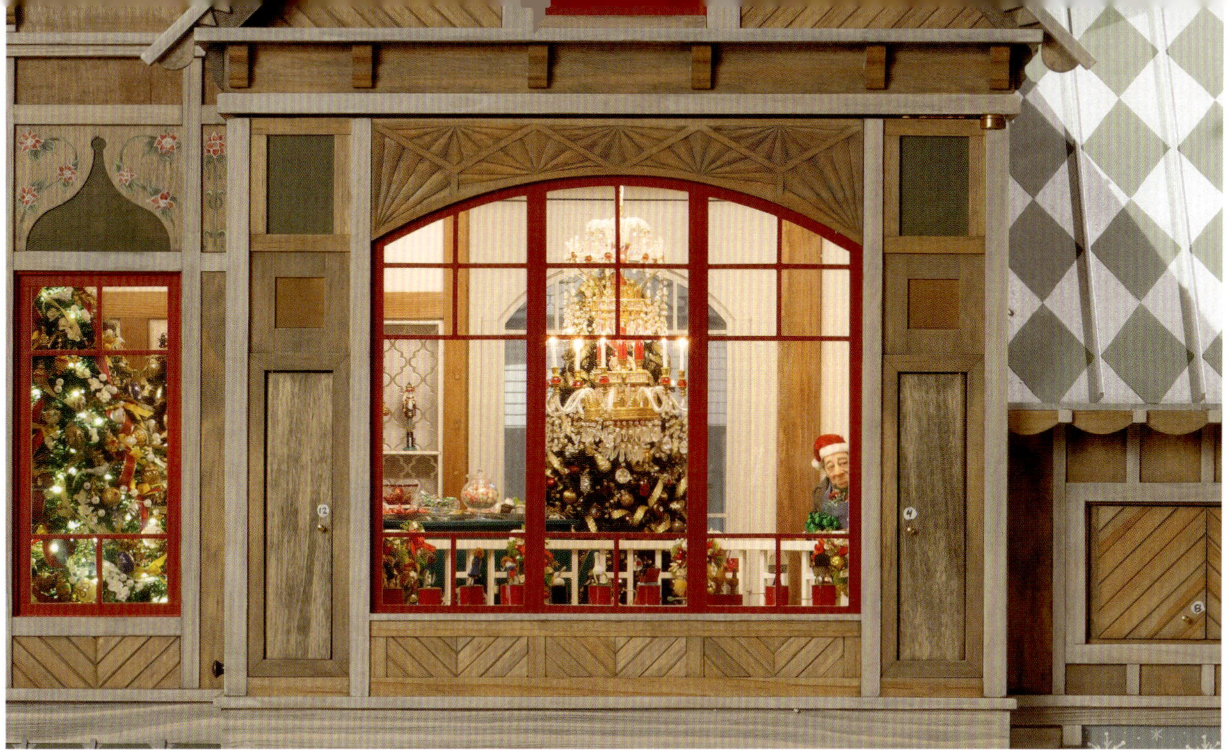

✳When the Emporium doors are closed, you're provided with the most magical view of the trees inside. Each tree, of which there are eighteen, is adorned with lights and ornaments. In fact, the Emporium boasts more than nine thousand ornaments and hundreds of tiny lights and sparkles throughout the shop.

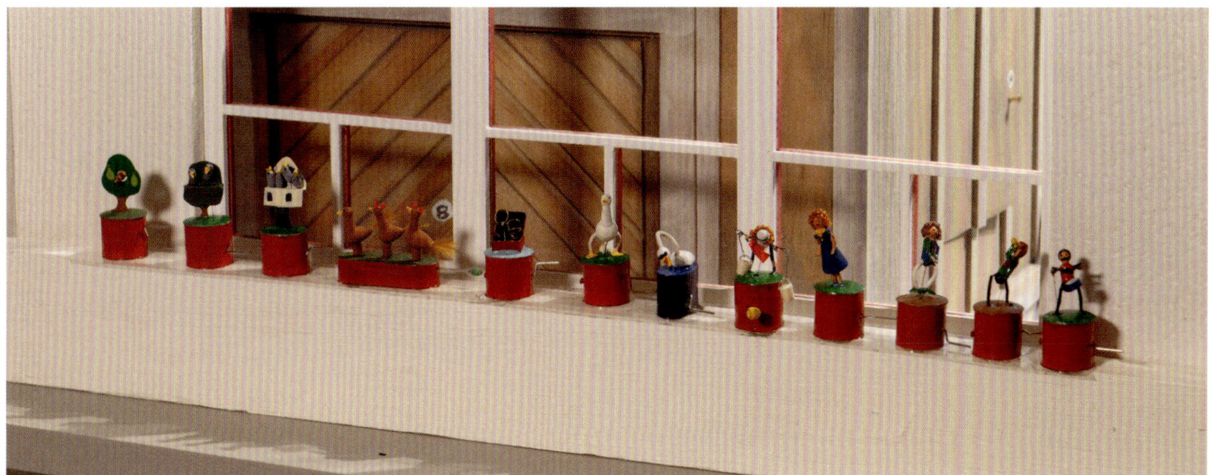

✳Upon one windowsill in the Emporium sits a line of toys re-created by the St. Leger company to represent the "Twelve Days of Christmas." Adorable, and also functional. Each of them has a crank and the toy moves.

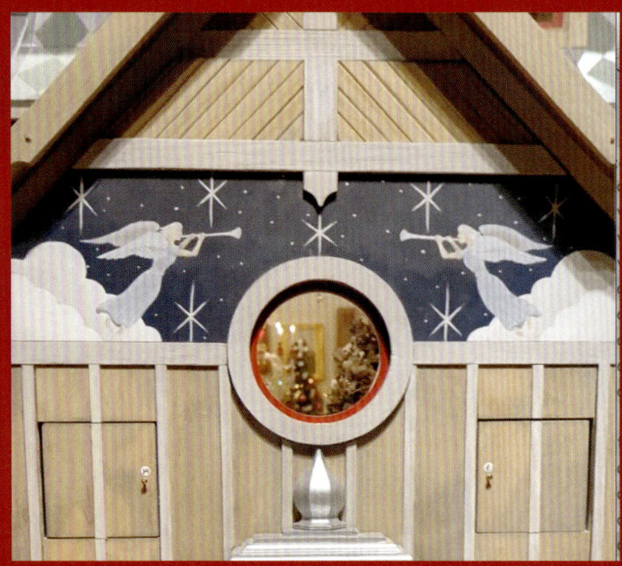

✳ The windows of the Emporium come in all shapes
and sizes: peep holes that show off the balcony trees;
stained glass representions of our faiths; and even large
bay windows that display trees and presents.

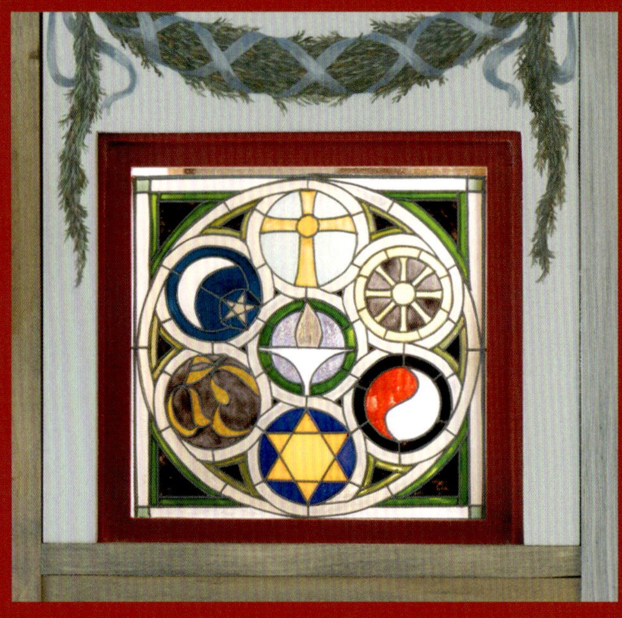

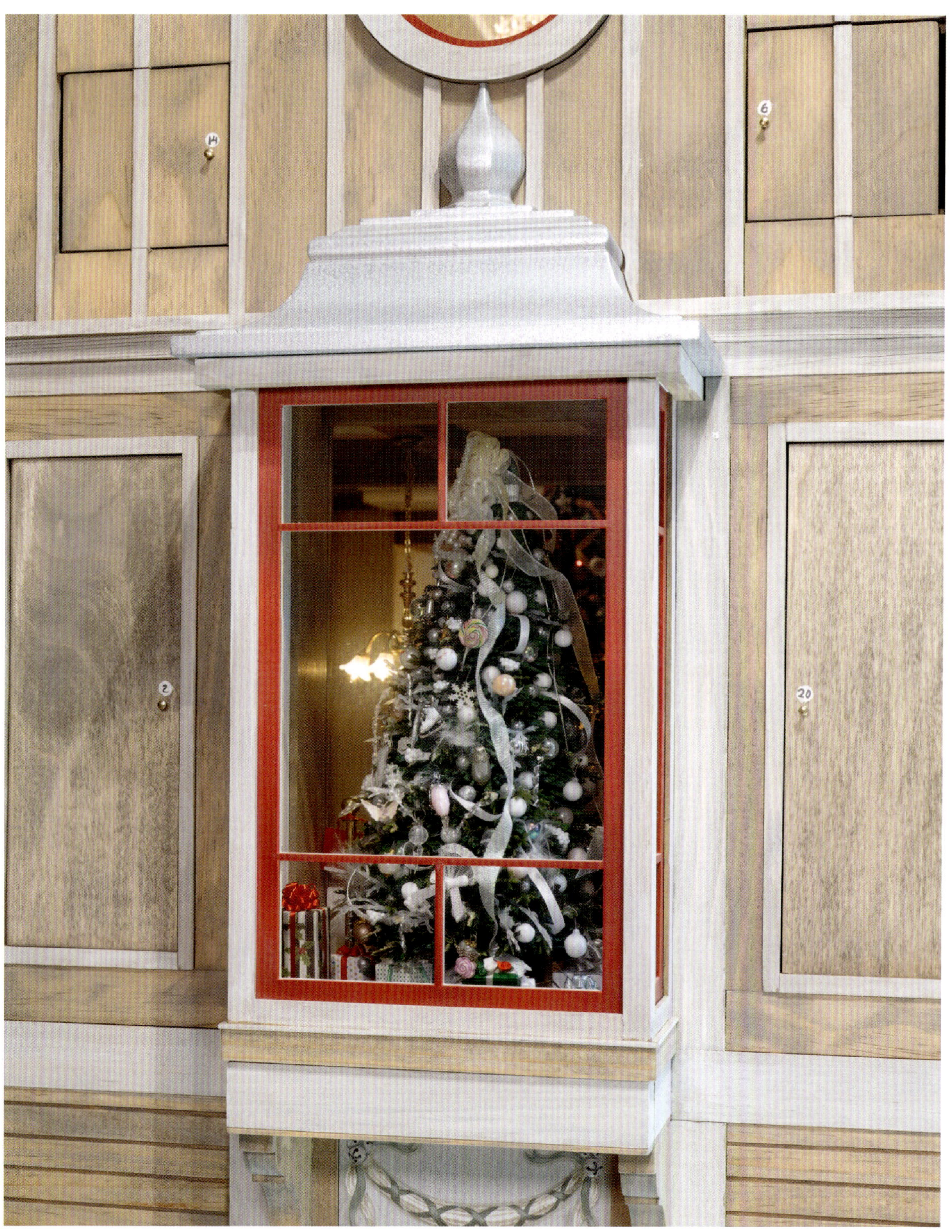

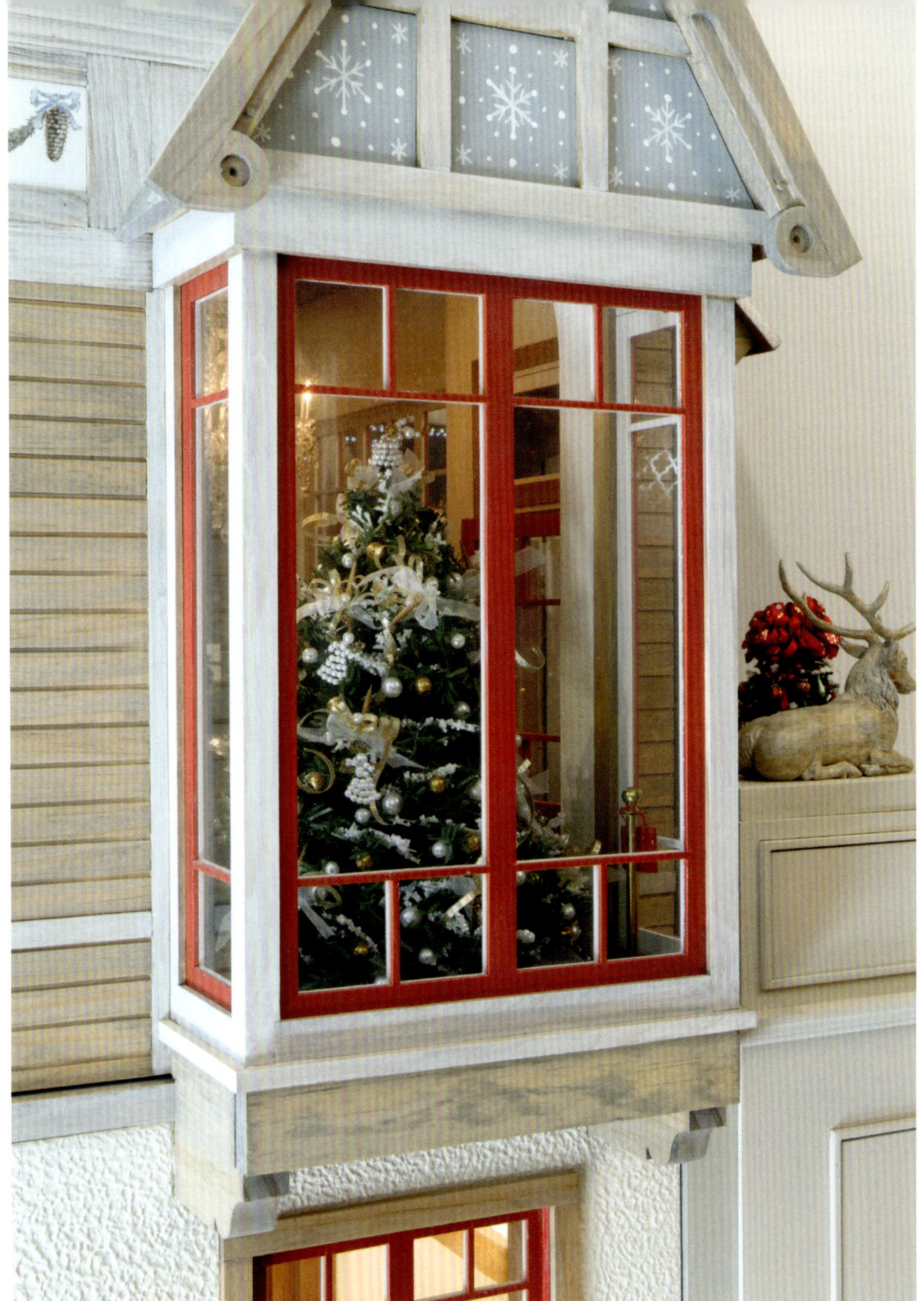

✳ The left side view of the Emporium showcases everything
from the sales counter to the magnificent chandeliers and
a little girl. It's impossible to miss the presents as there
are hundreds of presents under the trees.

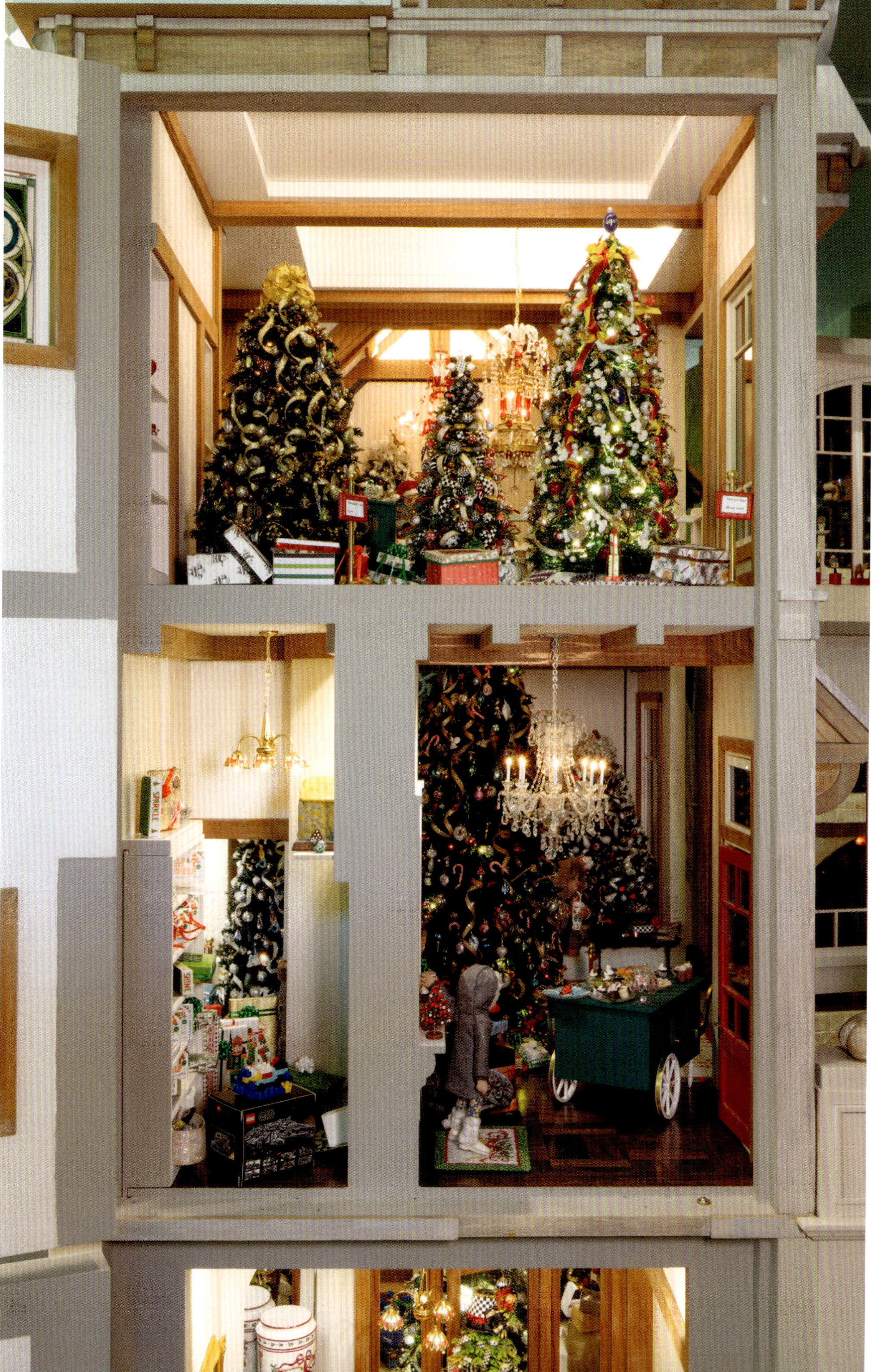

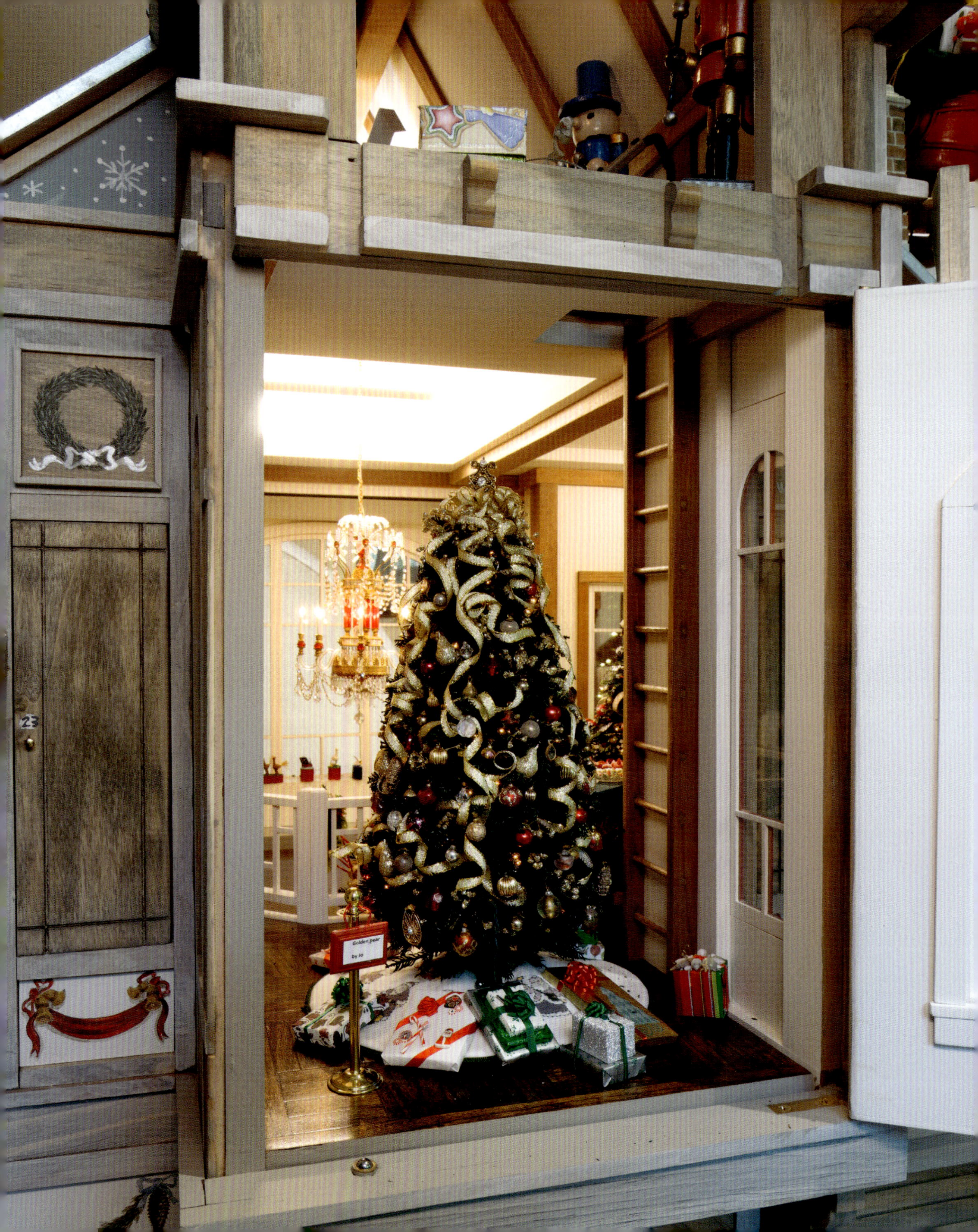
Golden pear
by Io

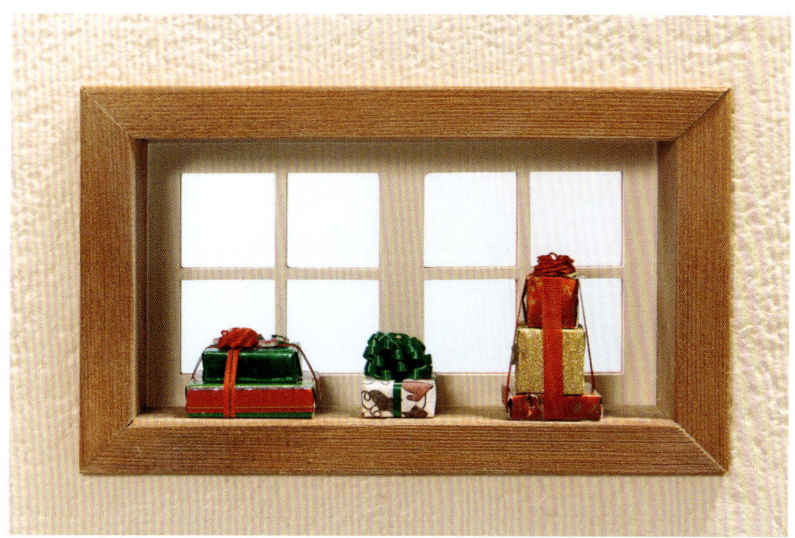

※Many of the windows have deep sills for presents
and treats. All the presents, stacked or individual, are
completely wrapped with bows ranging in size from
½ inch to 1 inch.

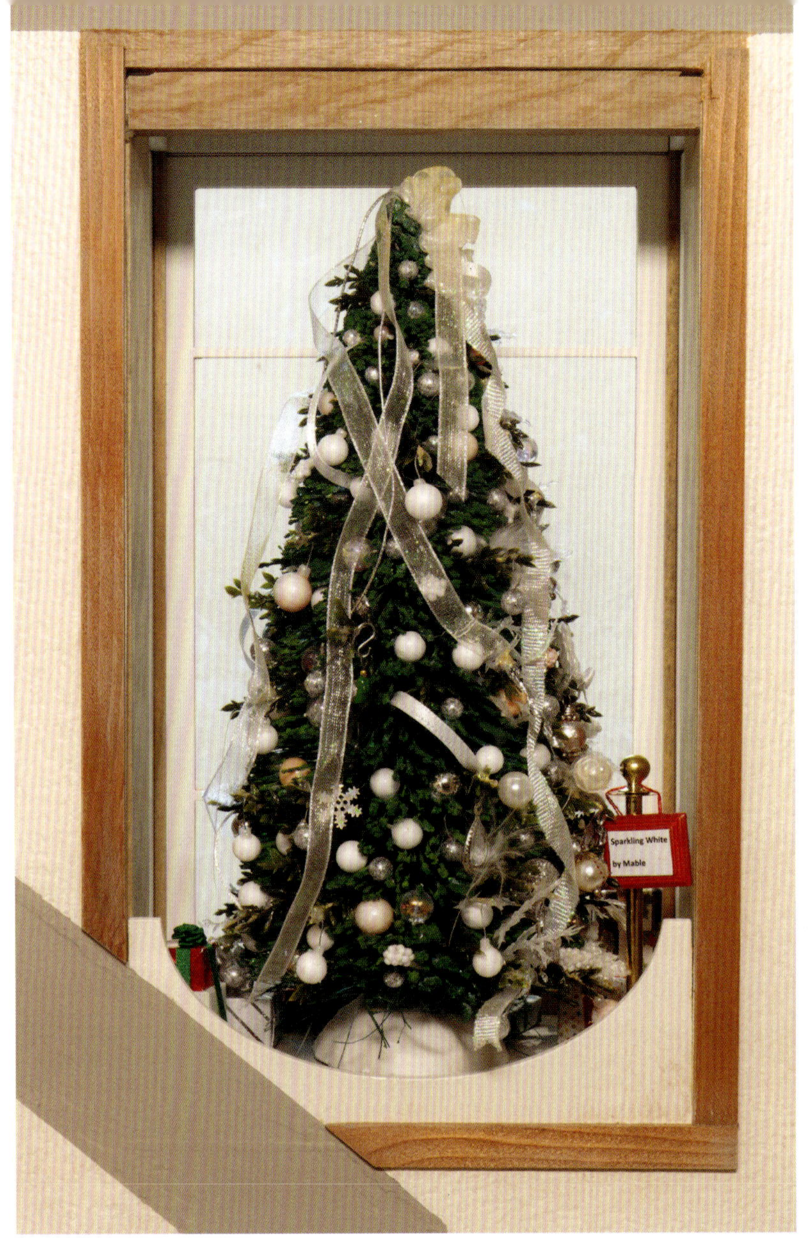

✳O Christmas tree, O Christmas tree . . . . This sparking white tree sits in a window bay (above); while the Coral Reef Tree (right) sits behind a sliding door. This ocean-inspired tree has over six hundred ornaments in a coral motif. And of course the packages below have been color coordinated, too. Elves are all over the Emporium, but this large elf carefully guards the mermaids on the tree.

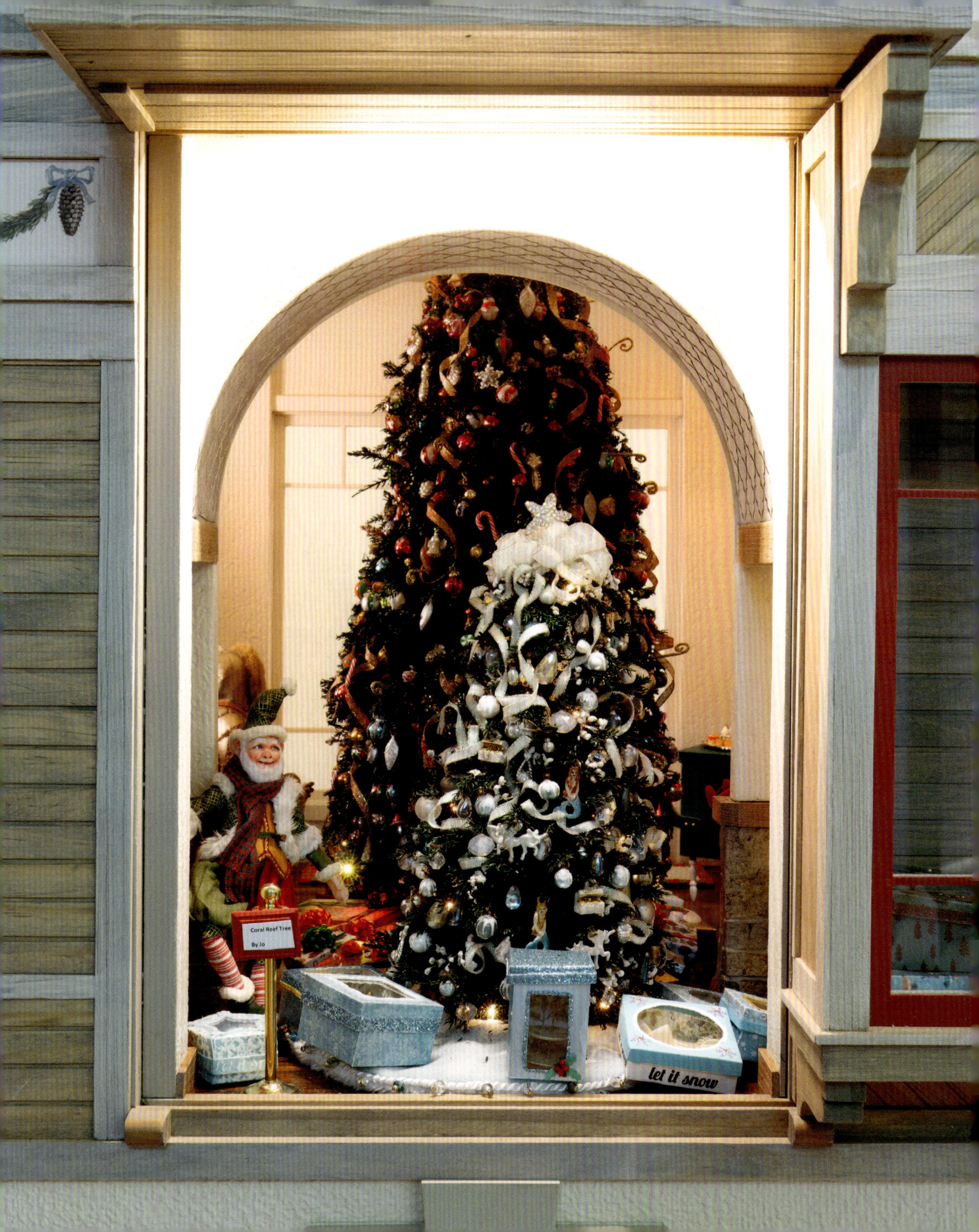

Coral Reef Tree
By Jo
let it snow

Each shining light,
each silver bell …
No one spreads
cheer so well.

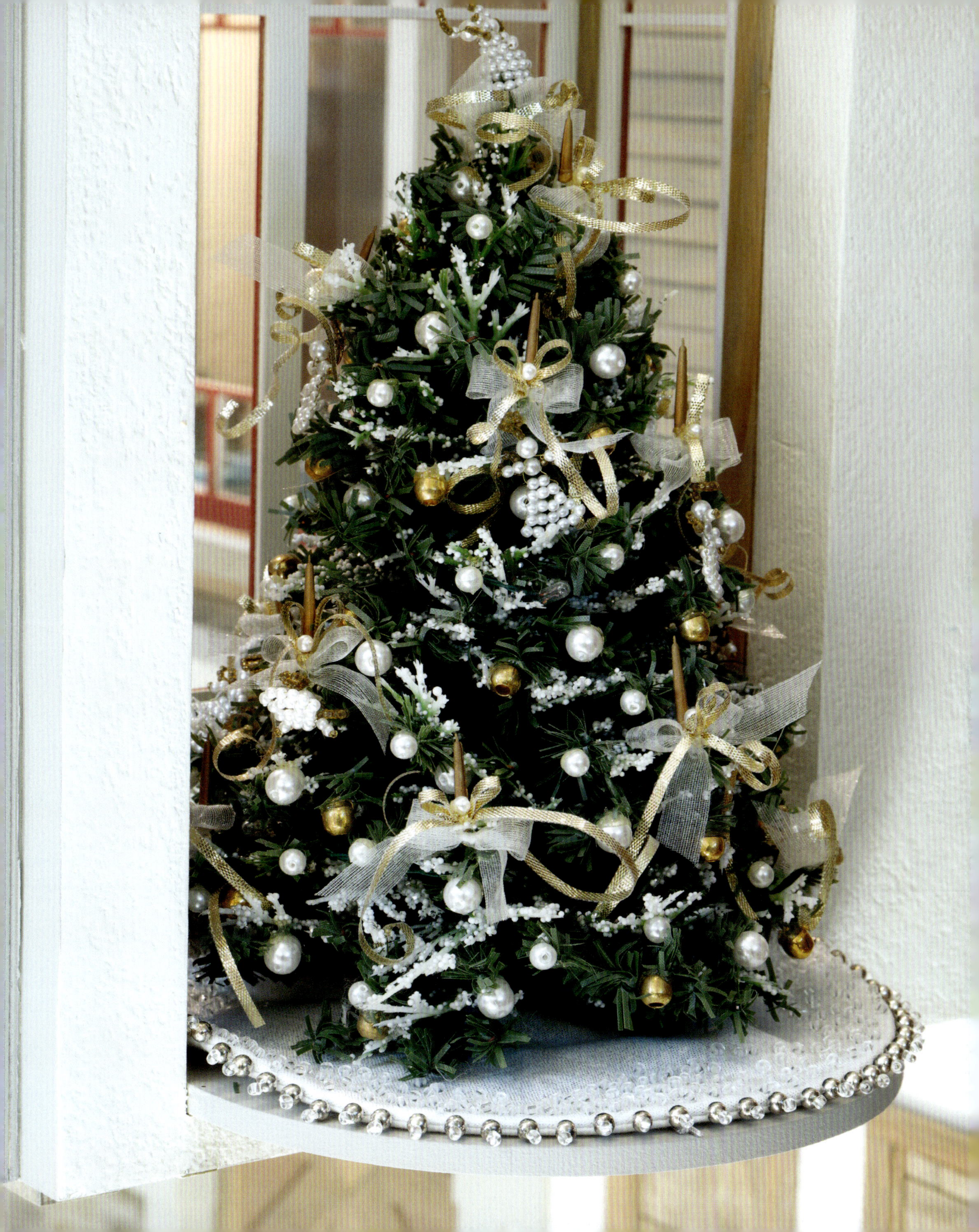

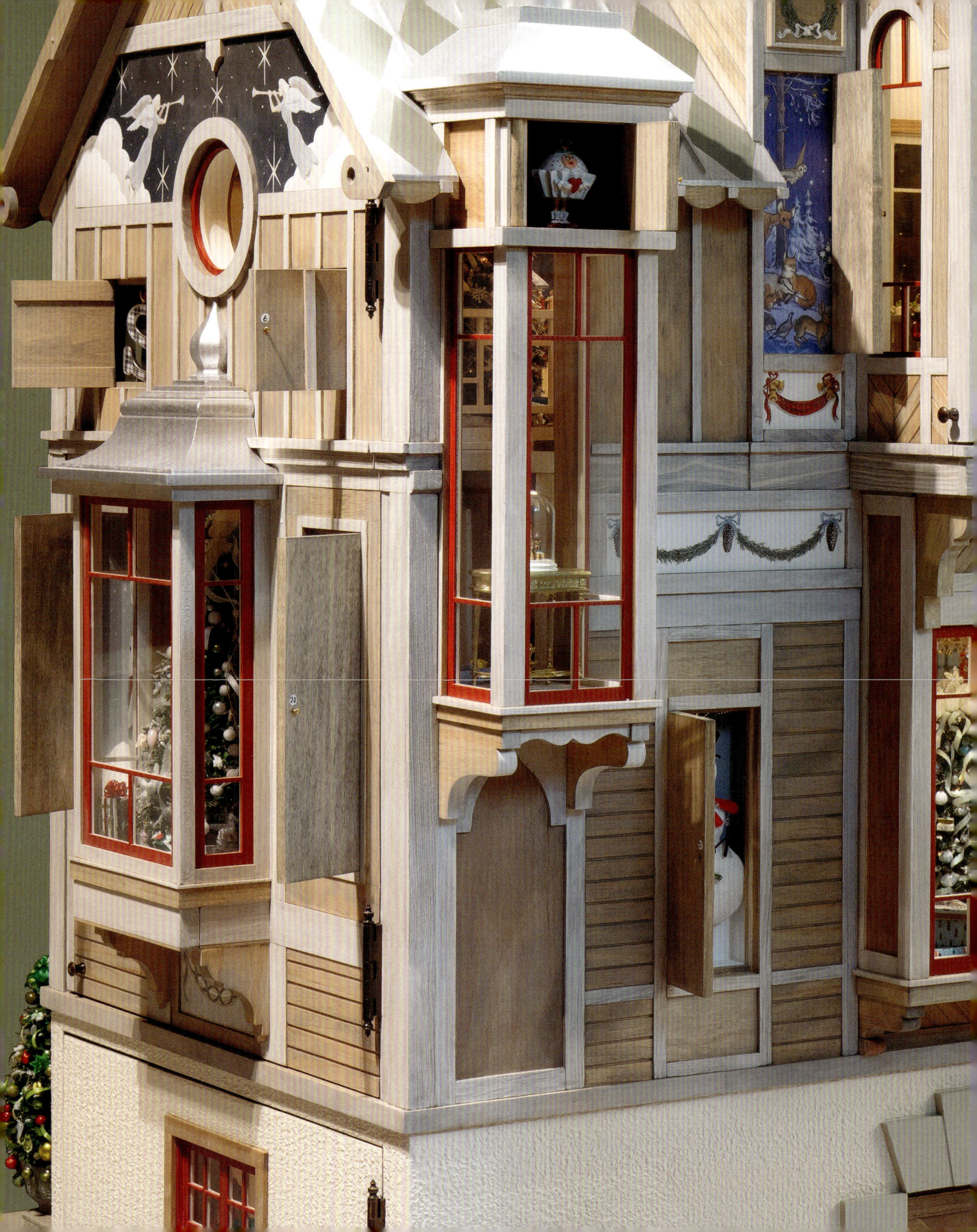

The Advent Doors: Exterior Delight

The most unique and imaginative parts of
the Christmas Emporium are the outside
Advent calendar doors.

The days are hidden and crisscrossed around
the house like a paper Advent calendar. Each
door opens into a surprise. The doors are
actually VERY small. Some are just $1^1/2$ inches
and some may be a little larger.

✳Each door is shown both open and closed on the
following pages.

Follow me in merry measure, while I tell of yuletide treasure.

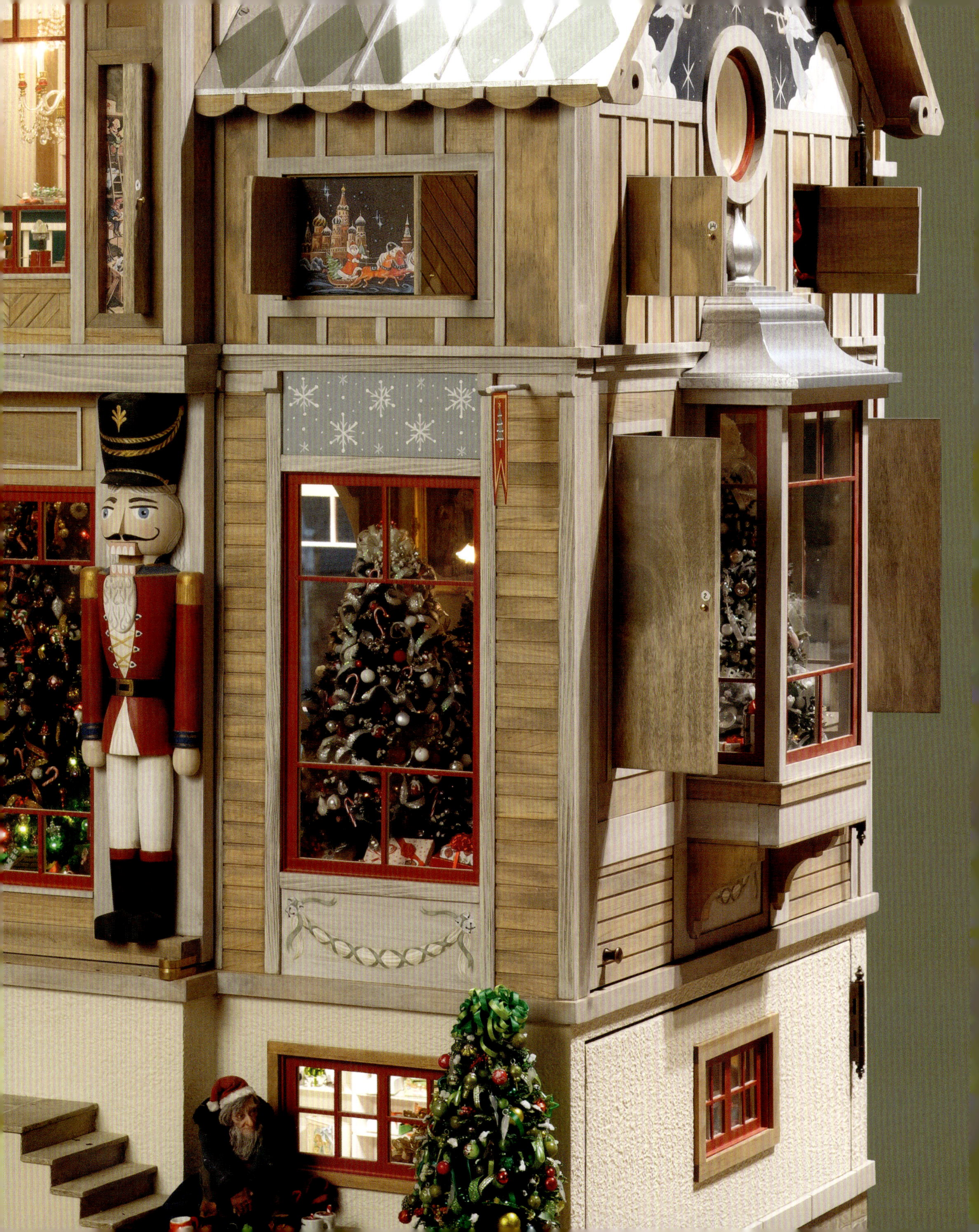

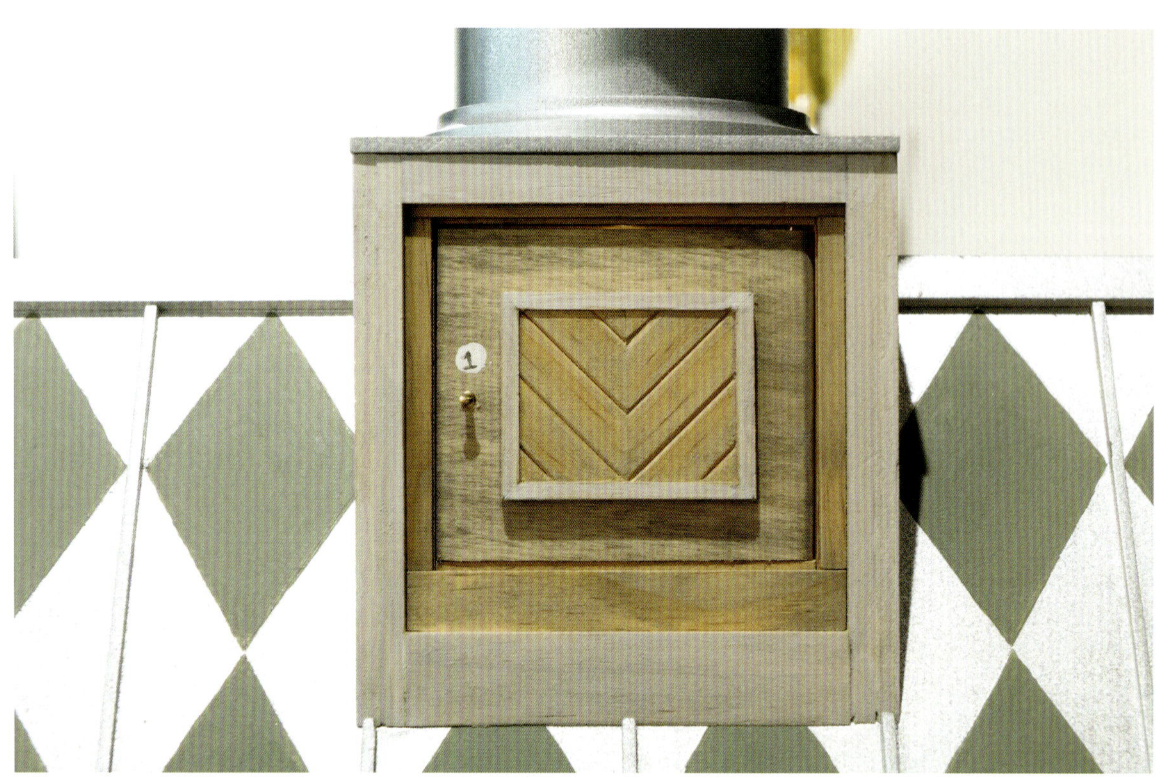

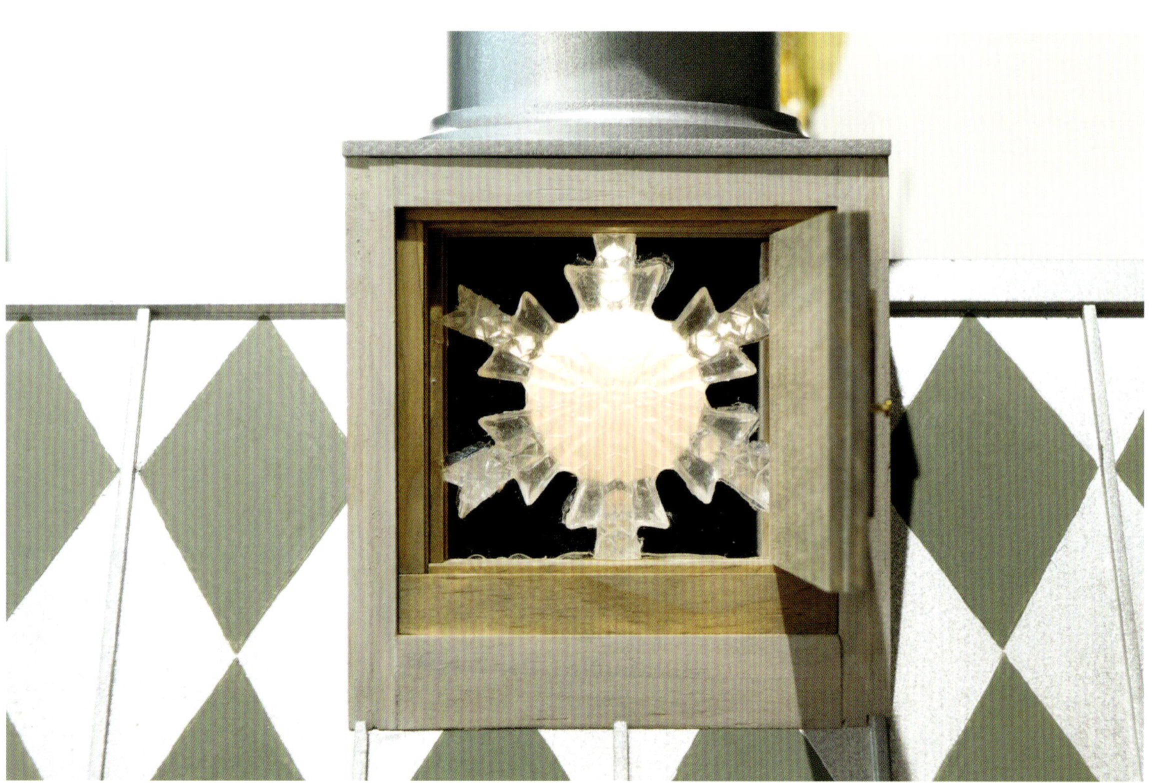

This door sits high atop the Emporium and has to be
opened with a special magnet. It contains a backlight
to start the Advent season.

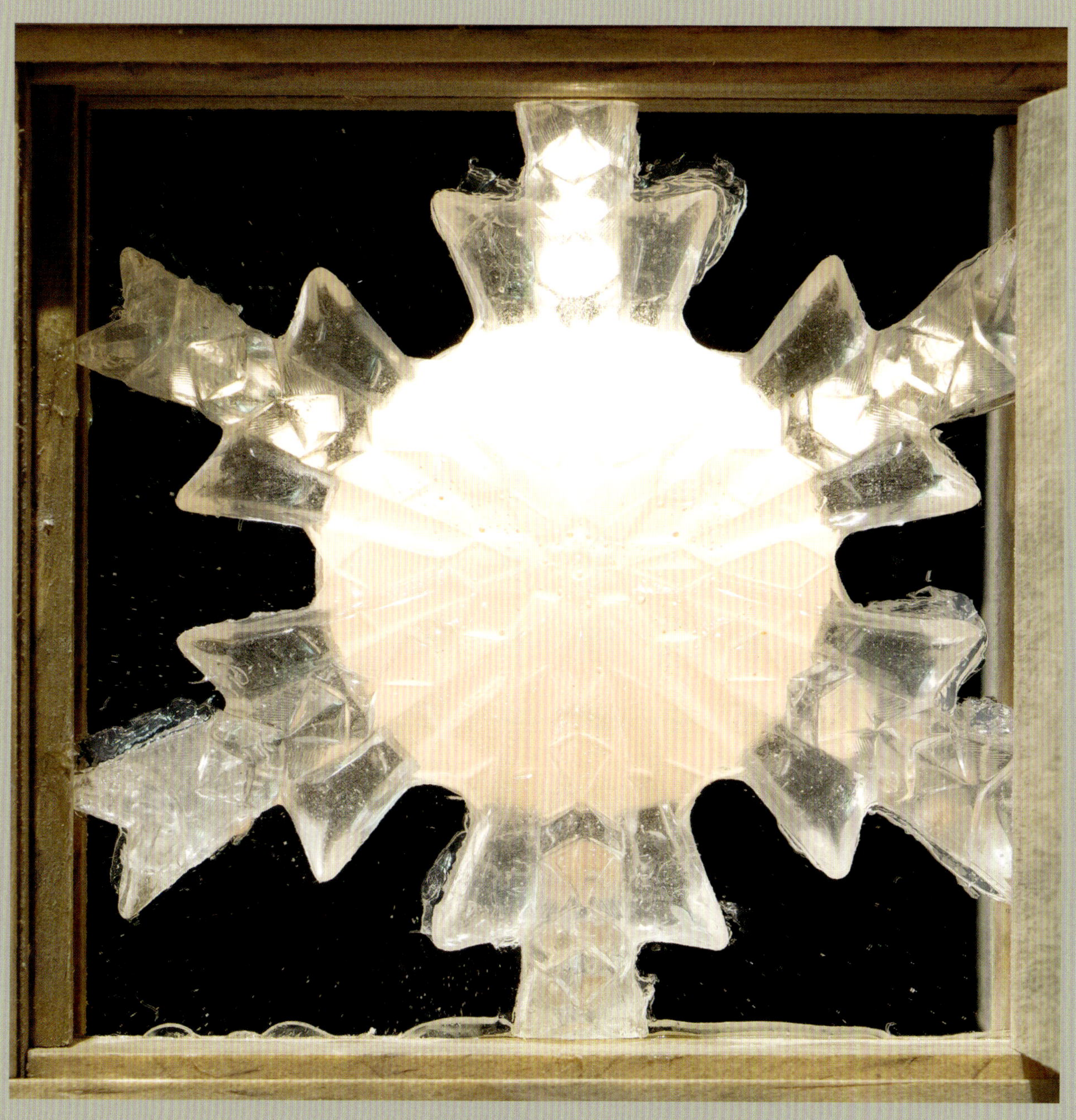

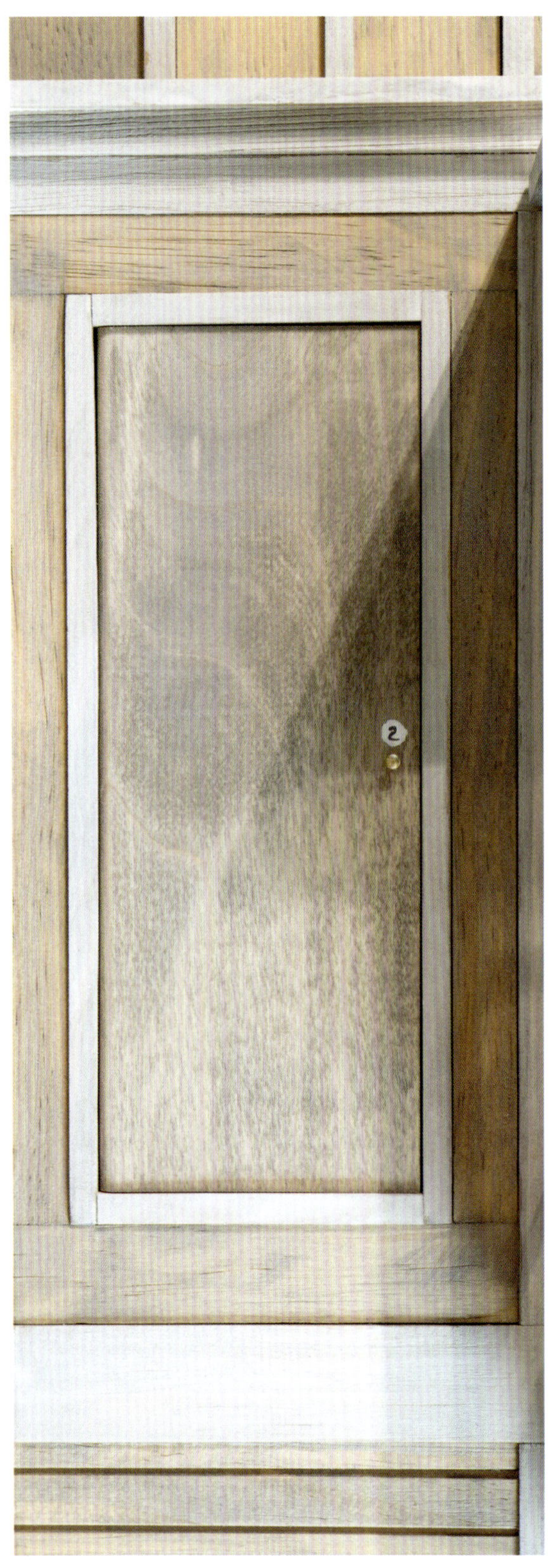
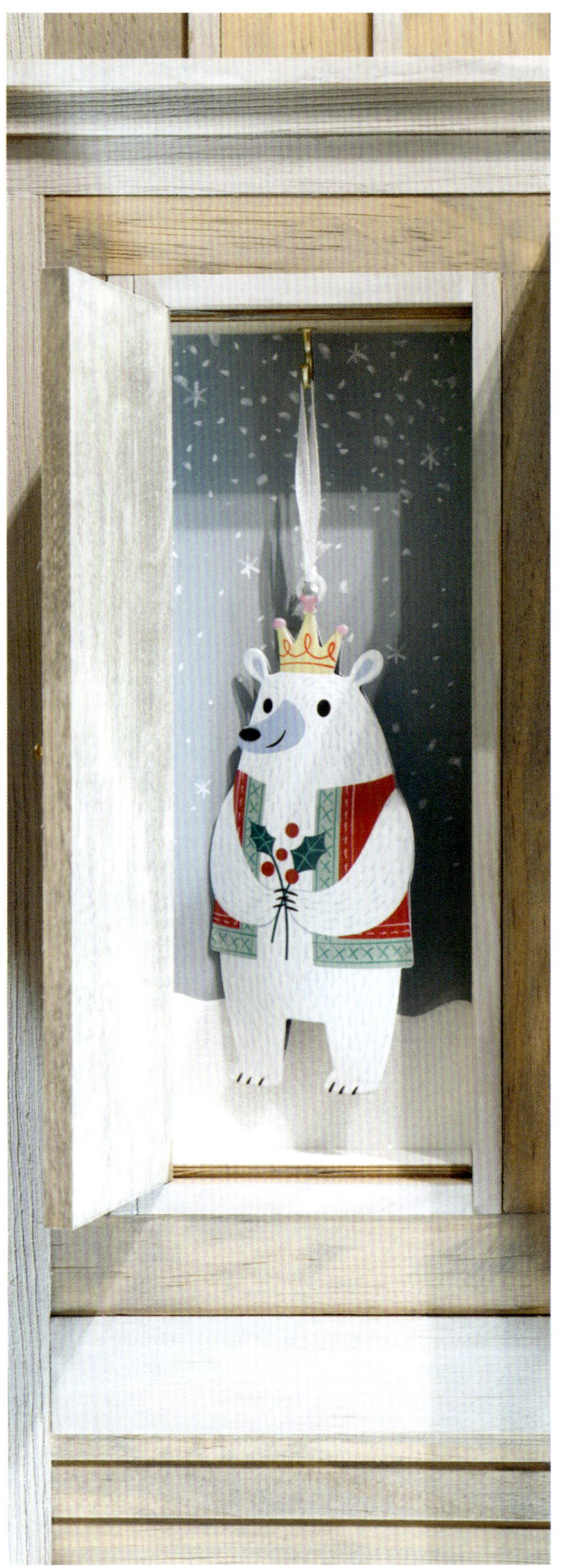

2.

This little bear is removable so it can
be hung on a tree and replaced with
another ornament if one desires.
He holds holiday ivy.

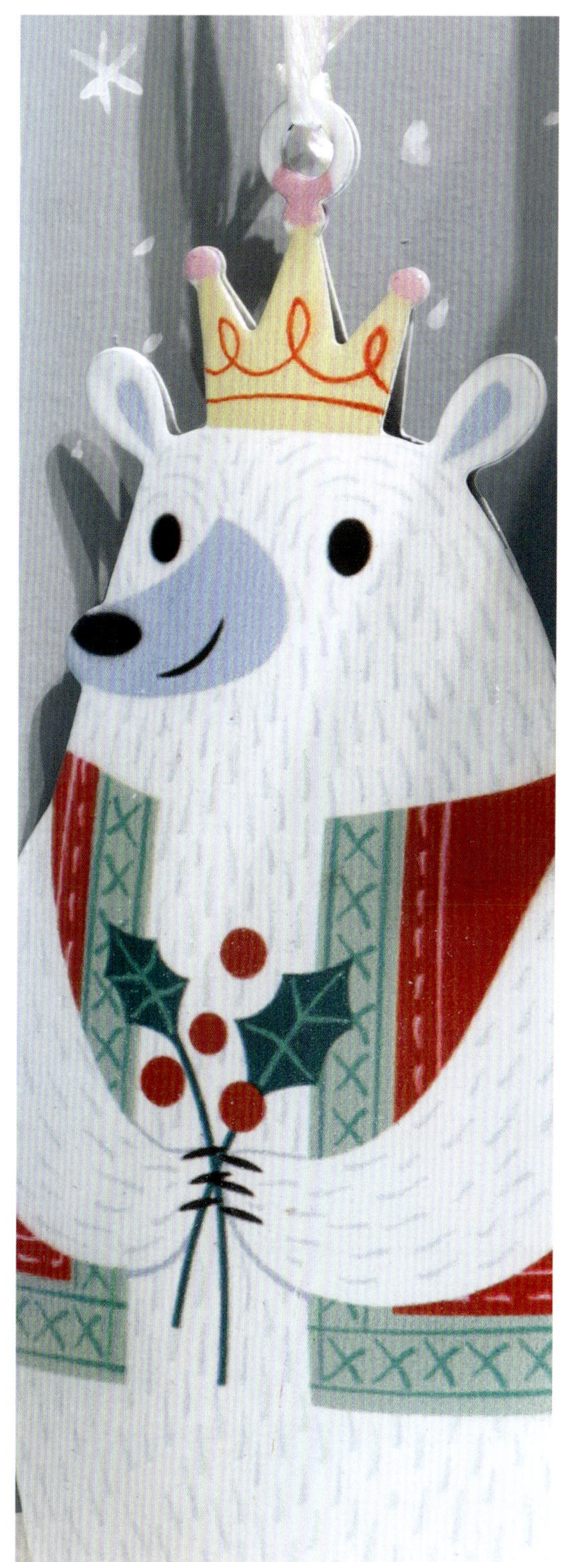

3.

This arrangement represents a
Buddhist holiday tradition.

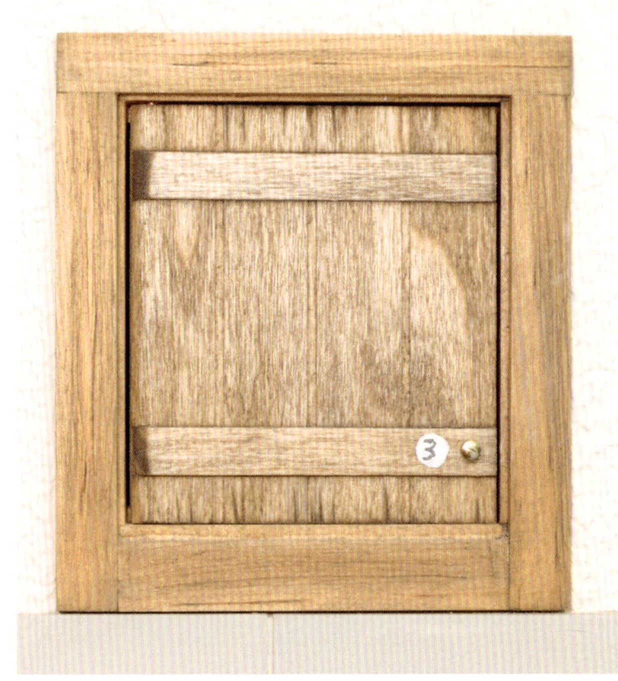

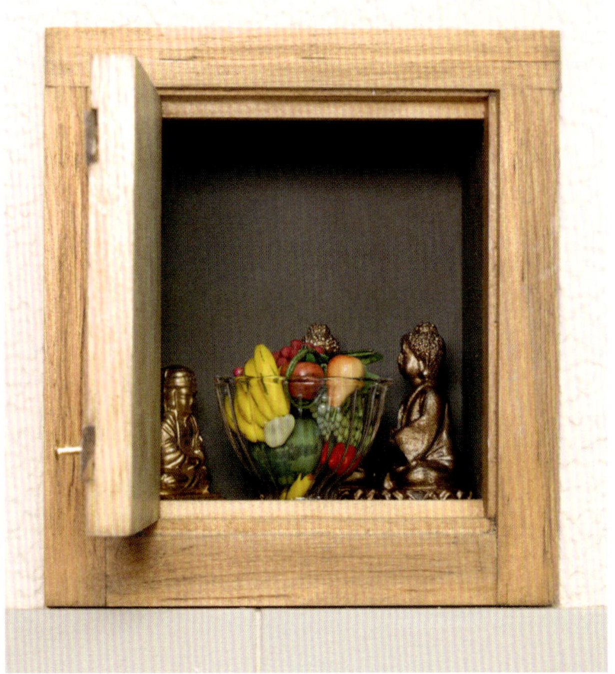

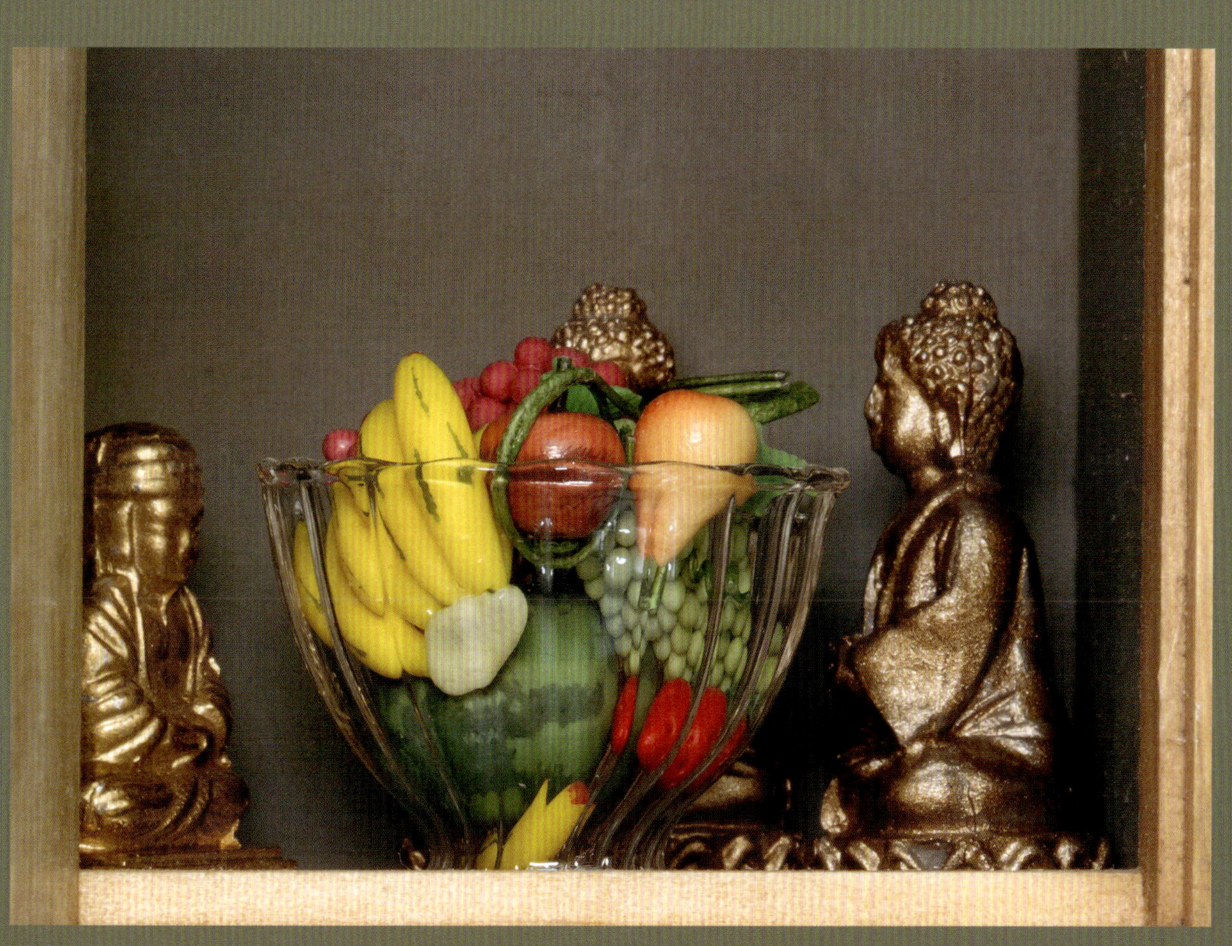

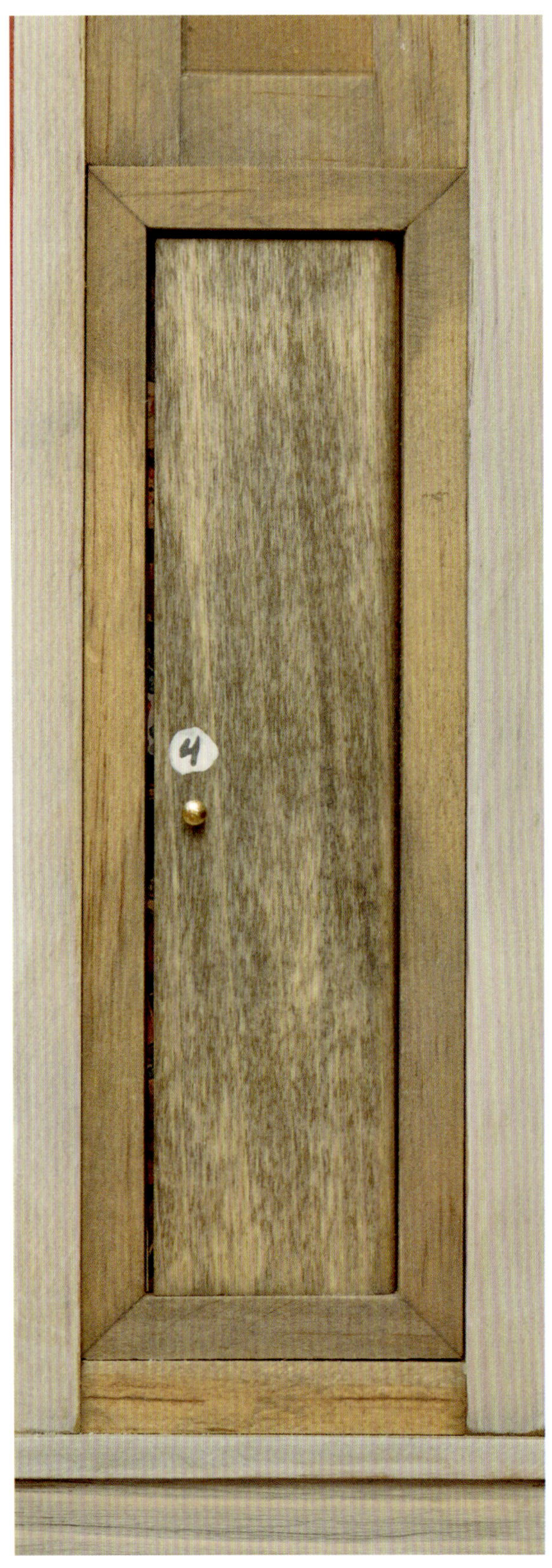
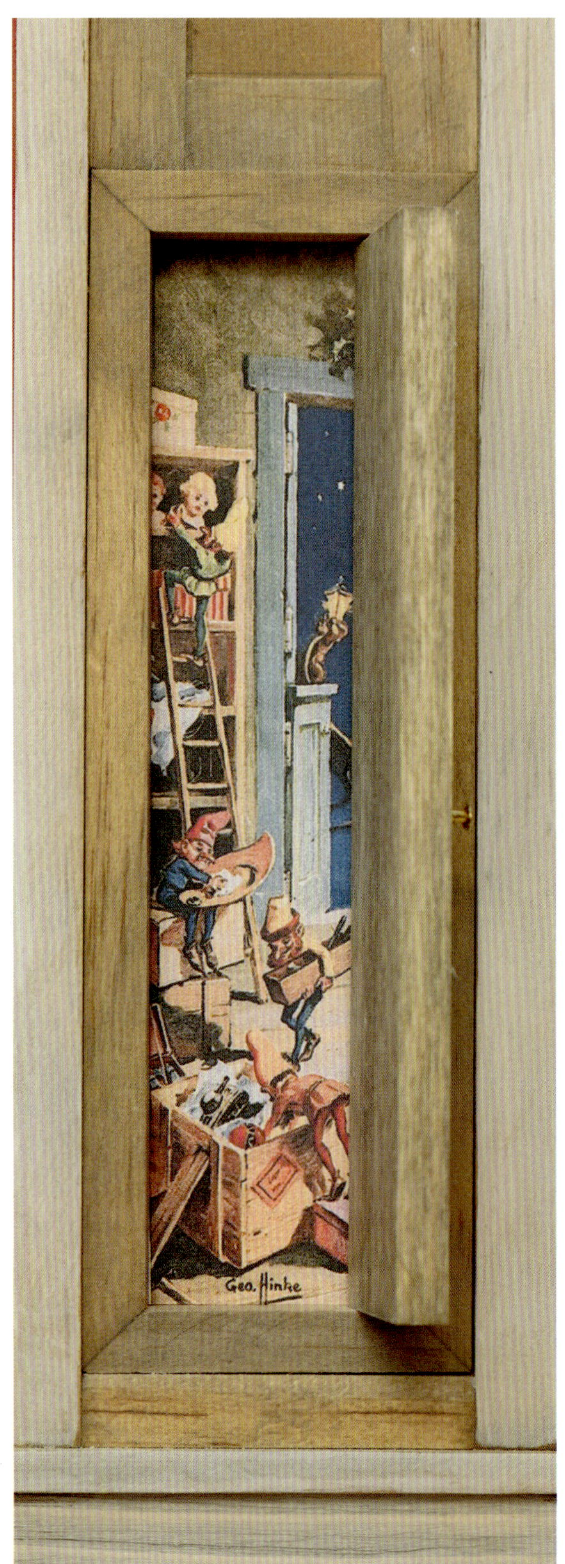

Geo. Hinke

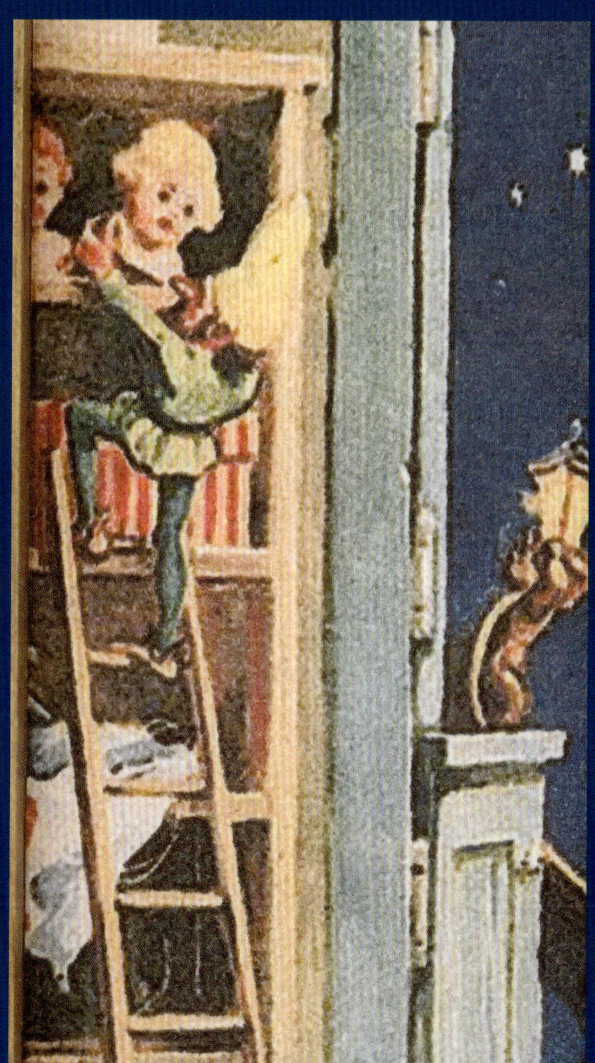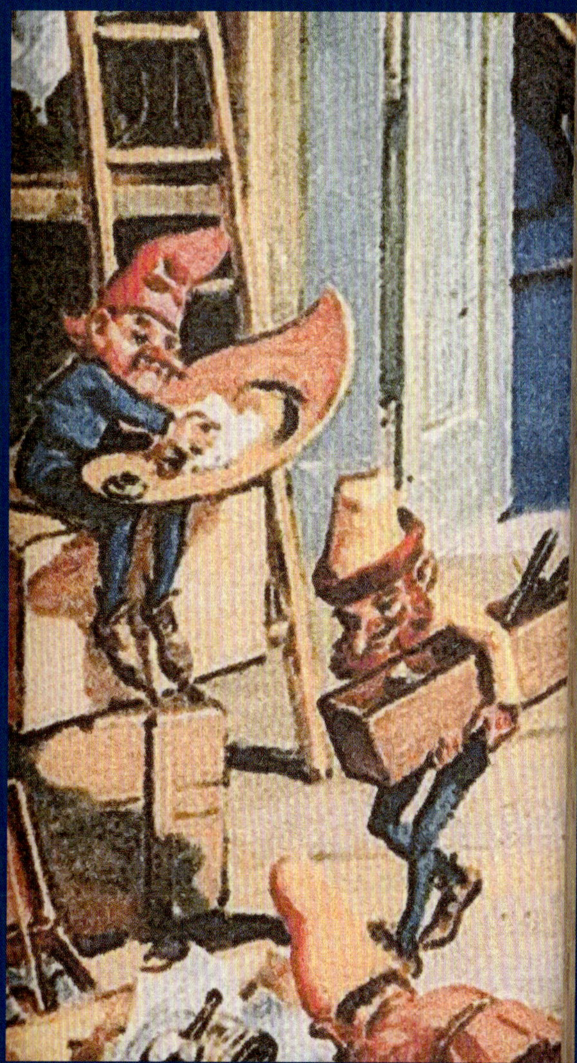

4.

This door is very narrow and contains an old-fashioned
print of the elves working very hard.

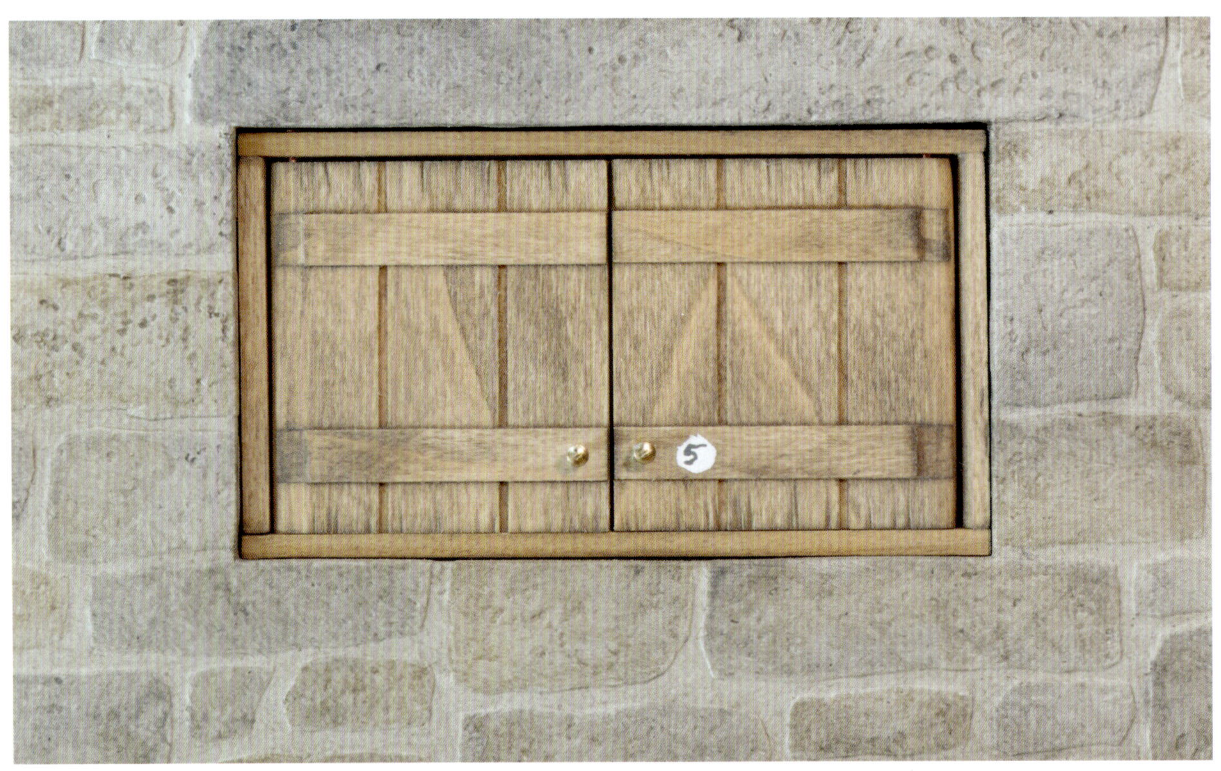

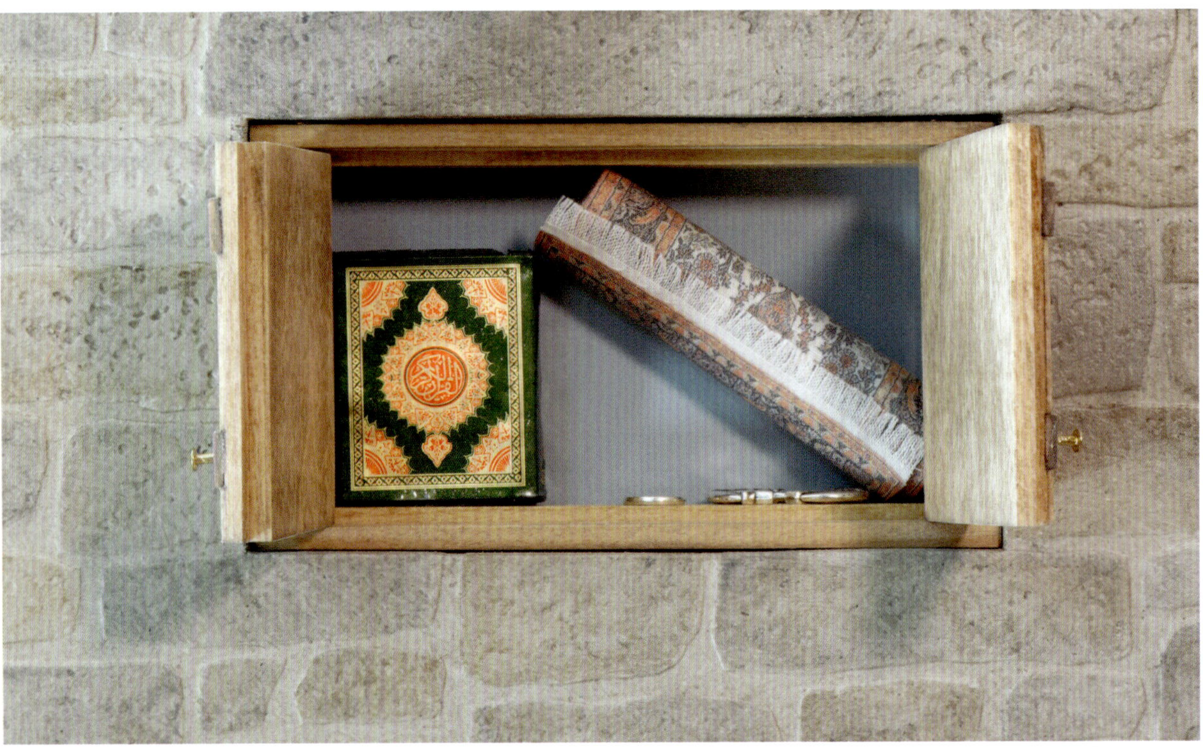

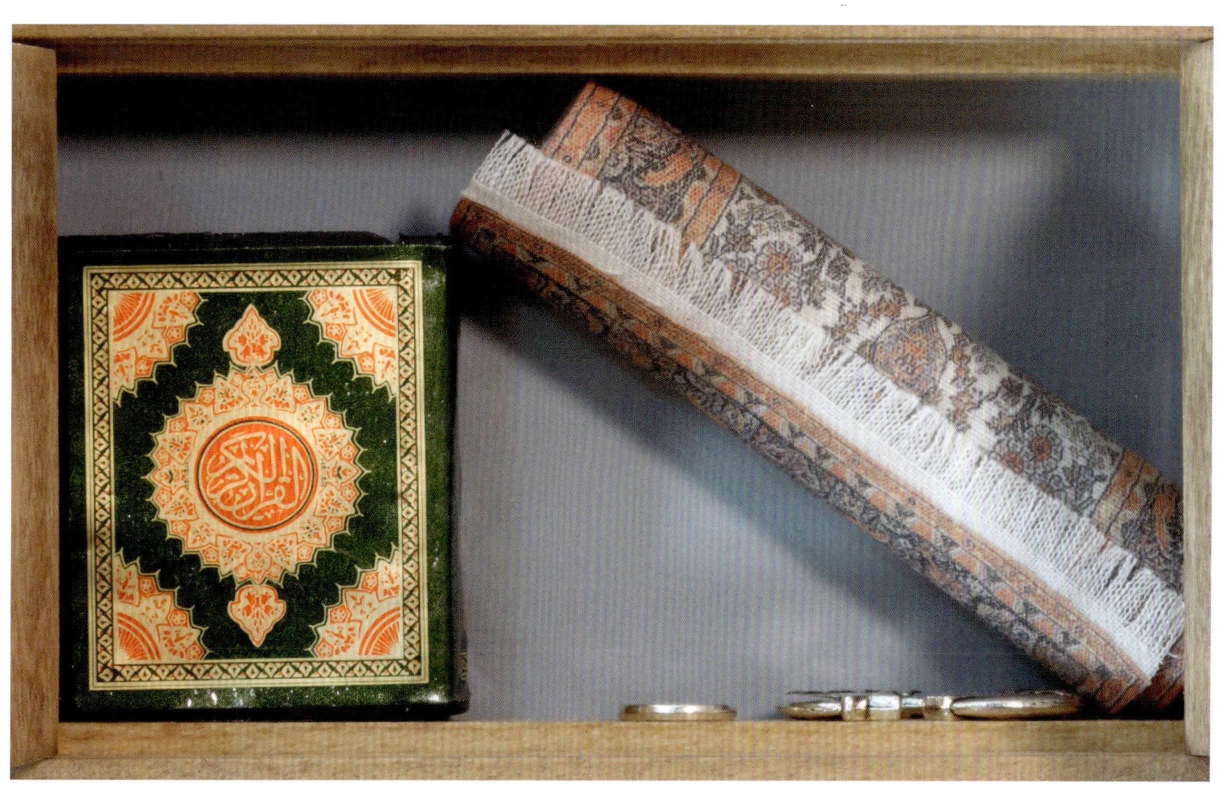

5.

Behind this door sits a dedication to the Islamic
devotion to prayer and the Quran.

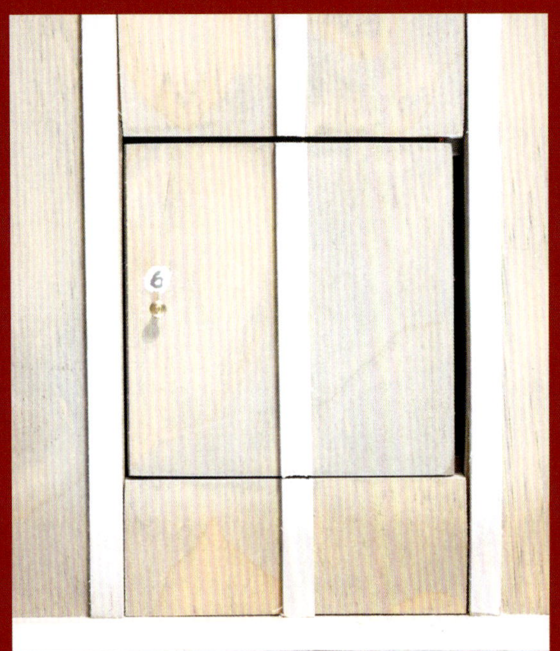 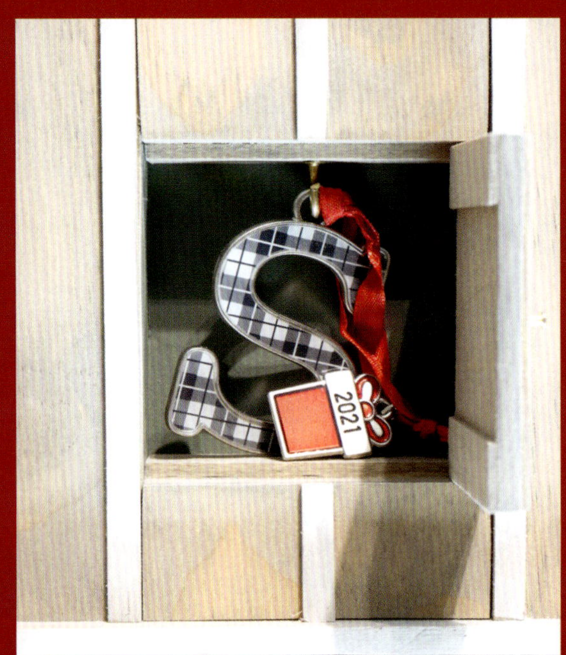

6.

Behind this door is a removable ornament to be placed
on our tree. The S stands for a family initial. The 2021
date signifies the year of completion.

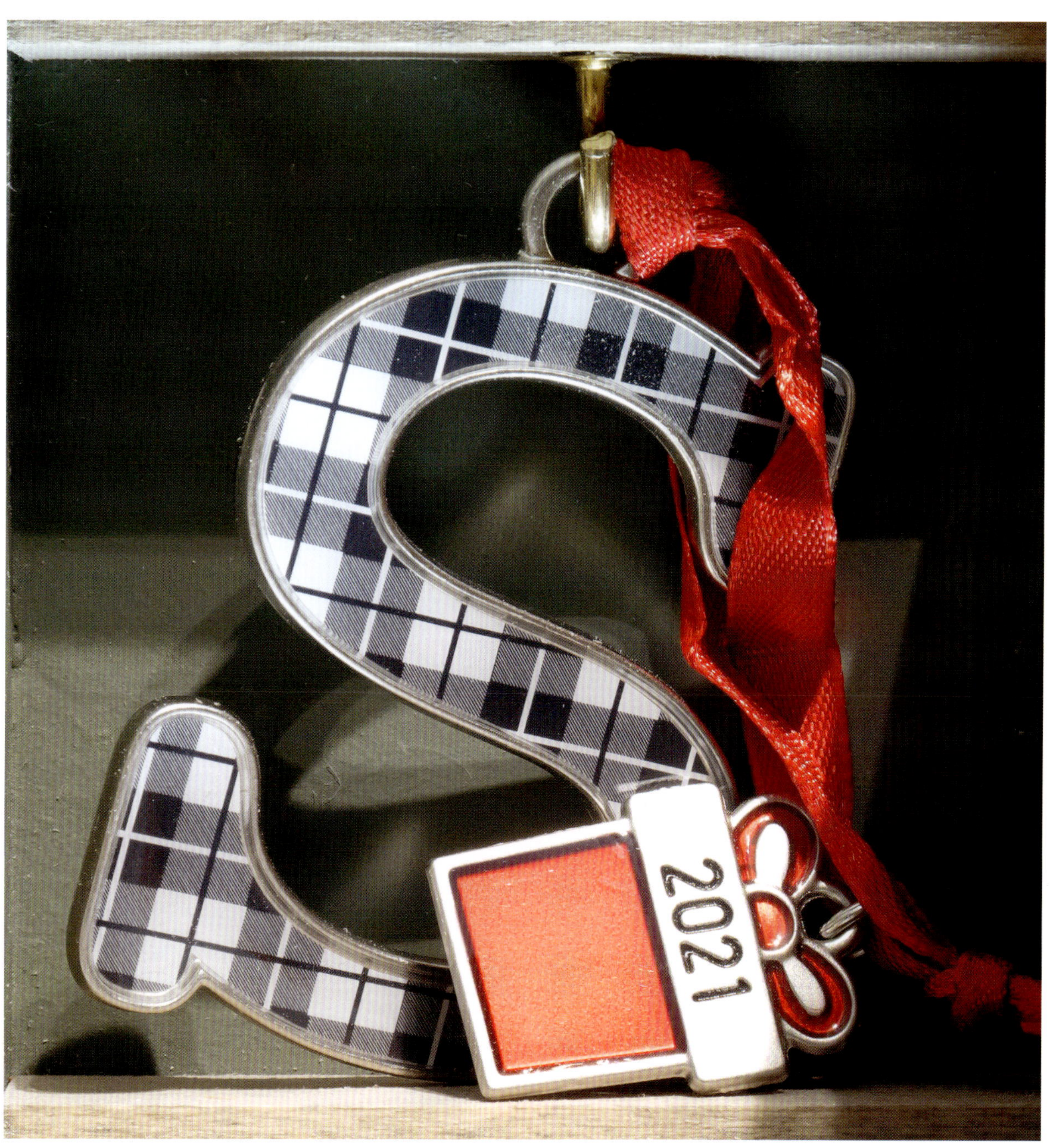2021

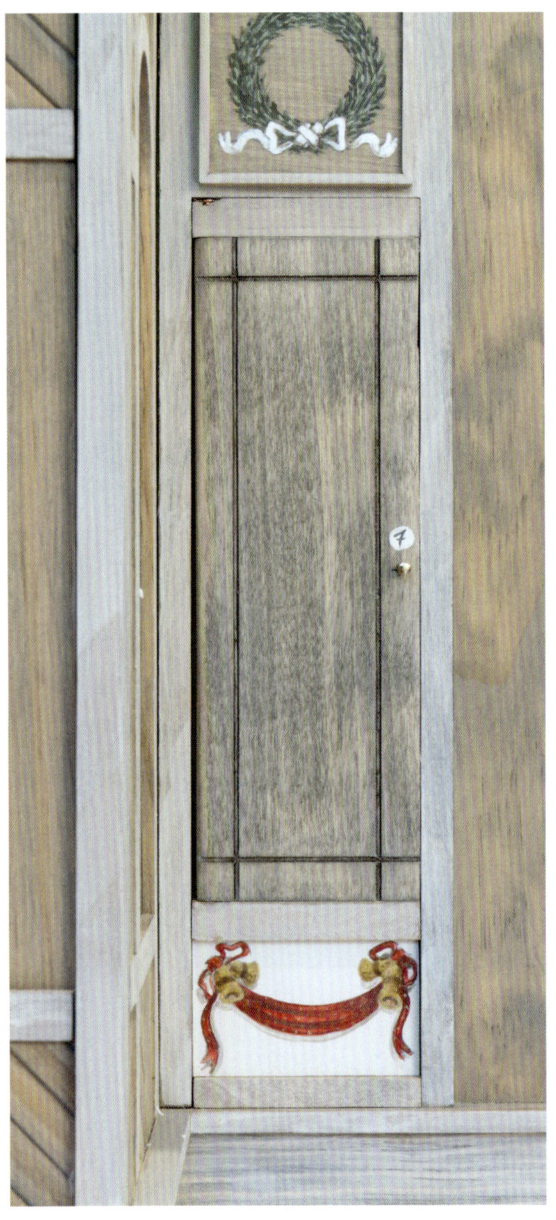 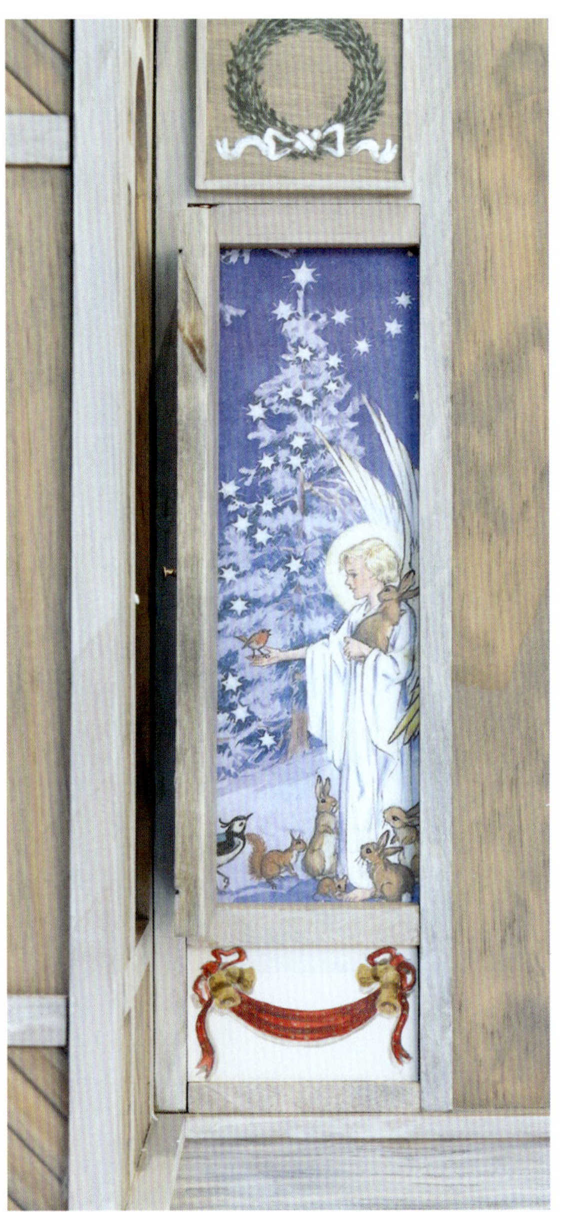

7.

This very narrow door opens into a
print of an angel and, of course,
a Christmas tree.

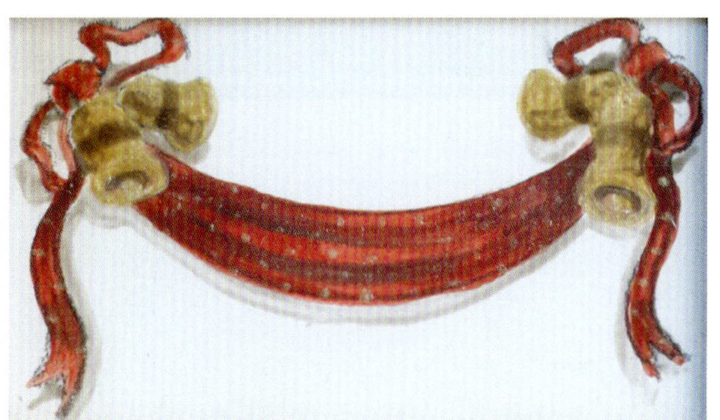

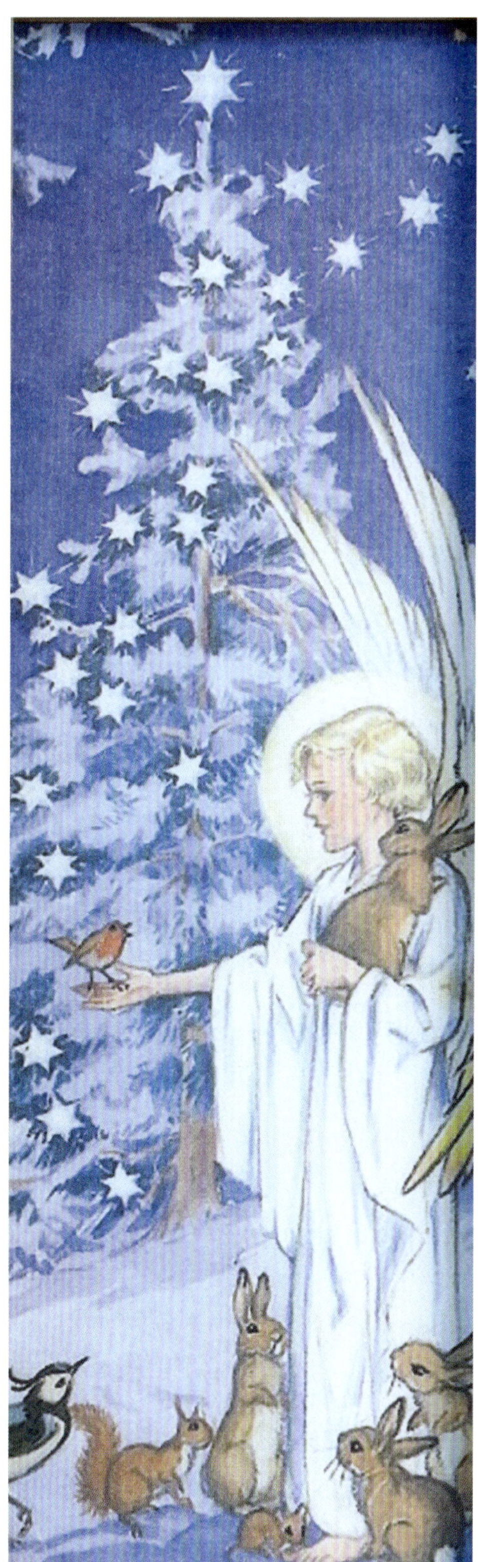

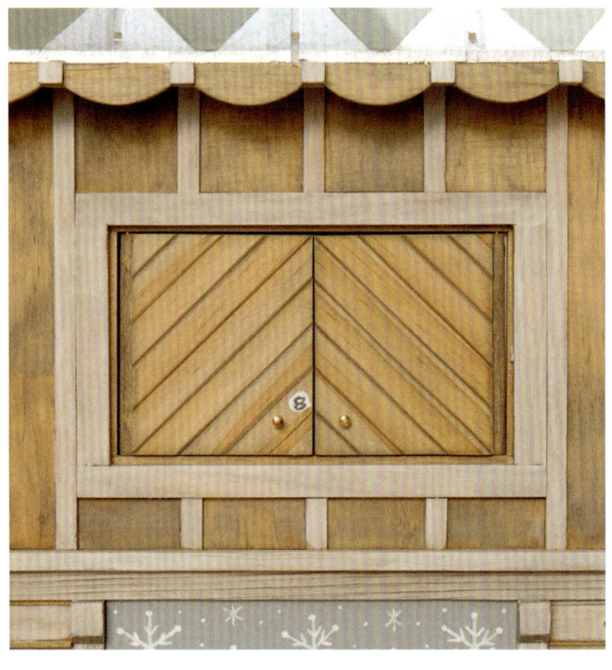

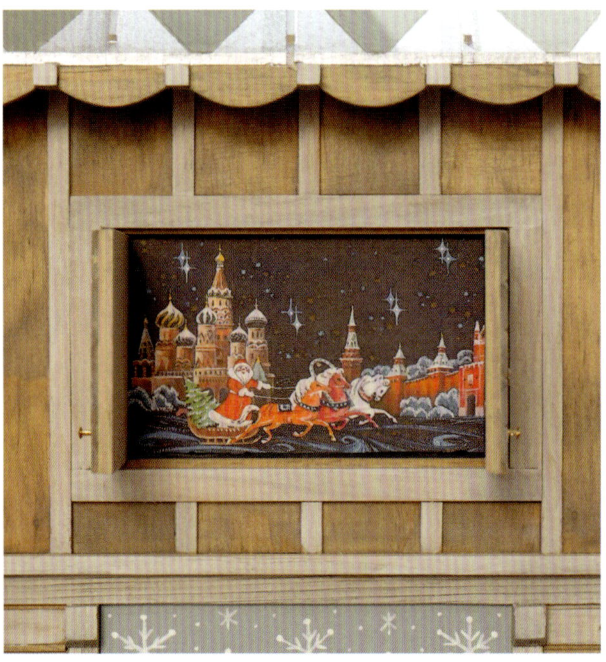

8.

These doors open wide to reveal Santa
in his sleigh in Russia riding
by Saint Basil's Cathedral—a very
special place.

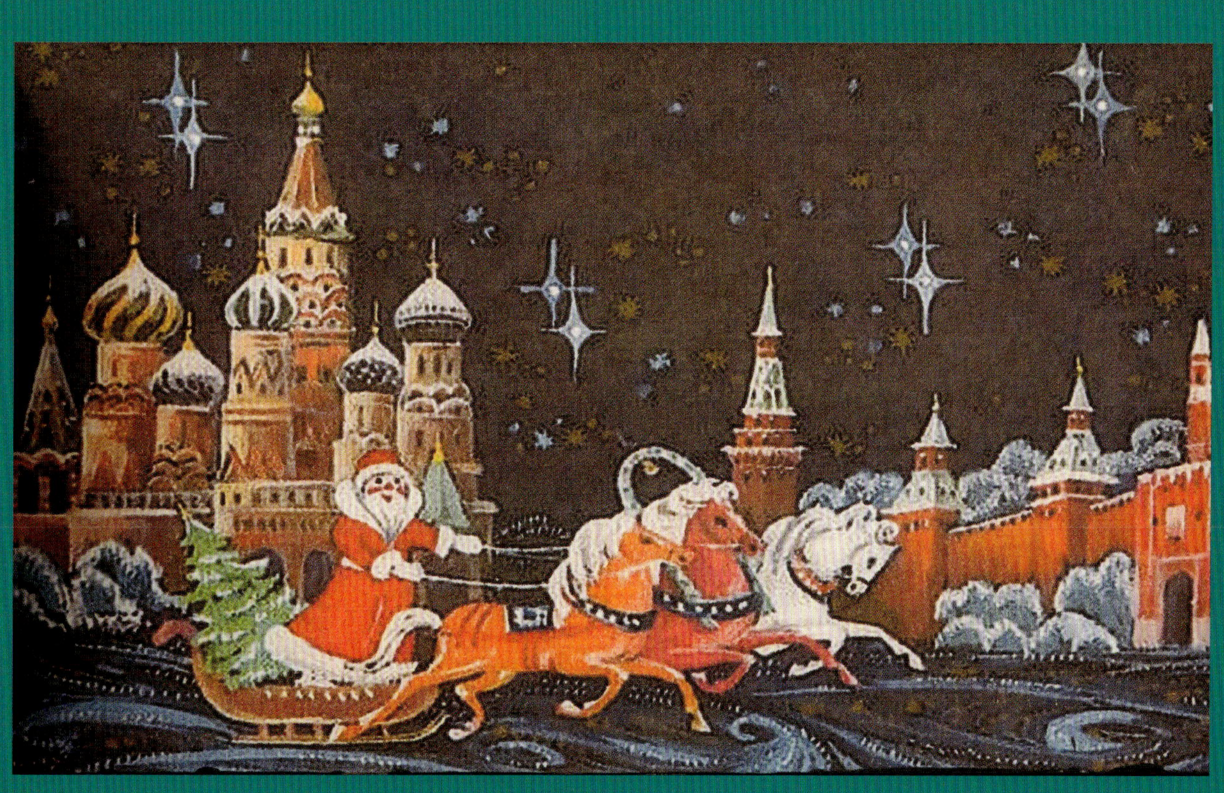

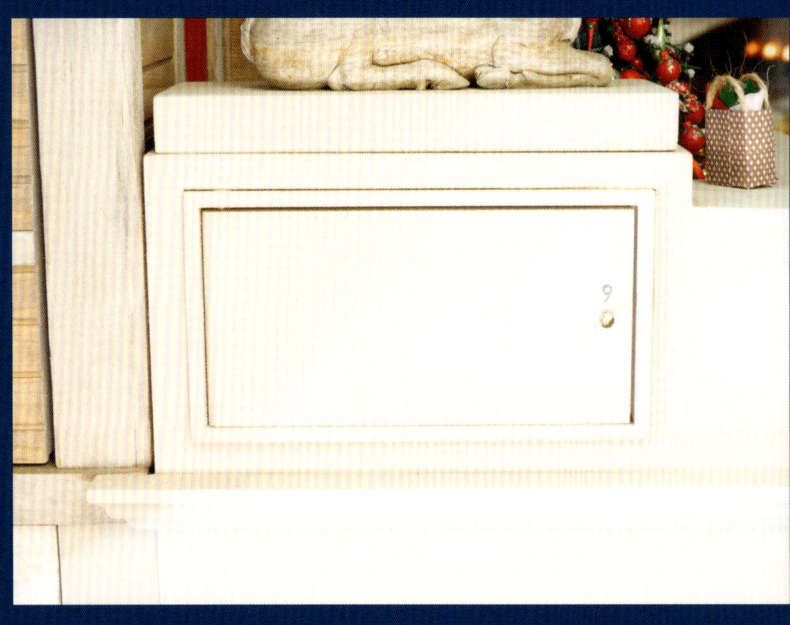

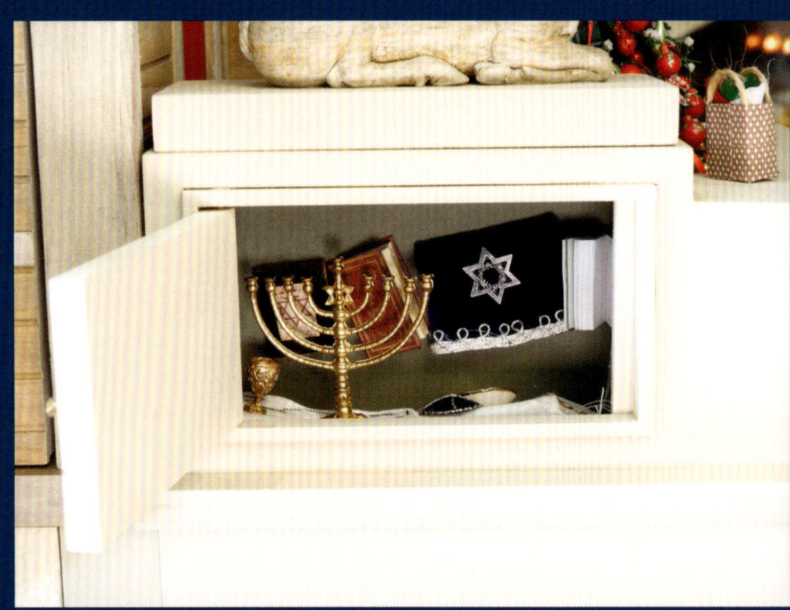

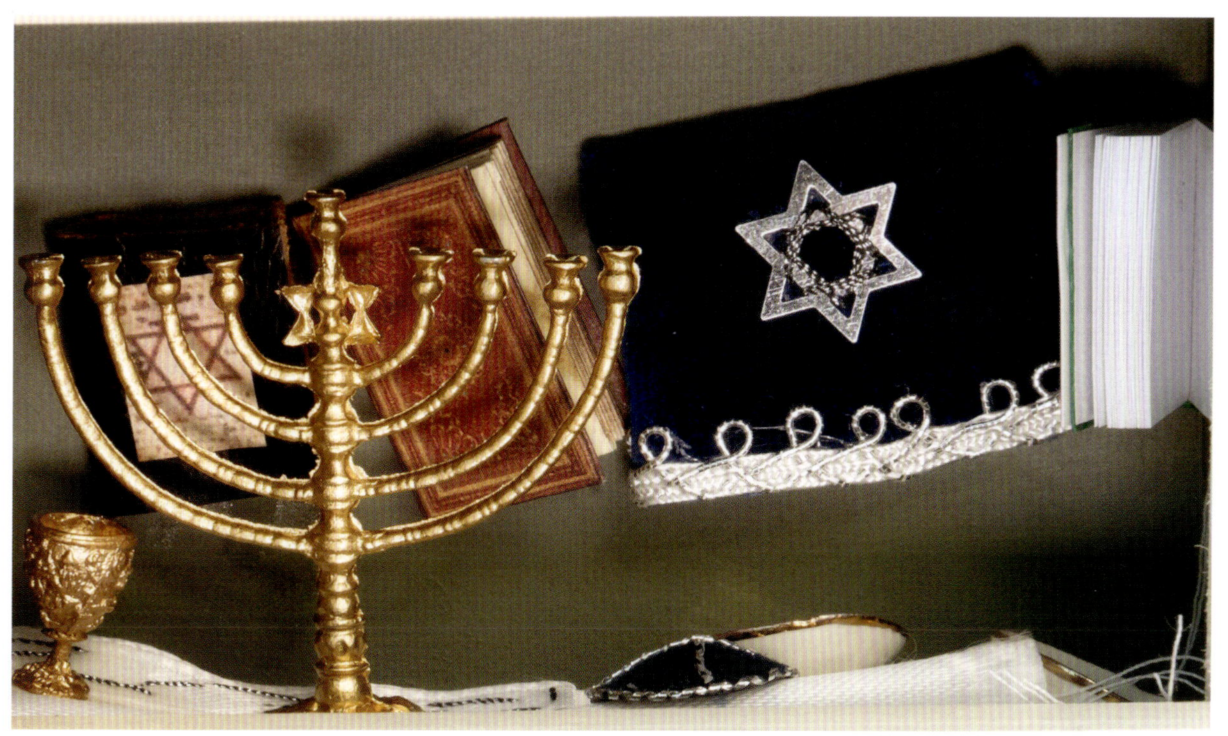

9.

This little white door opens to showcase Jewish
traditions and faith.

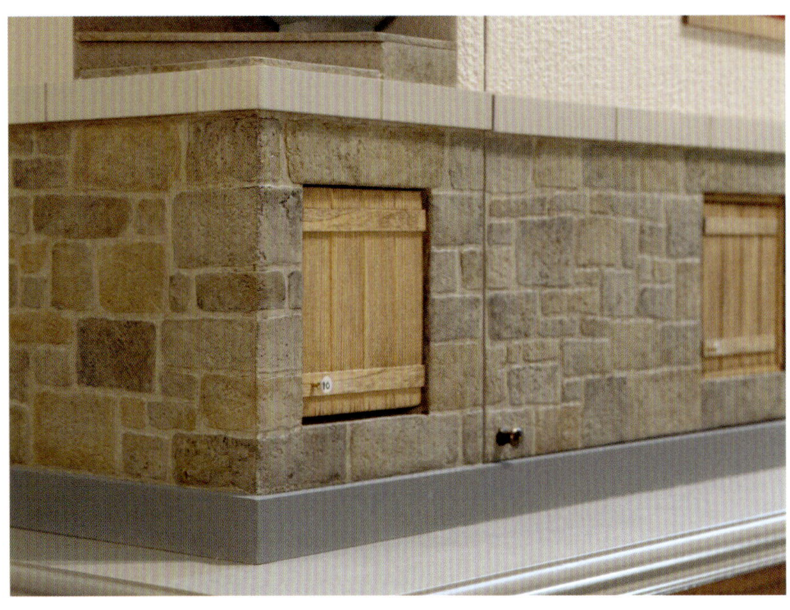

10.

This door actually slides open. You'll find Santa on a tricycle
wagon transporting a tree and a present, of course.

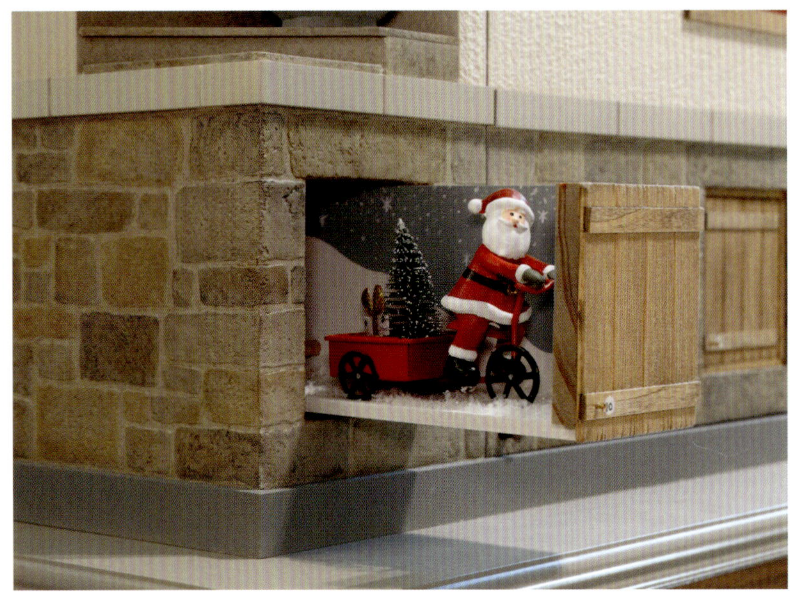

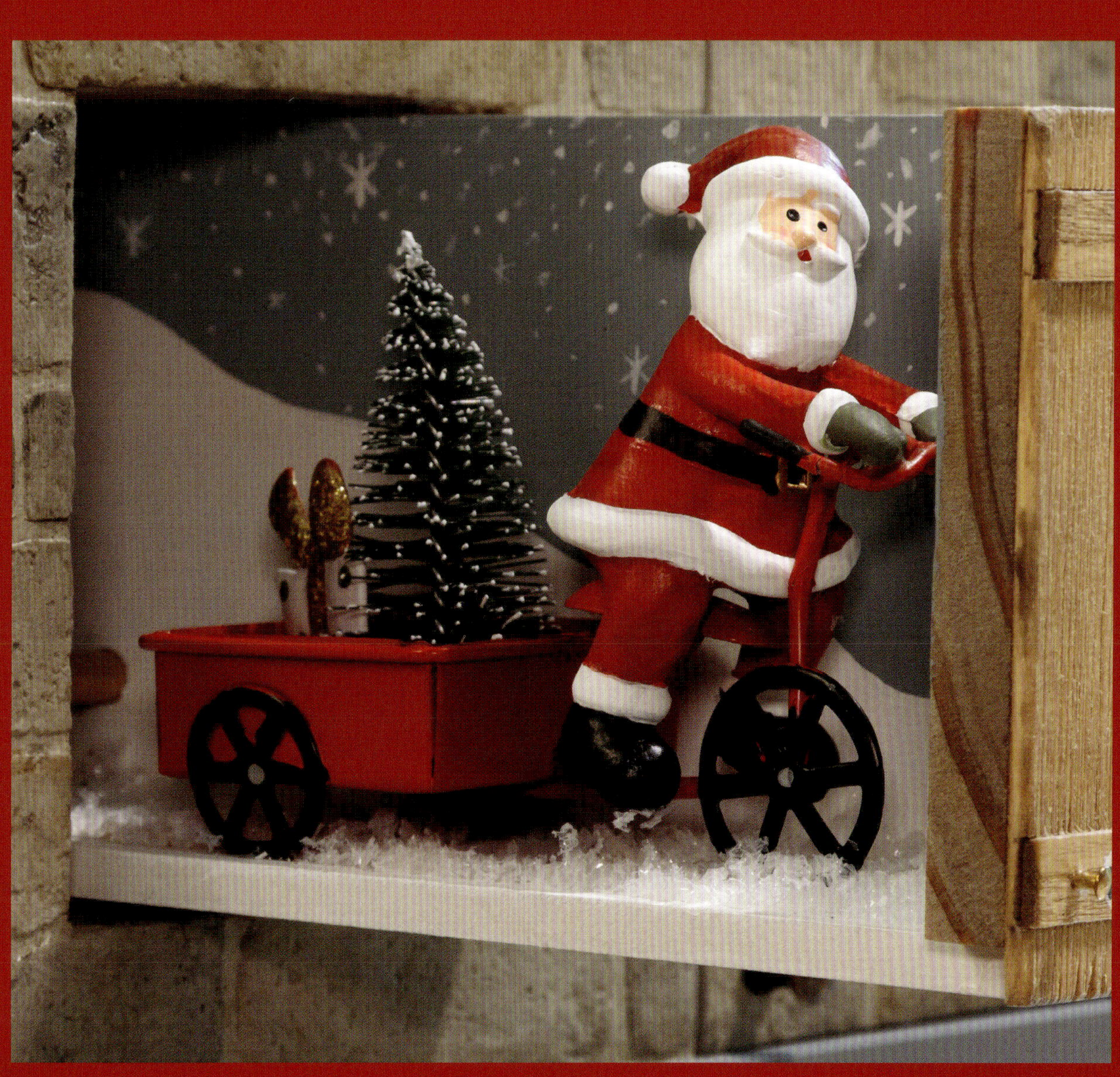

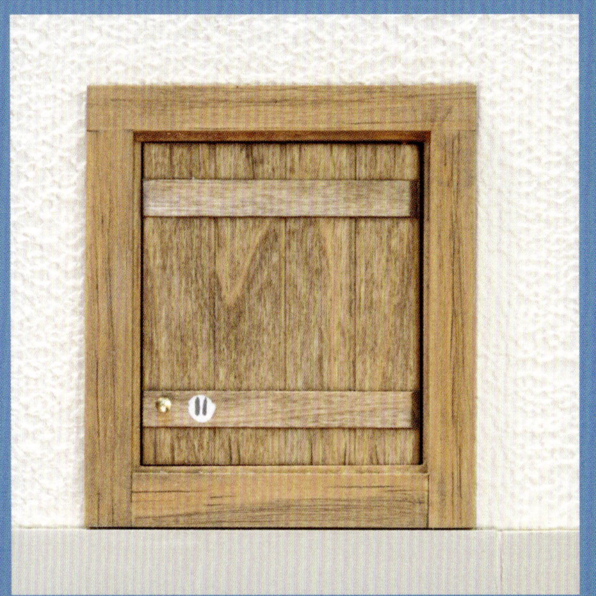 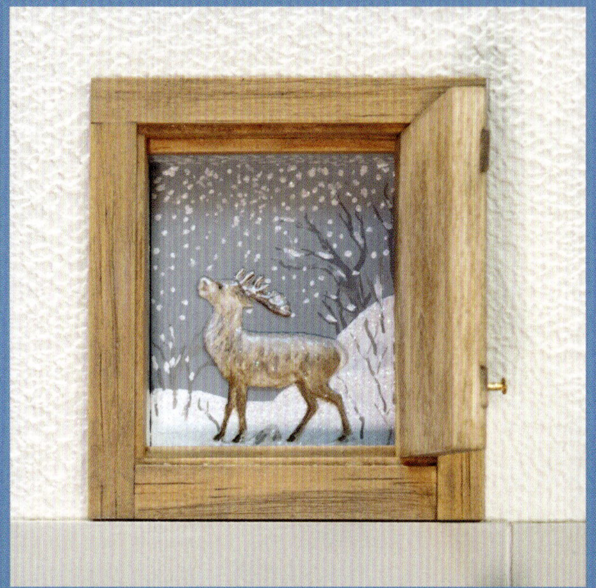

11.

Behind this itsy bitsy wooden door is a three-dimensional
deer basking in freshly fallen snow.

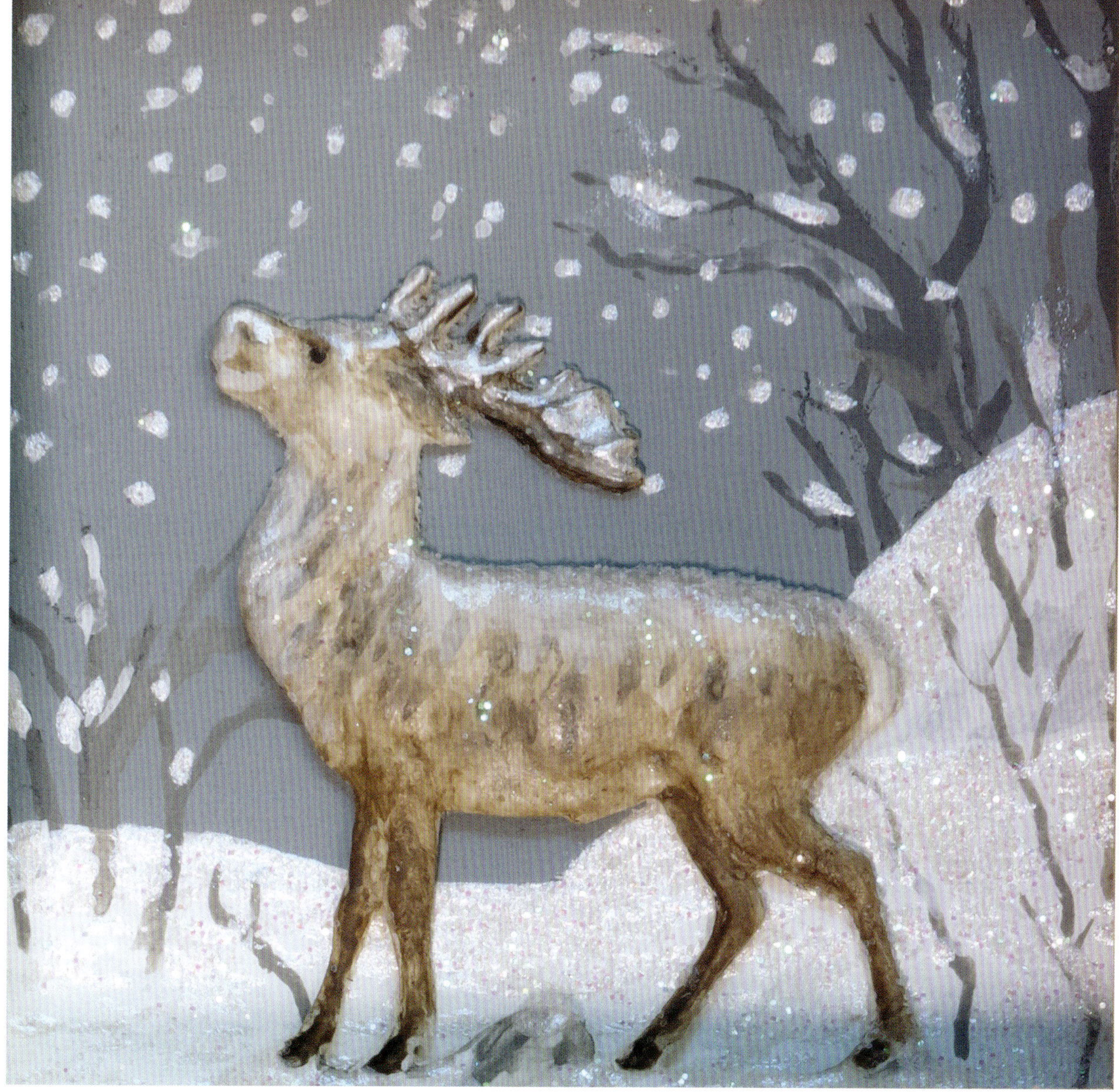

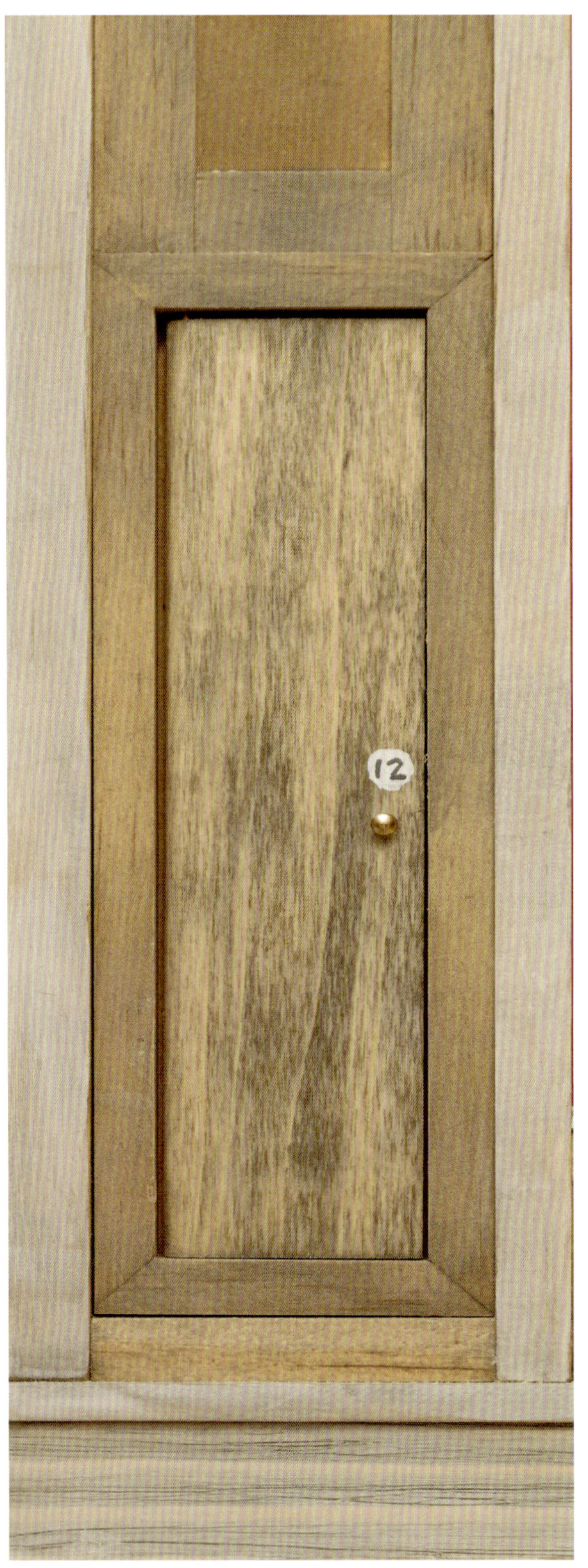
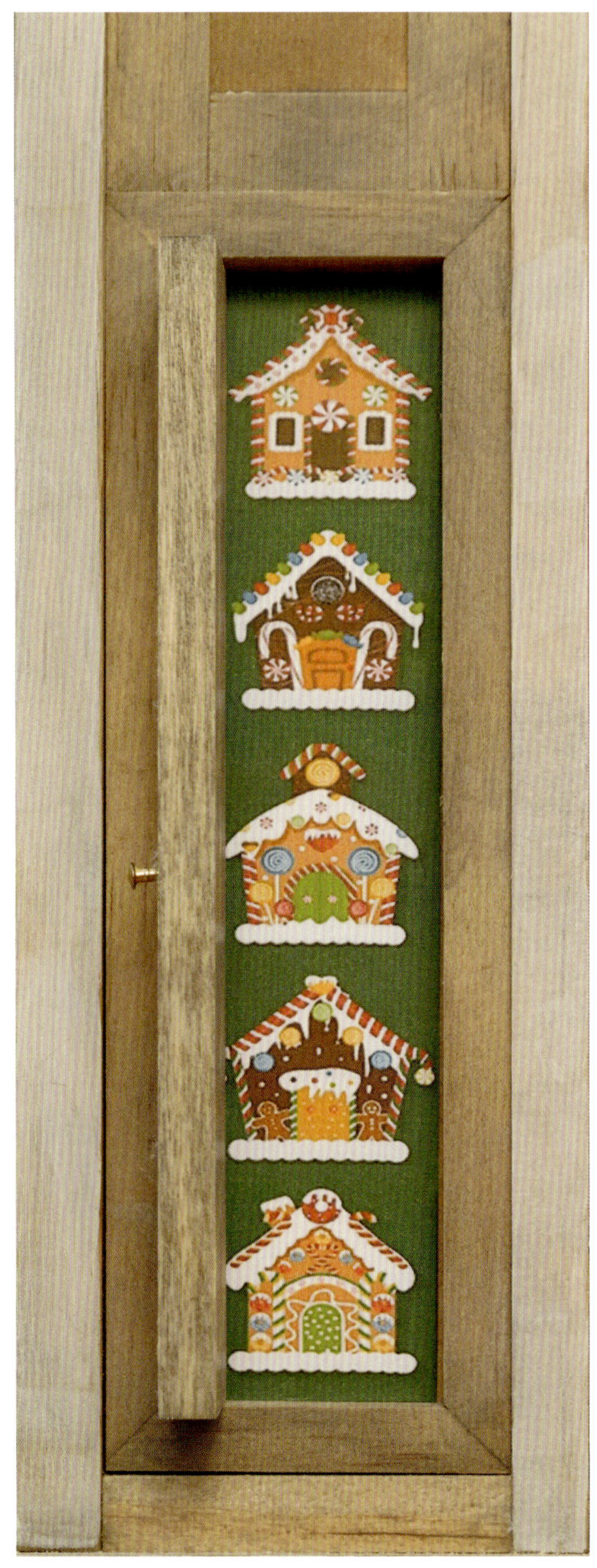

12.

What's better than gingerbread houses?
A visual treat.

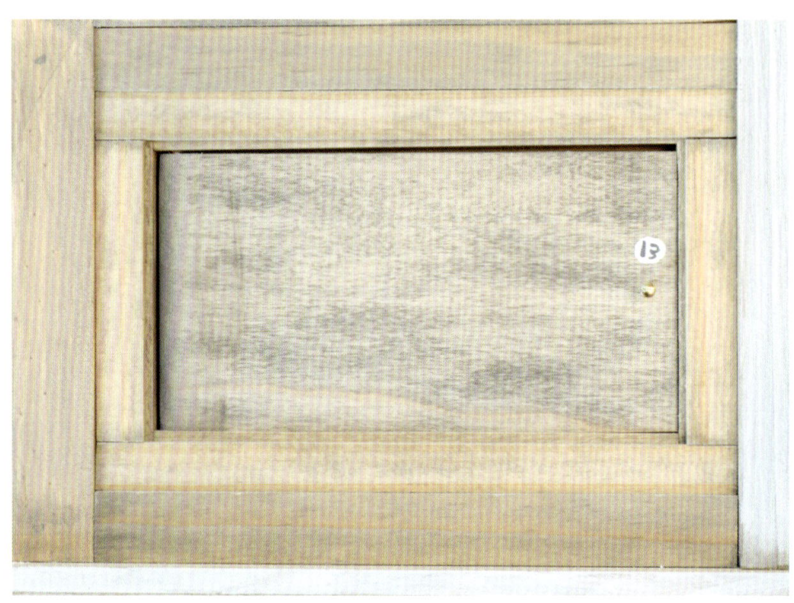

13.

This door holds a stained glass Santa, which can be removed and hung anywhere you like as well as a few $1/4$- and $3/8$-inch ornaments just for fun.

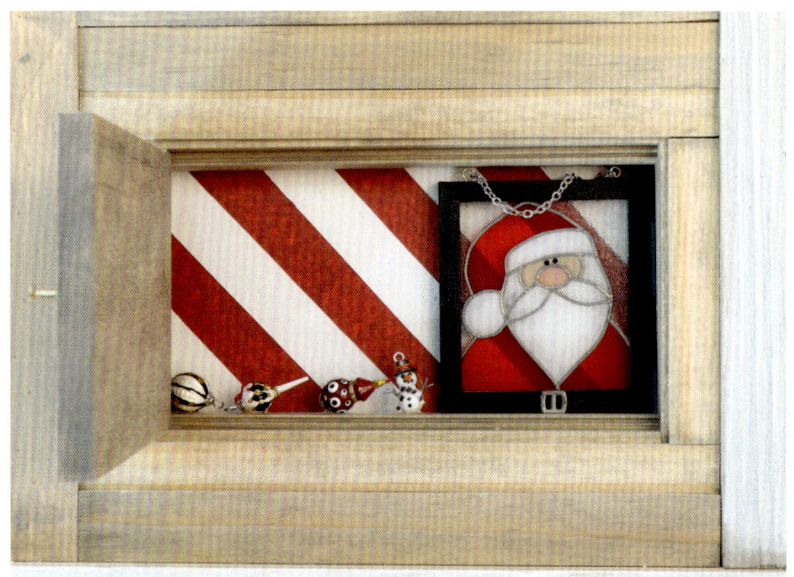

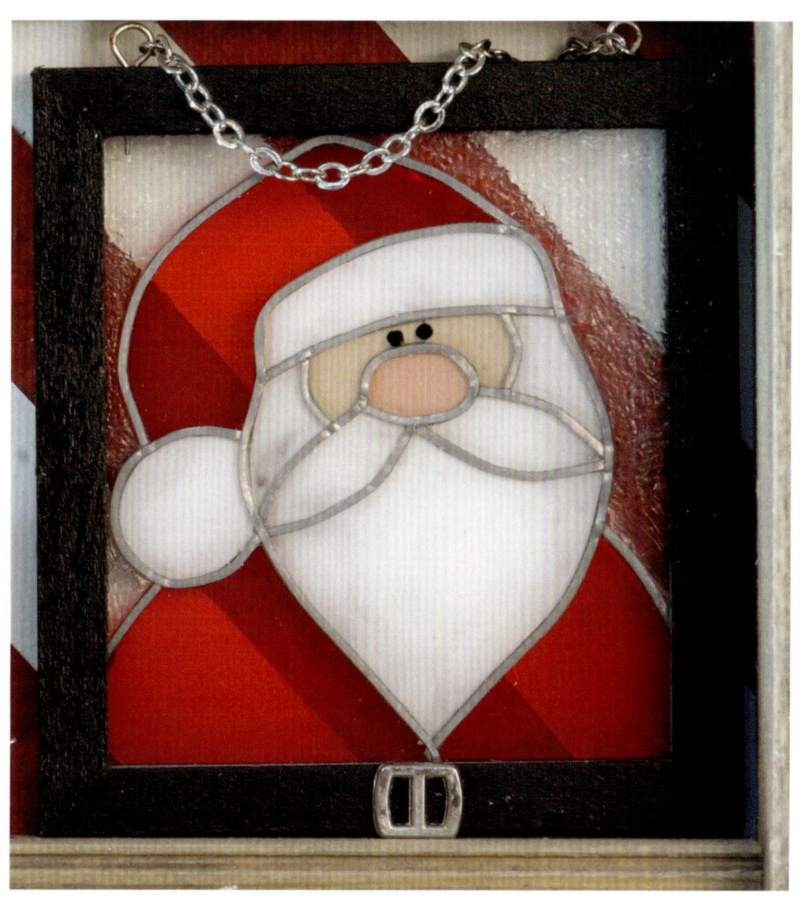

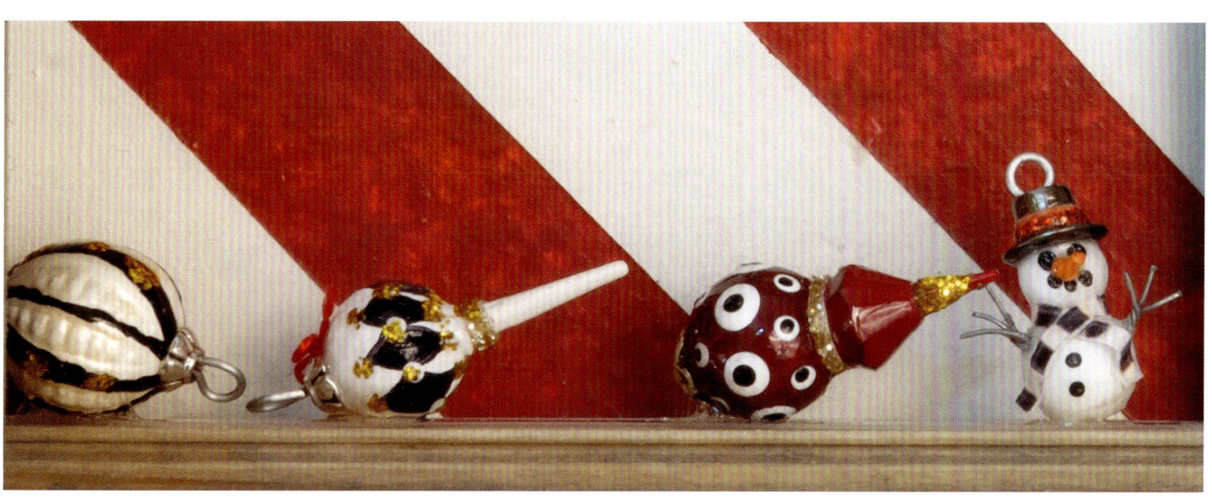

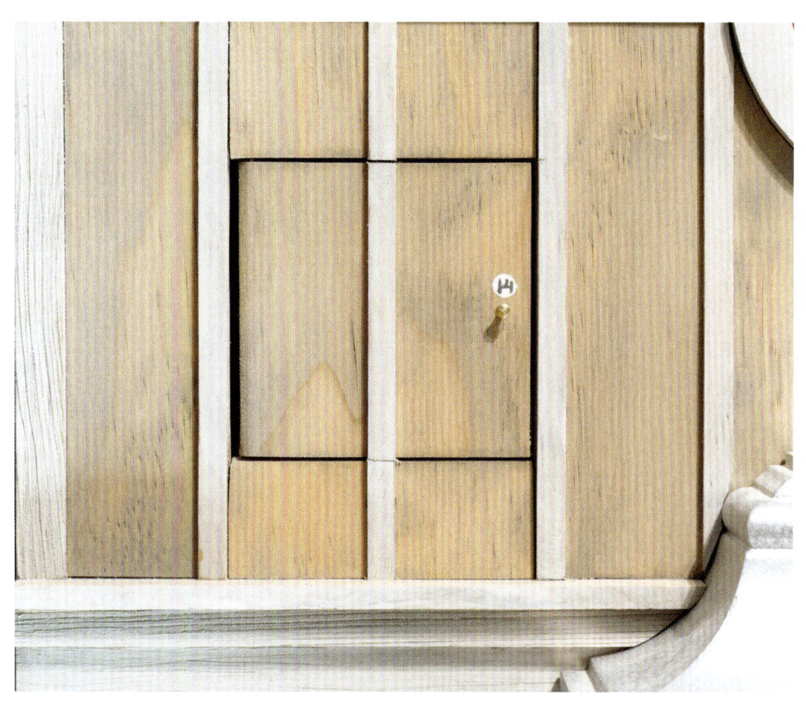

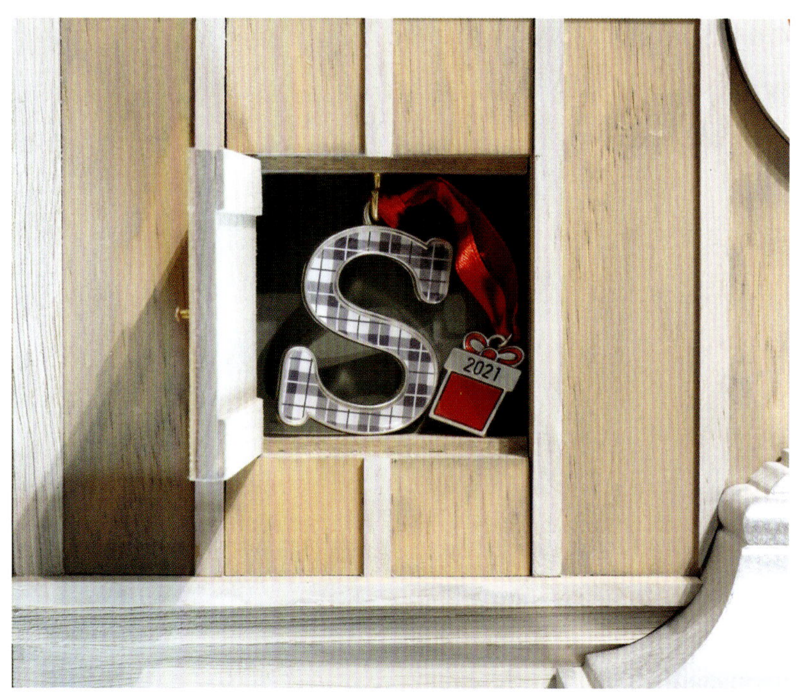

<h1 style="text-align:center">14.</h1>

This may look familiar, and that's because this is the second S in the family initials. This ornament can be hung on the tree and replaced with something else for this Advent calendar, but for now, it stays where it is. It's a lovely reminder each time the door is opened.

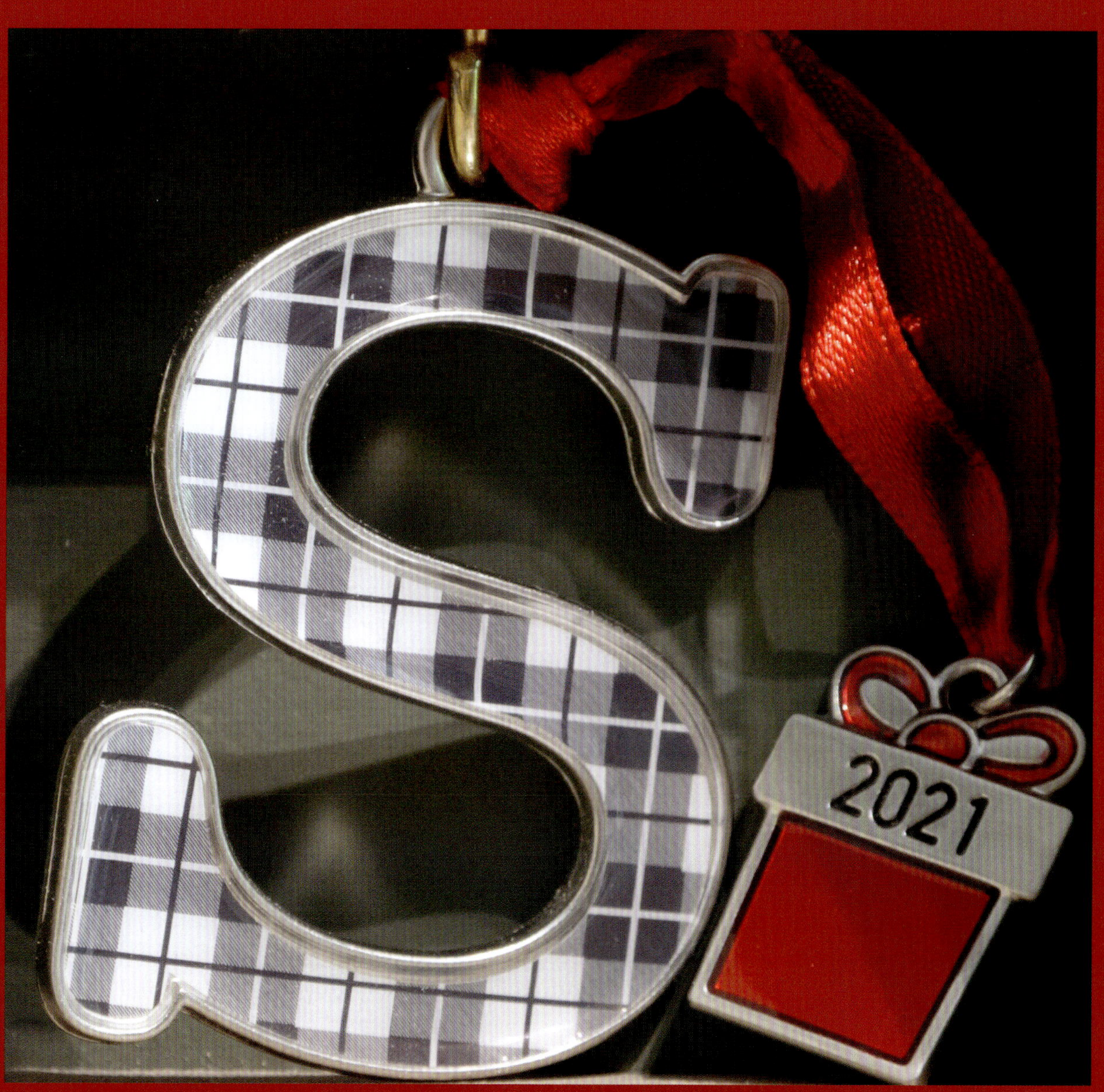

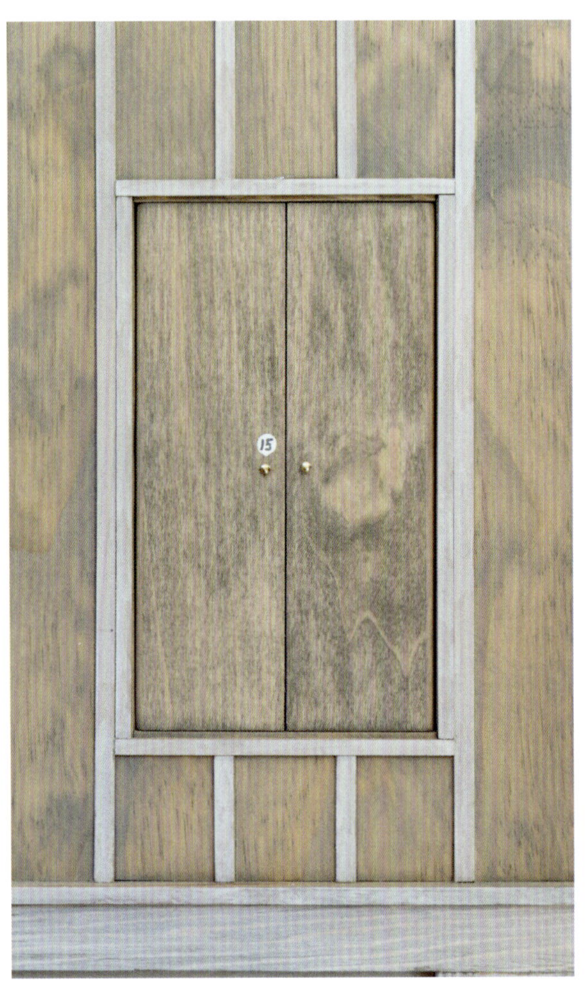 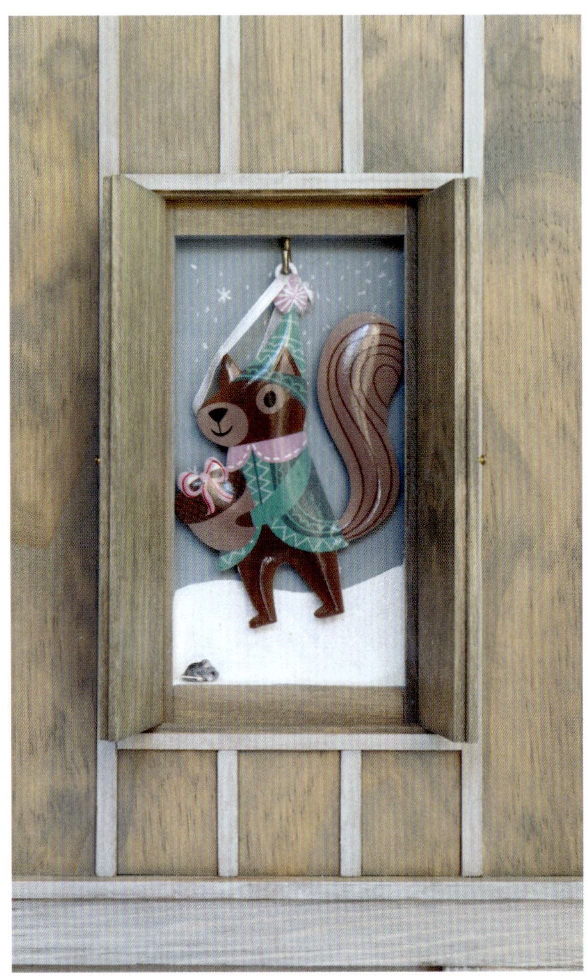

15.

Another ornament meant to be hung on any tree.
It can be replaced with any ornament—as long as it's flat
and less than 2 inches tall. For now, the squirrel stays here.

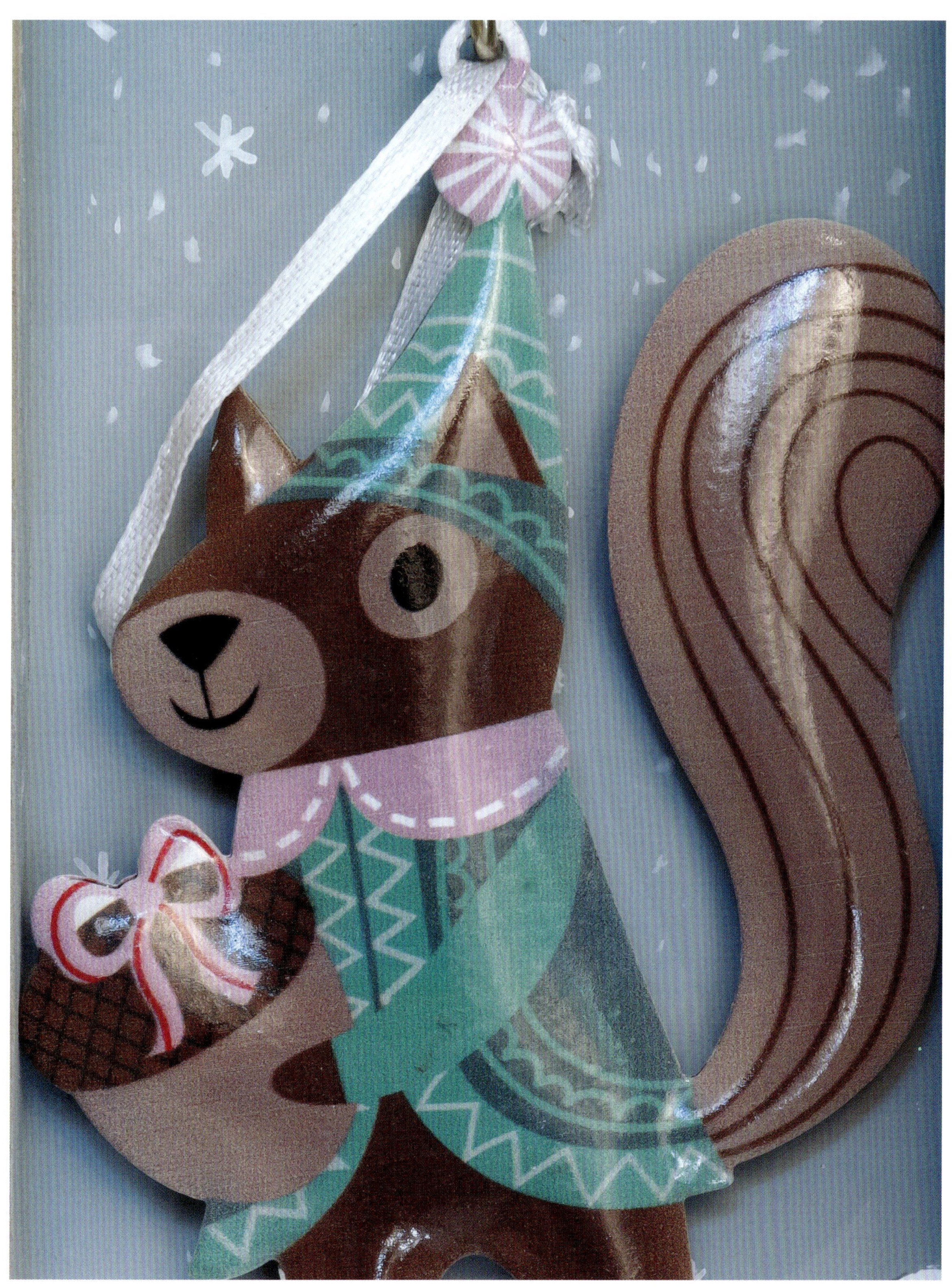

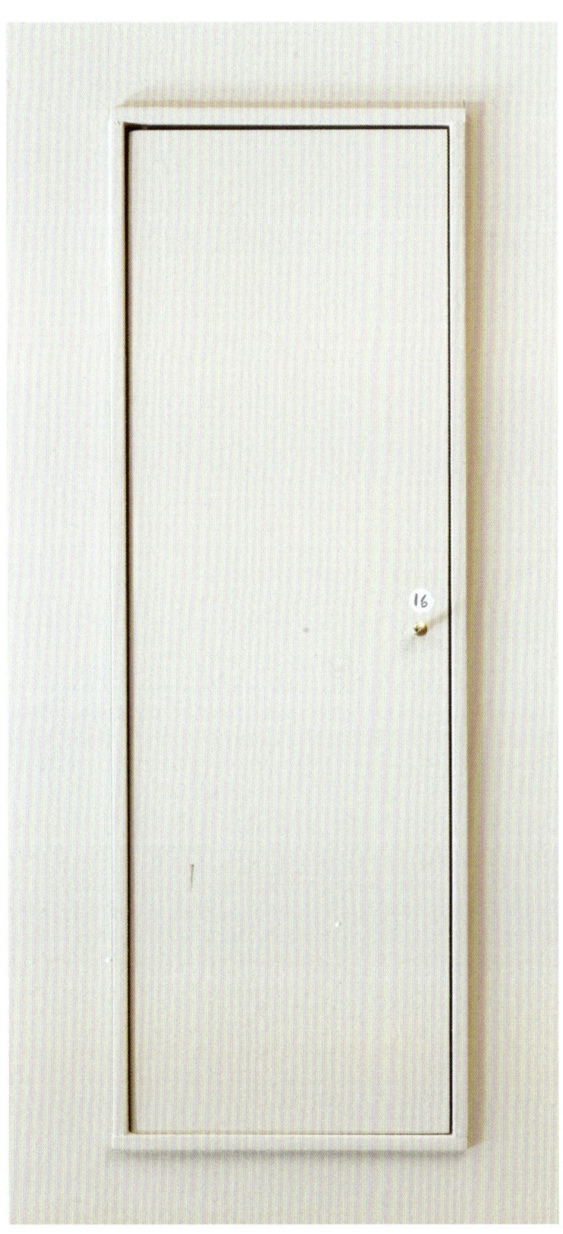 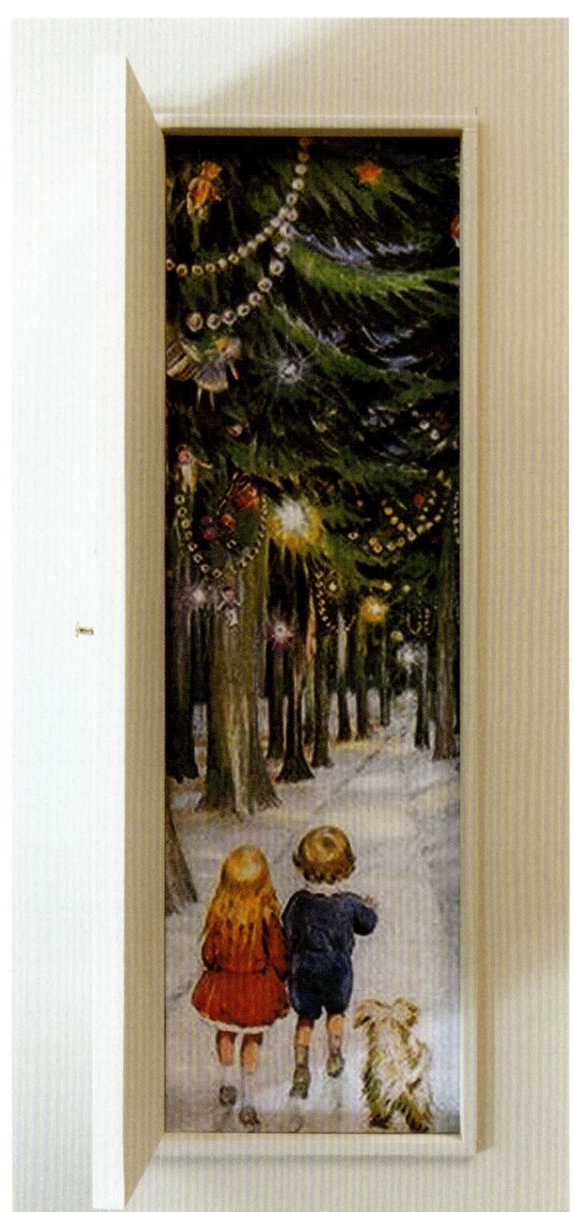

16.

With only nine days left until Christmas, this door opens to a print of two children in
a winter wonderland—with, of course, trees.

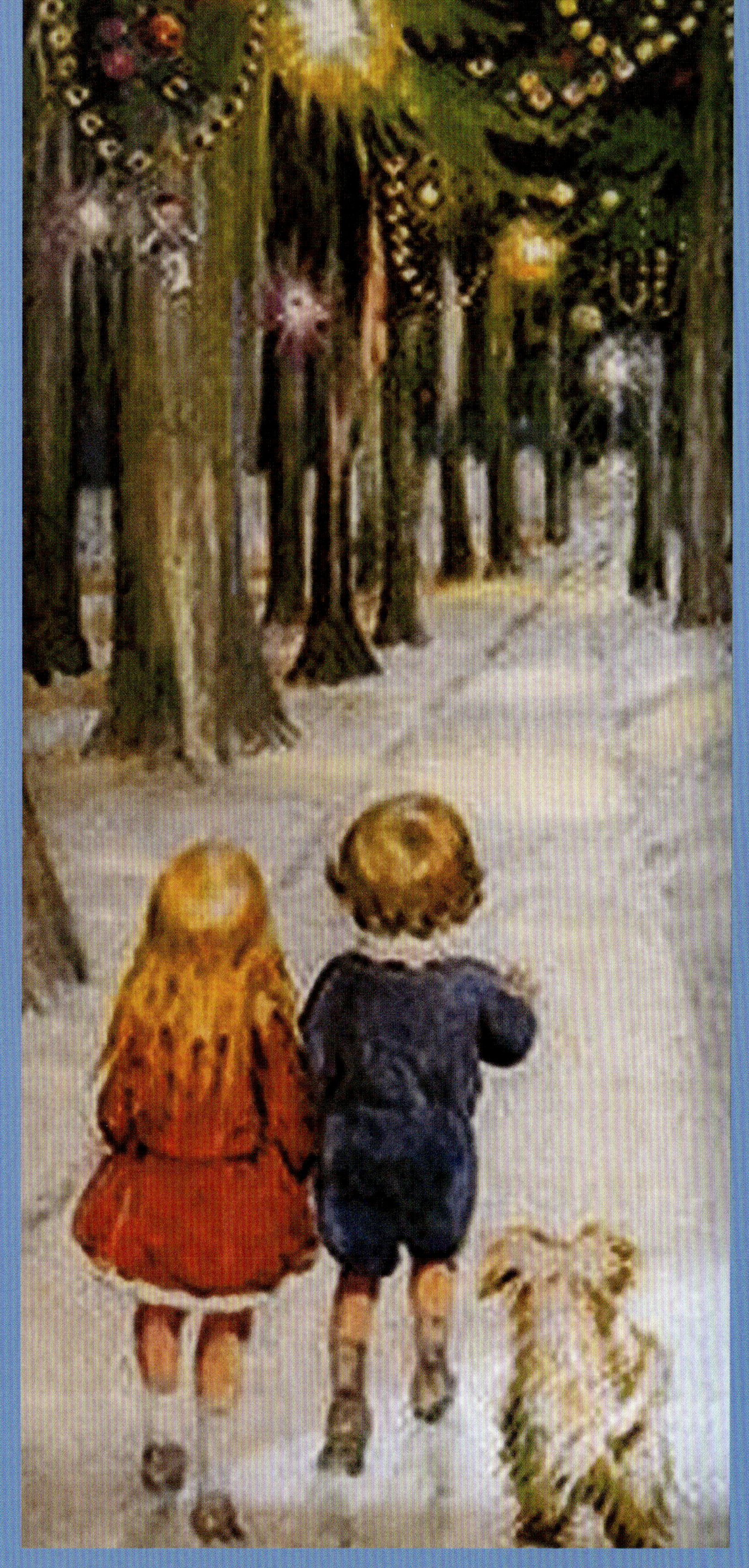

17.

This tiny door opens to the last of the family initials to be placed on the Christmas tree to commemorate this Advent house.

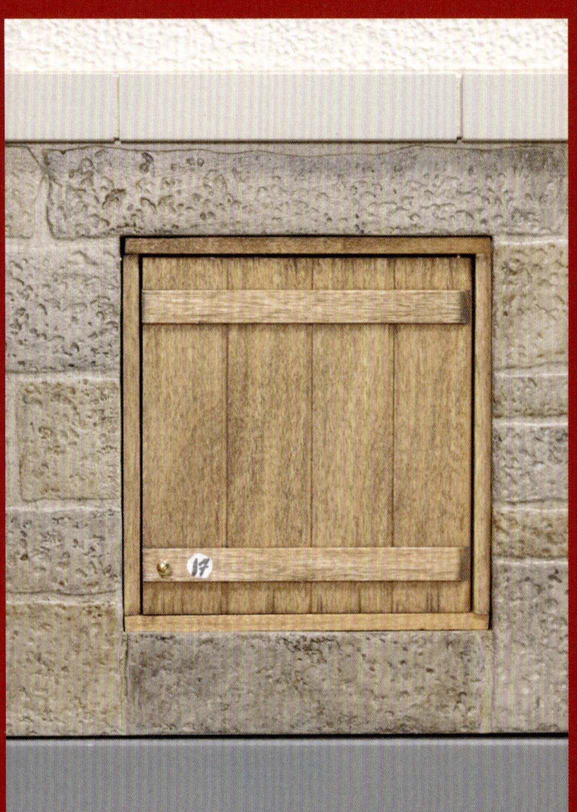

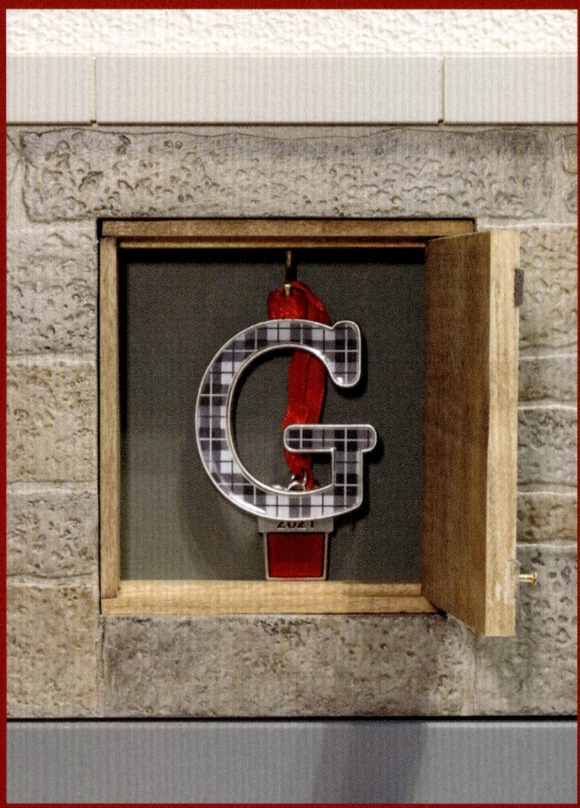

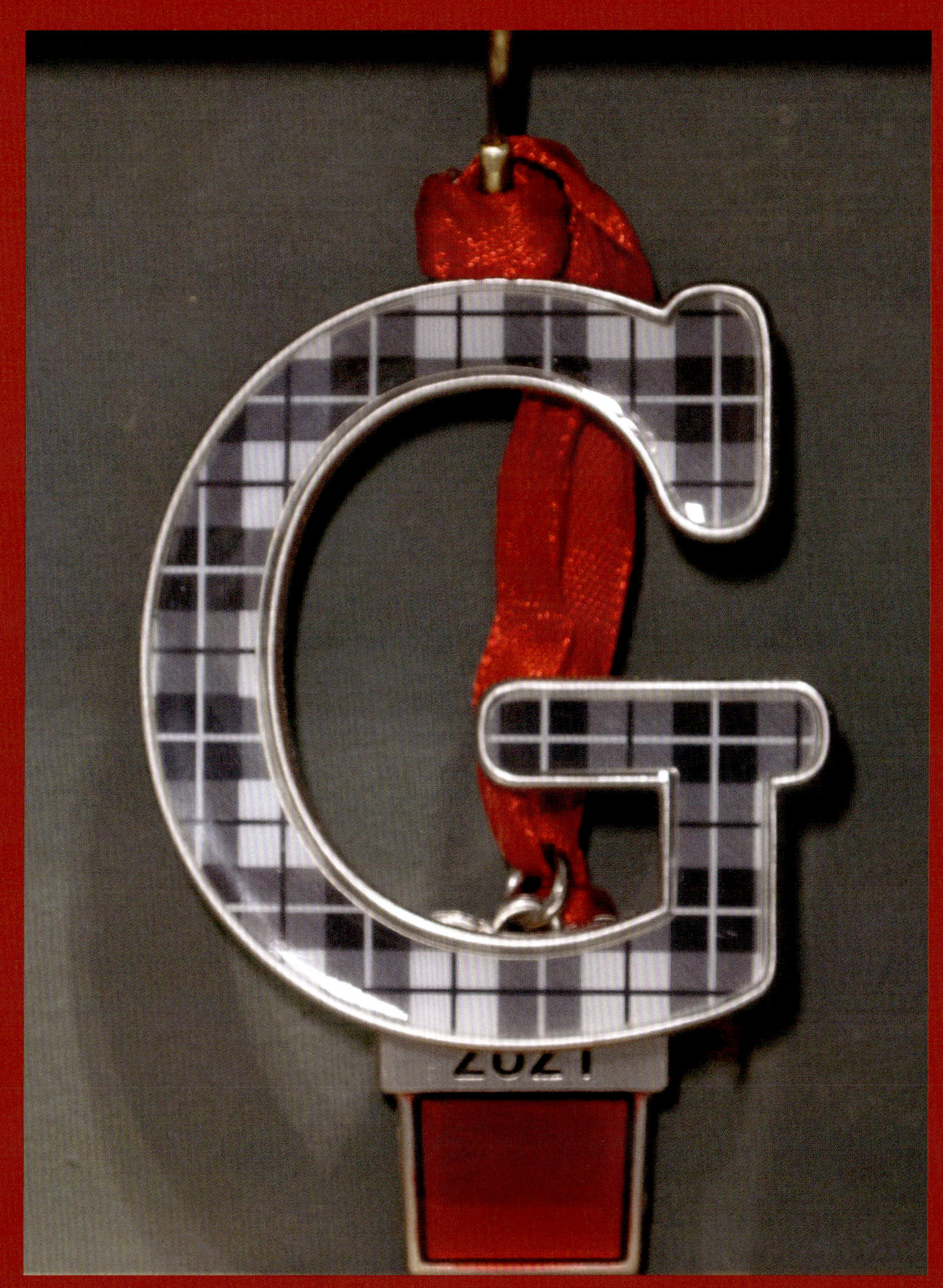

2021

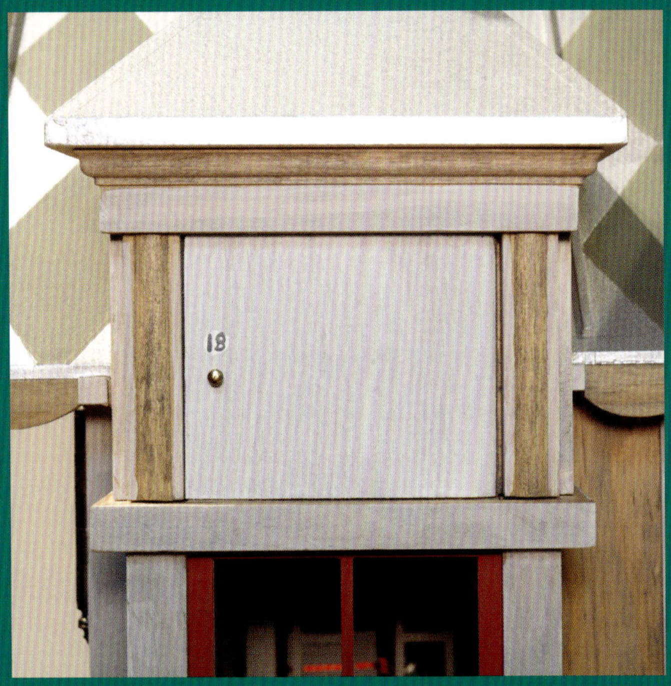

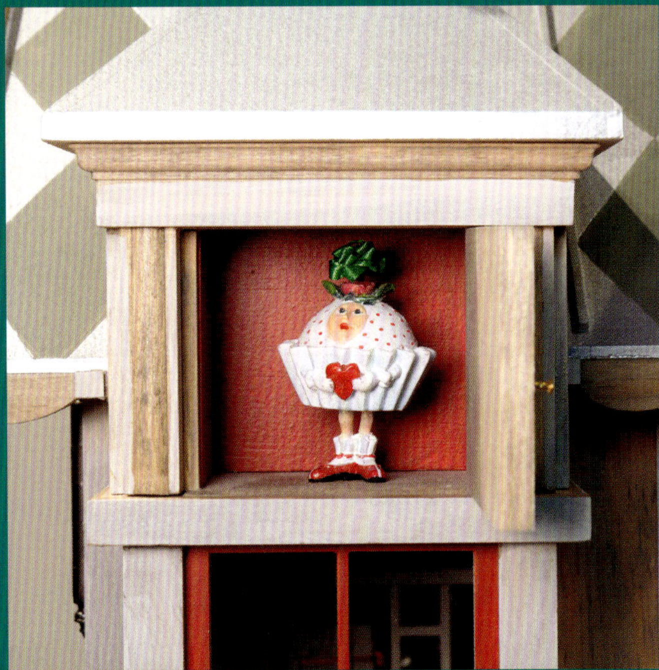

18.

This door is one of the hardest
to locate on the Emporium.
Once found (tucked above
a window), it opens to reveal a
vintage holiday cupcake.

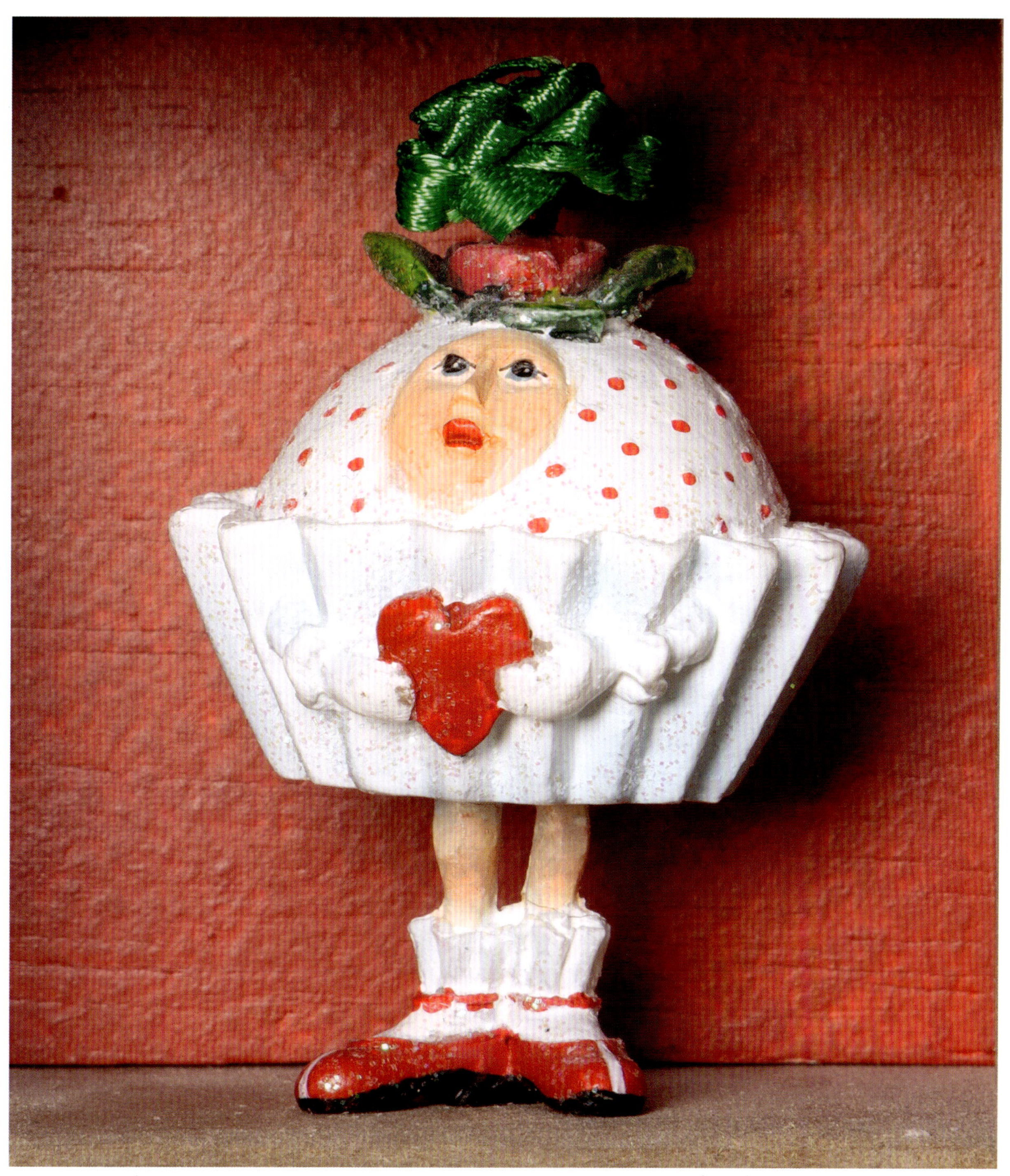

19.

Two sneaky elves are tucked into this doorway. They
each measure an inch tall, at most.

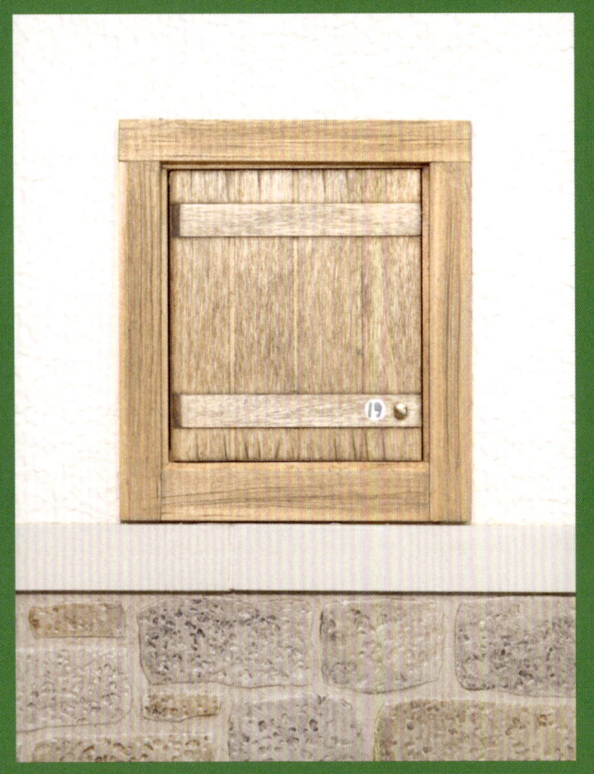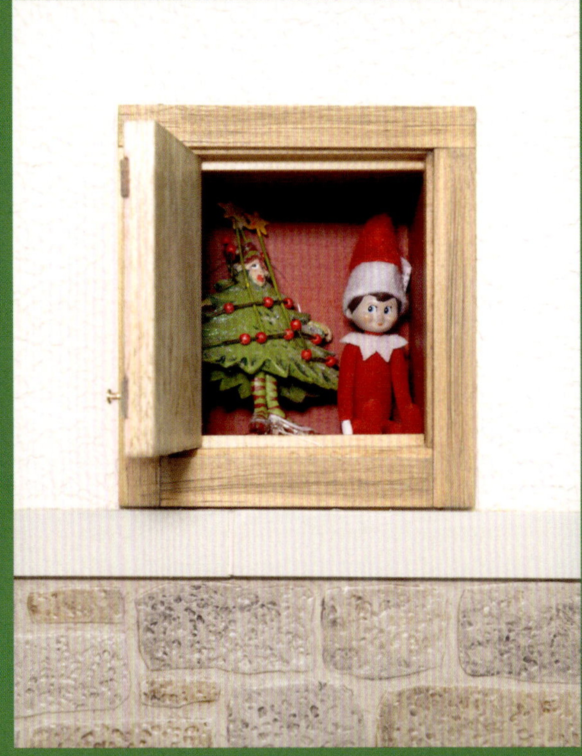

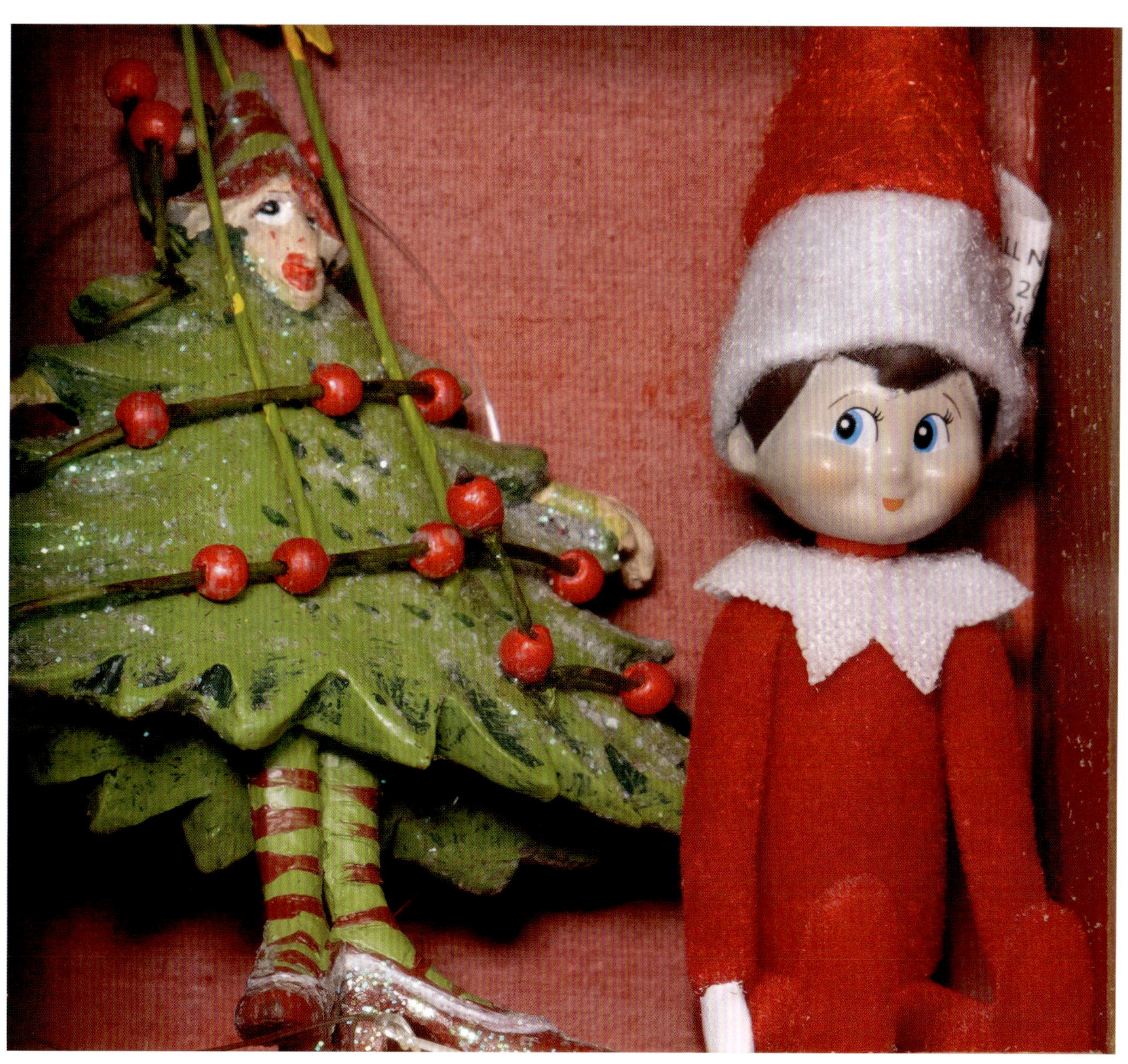

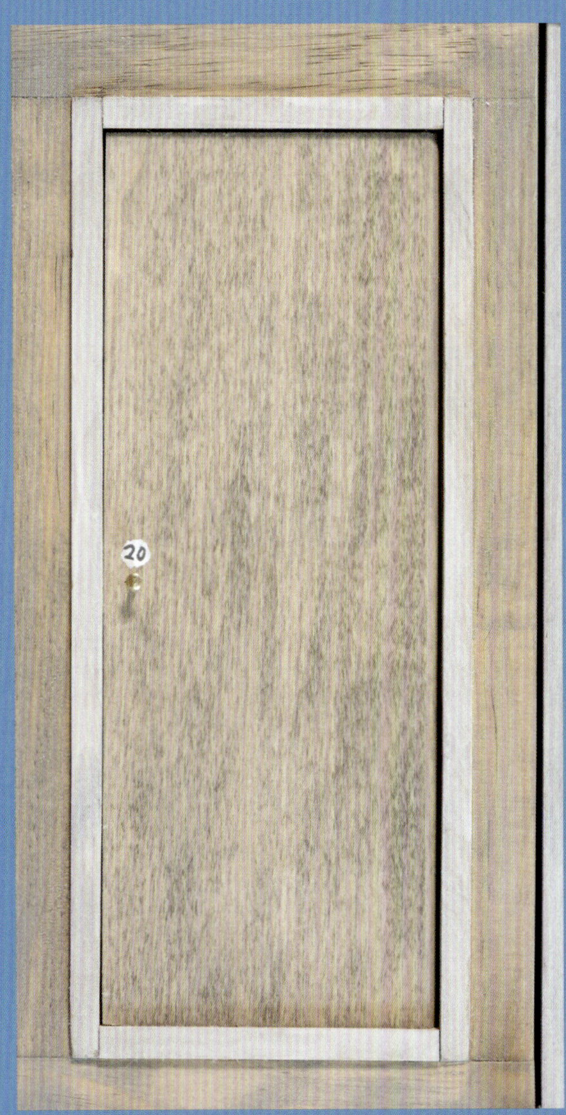 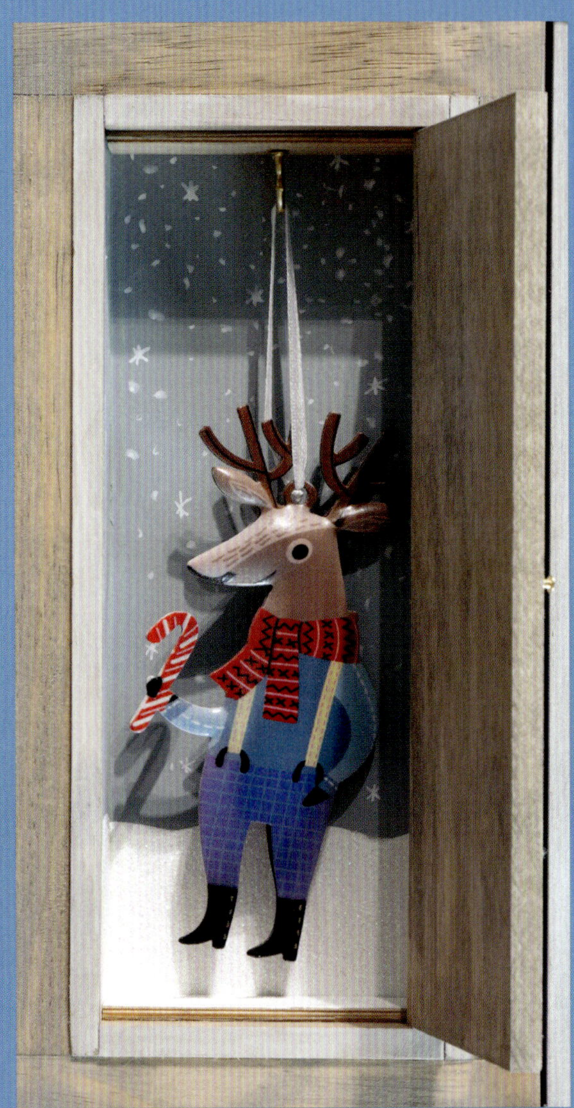

20.

This reindeer can be removed and placed on a large tree.
I must admit, though, that I have left these ornaments in
their doors for sentimental reasons. But maybe next year
the doors will open to reveal new items . . . .

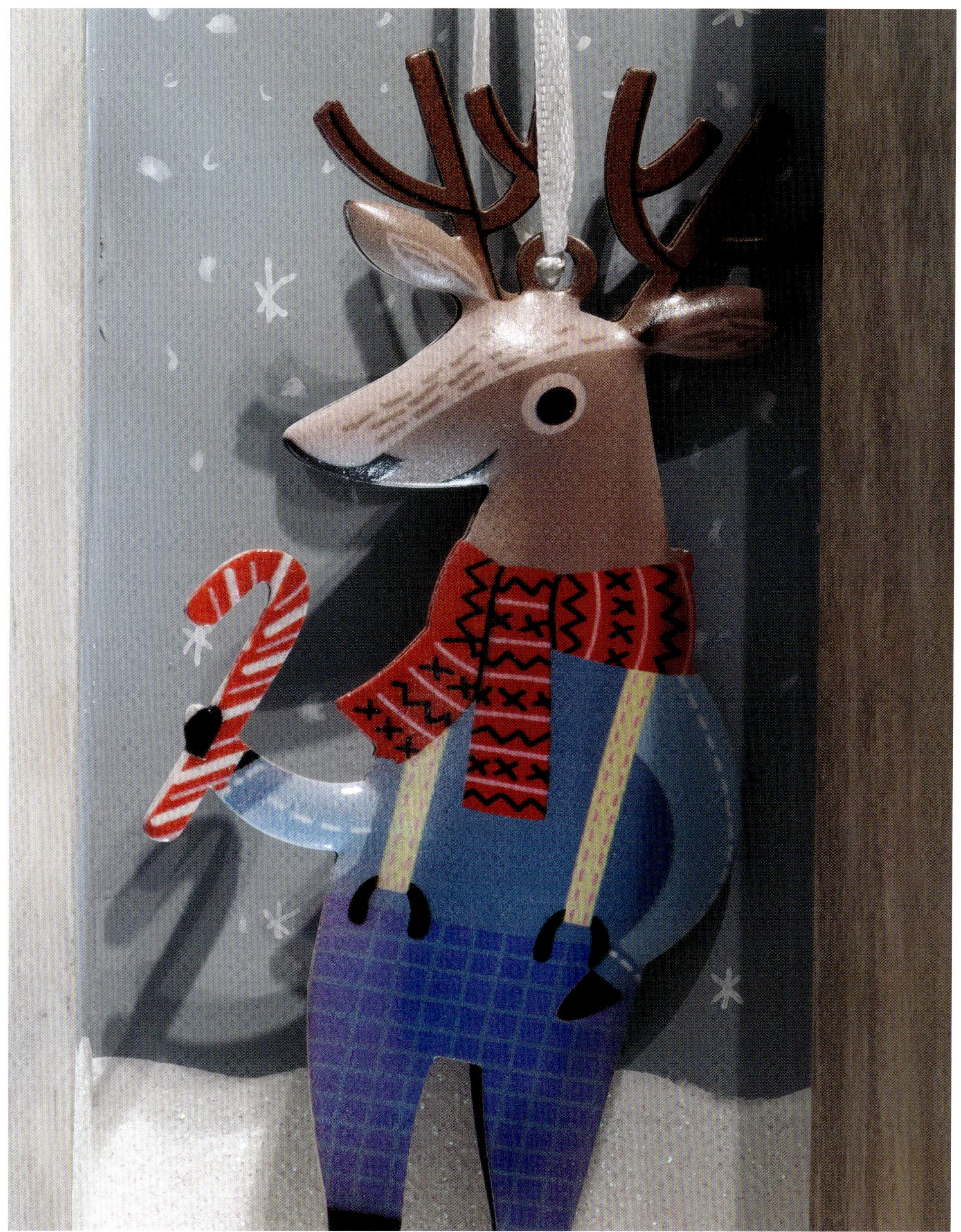

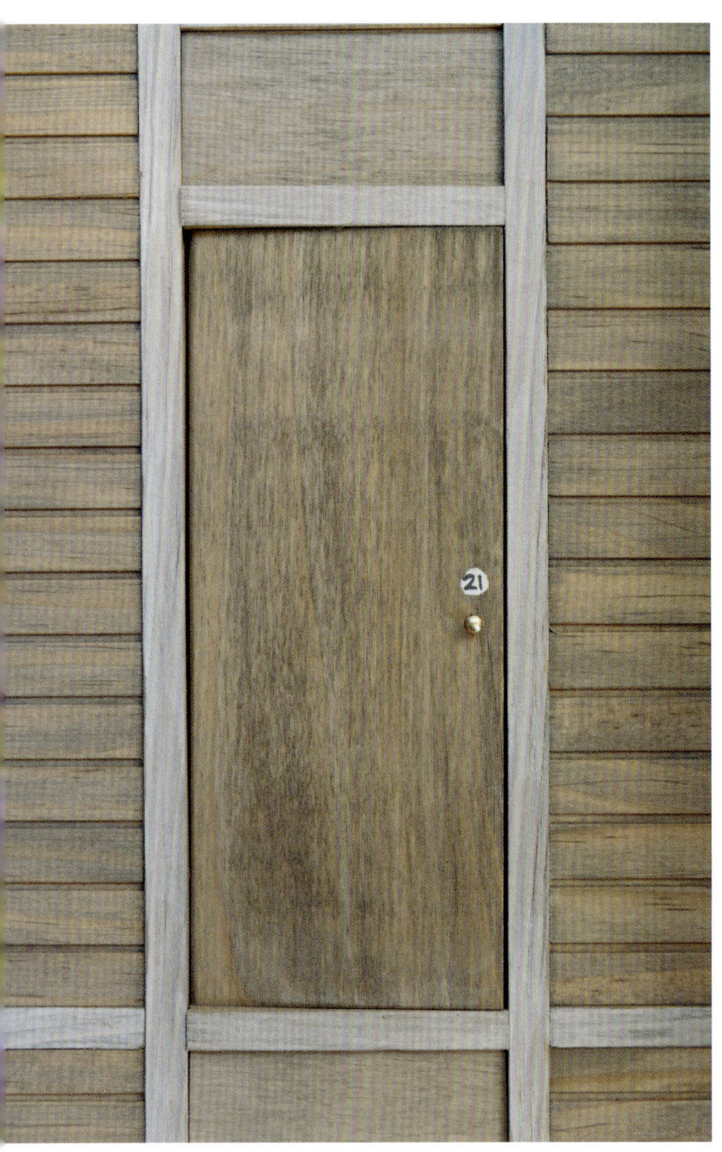 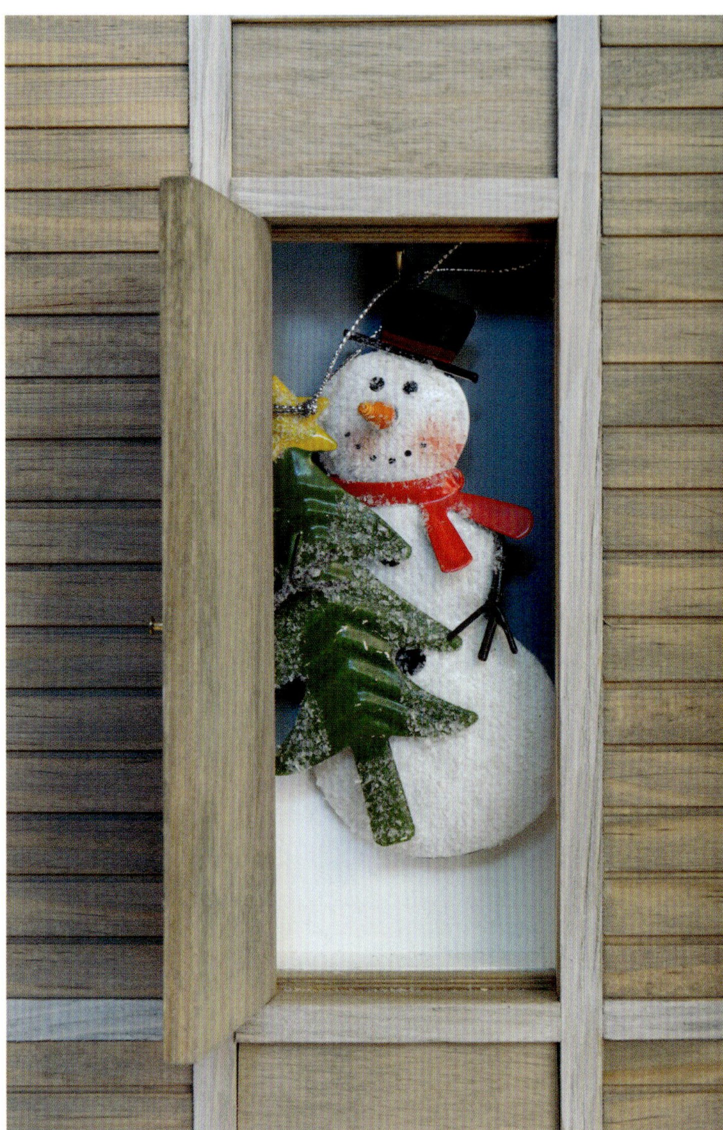

21.

A snowman fit for a large tree. Just like the other
ornaments, though, this one is staying put for now.

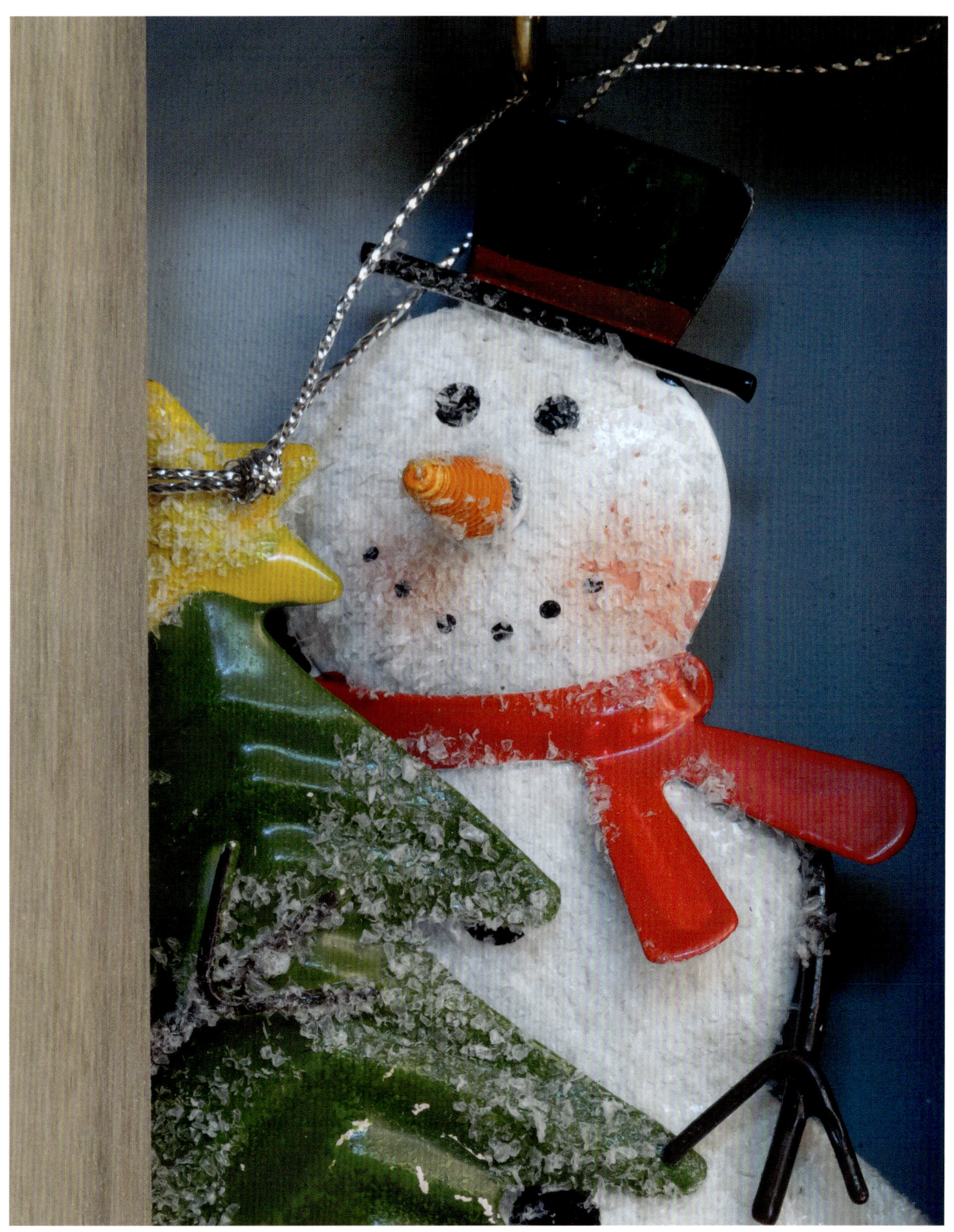

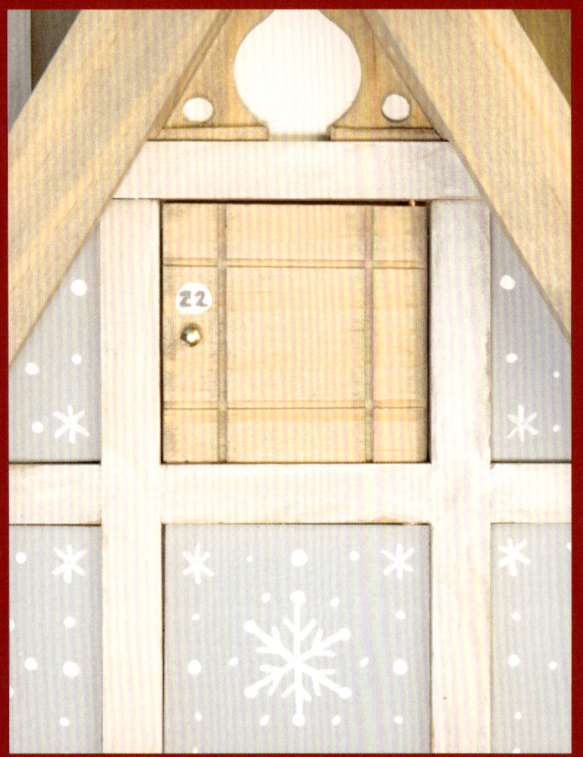 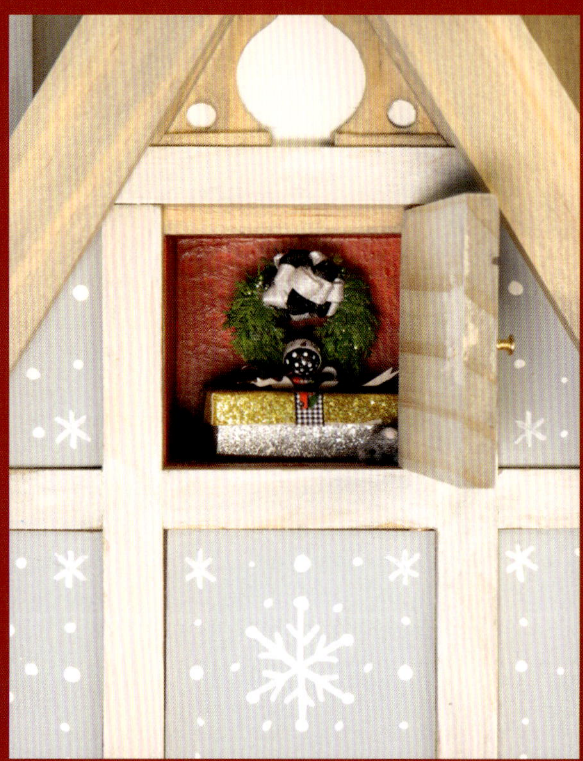

22.

A cute little stack of Christmas cheer sits behind door 22.
The package, wreath, and ornament are minis, of course,
but to give this some perspective, consider that the
ornament's size is only $3/8$ inch.

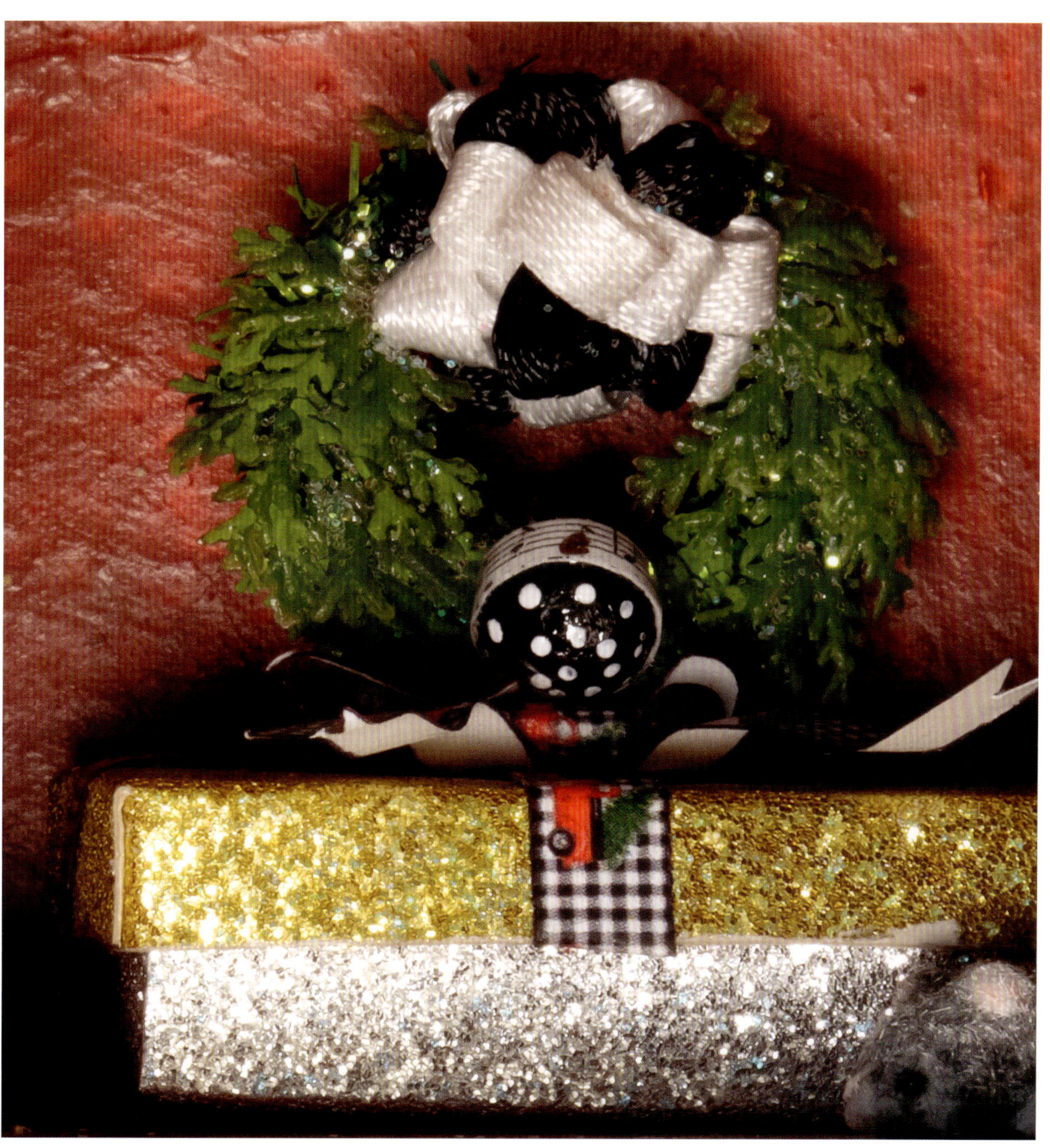

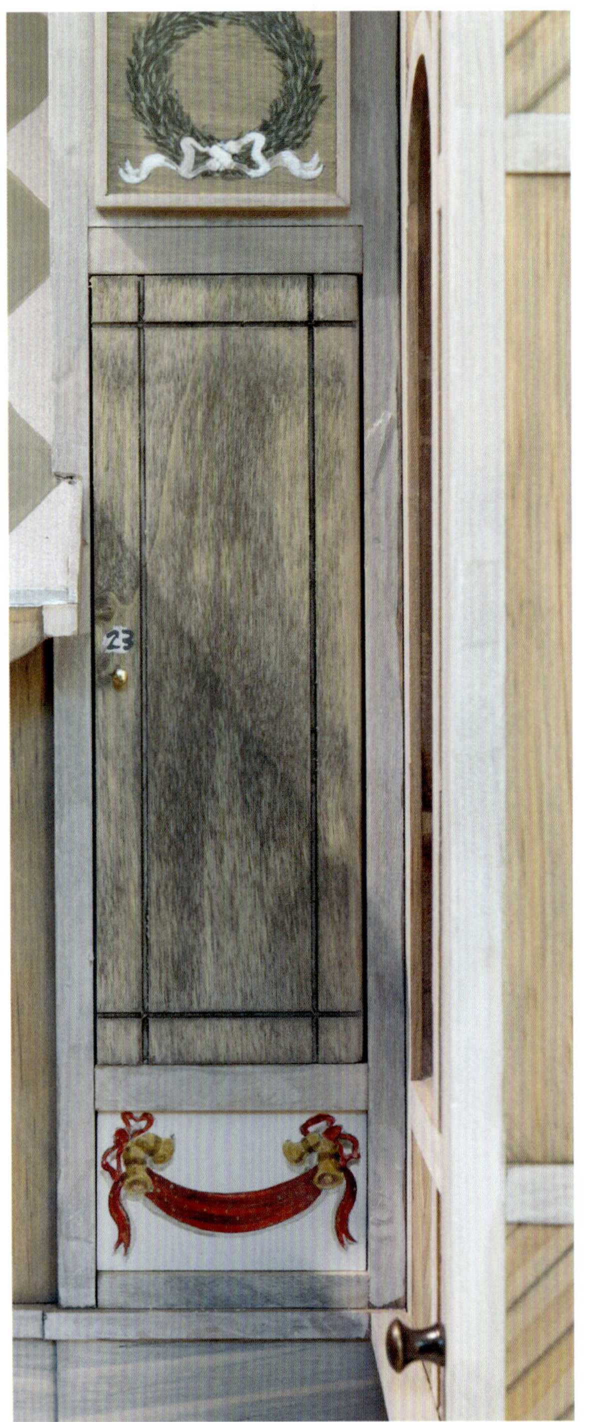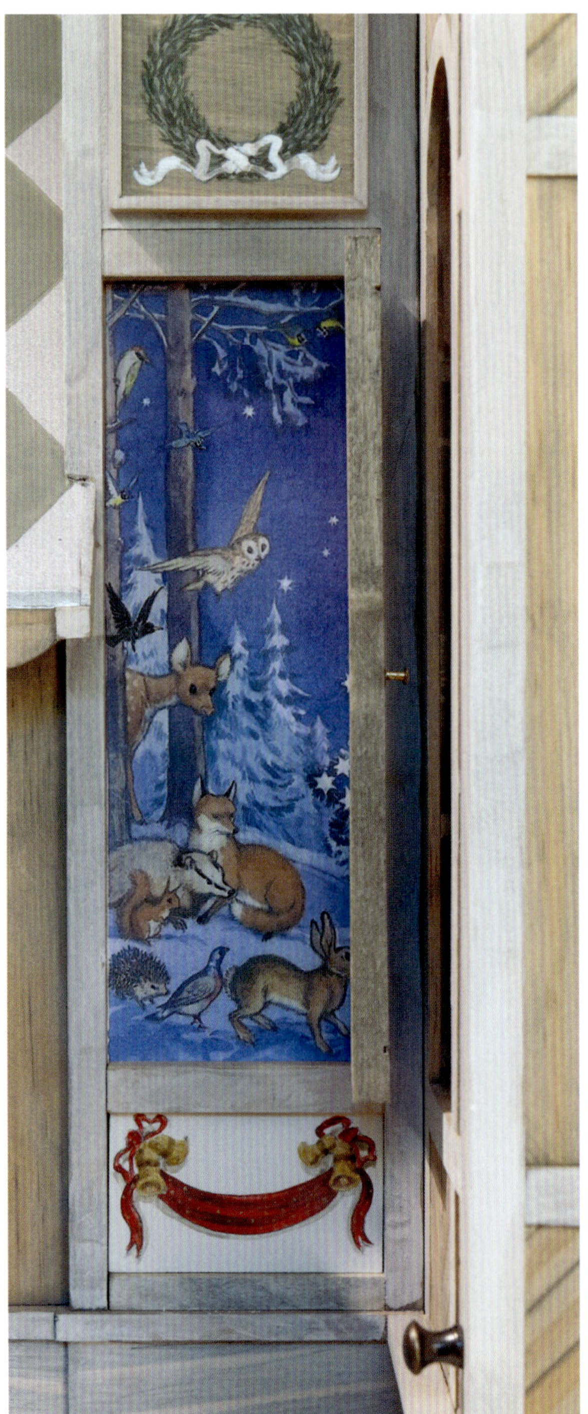

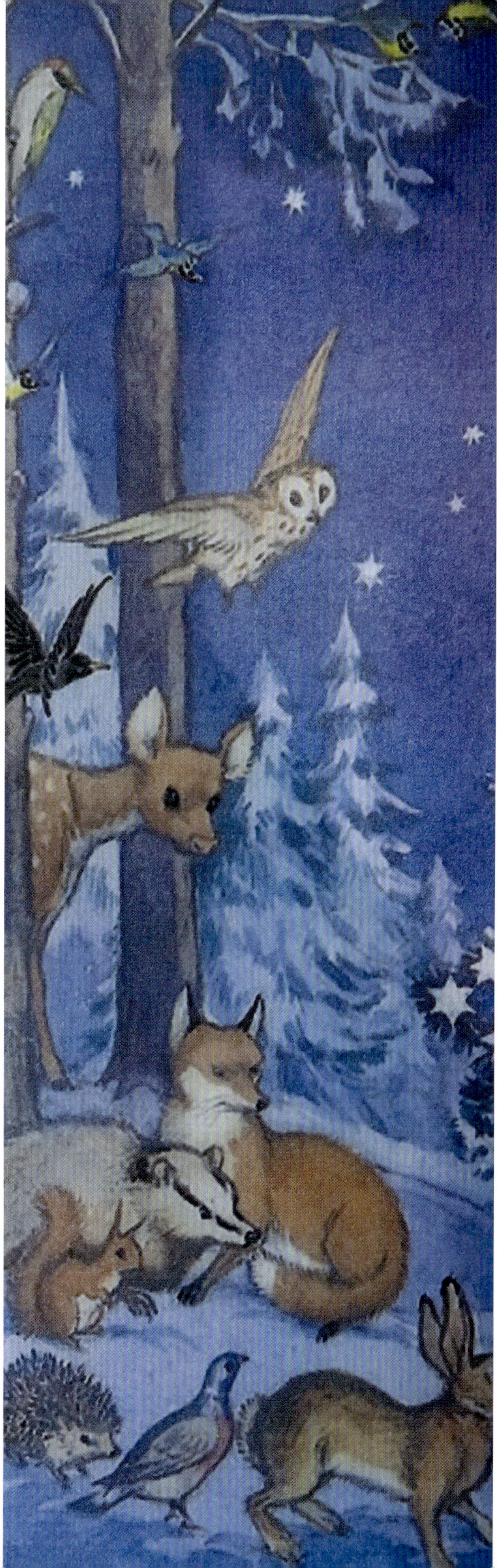

23.

This forest scene depicts the animals eagerly waiting for Christmas. And, of course, we see snow-covered trees.

24.

Hark! The Herald Angels Sing!

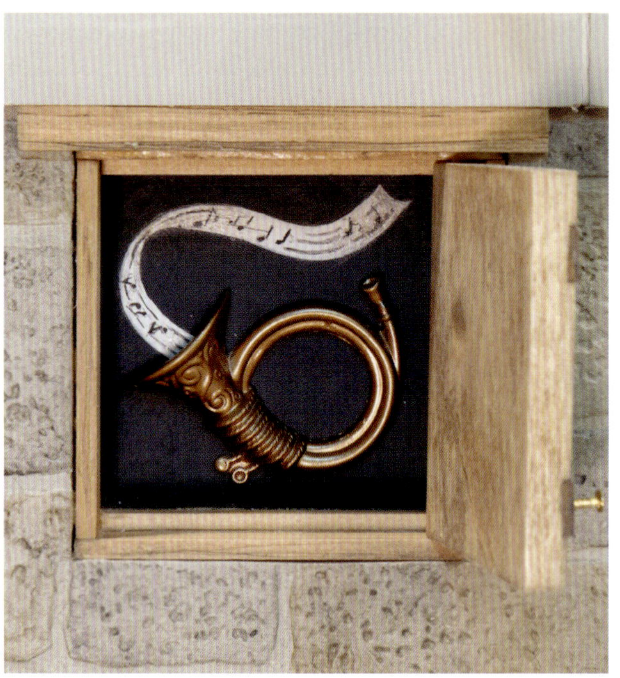

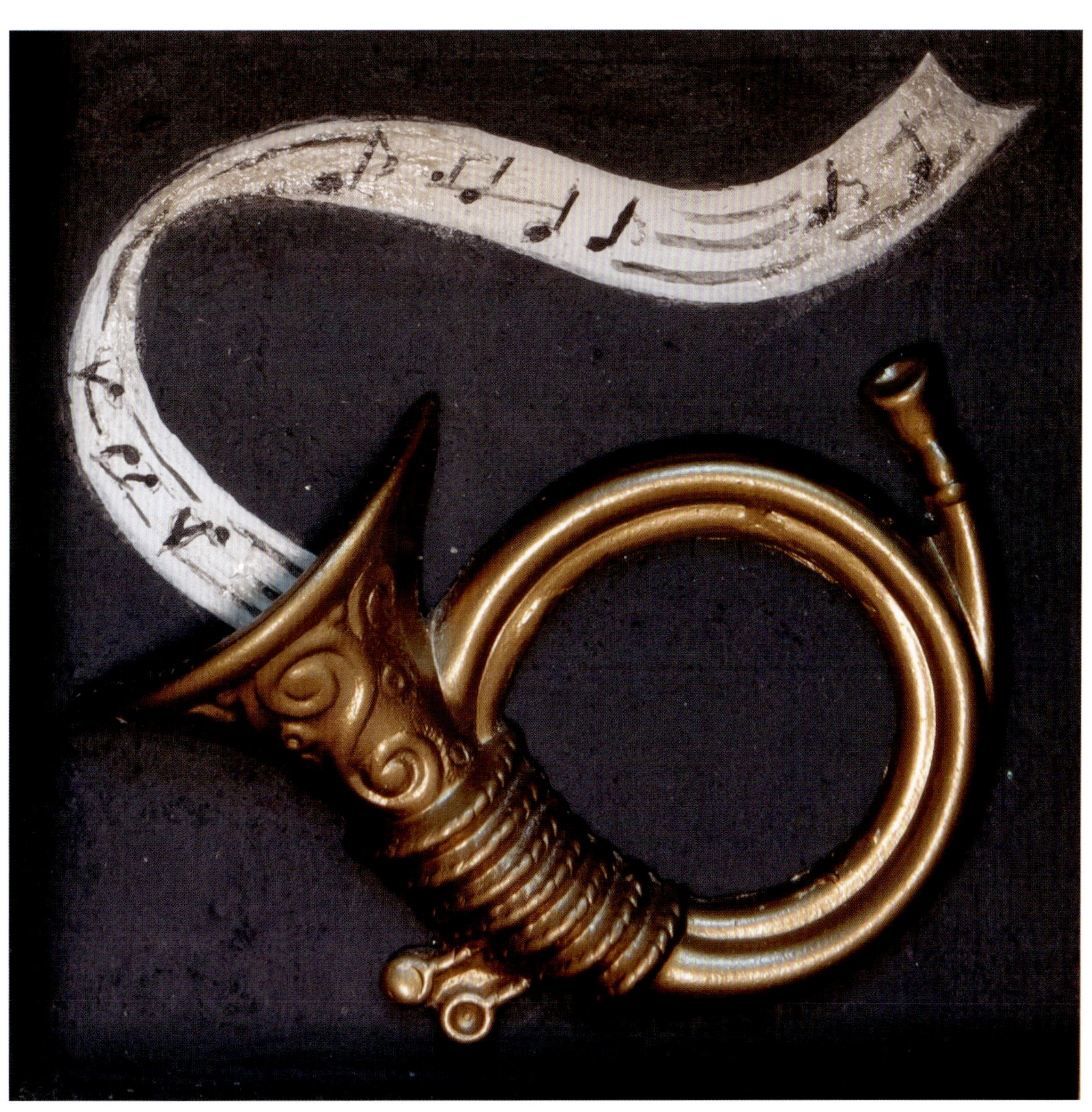

25.

The final day of the Advent calendar is positioned at the front of the Emporium and opens to a lighted nativity scene, beautifully handcrafted by Jon Fish.

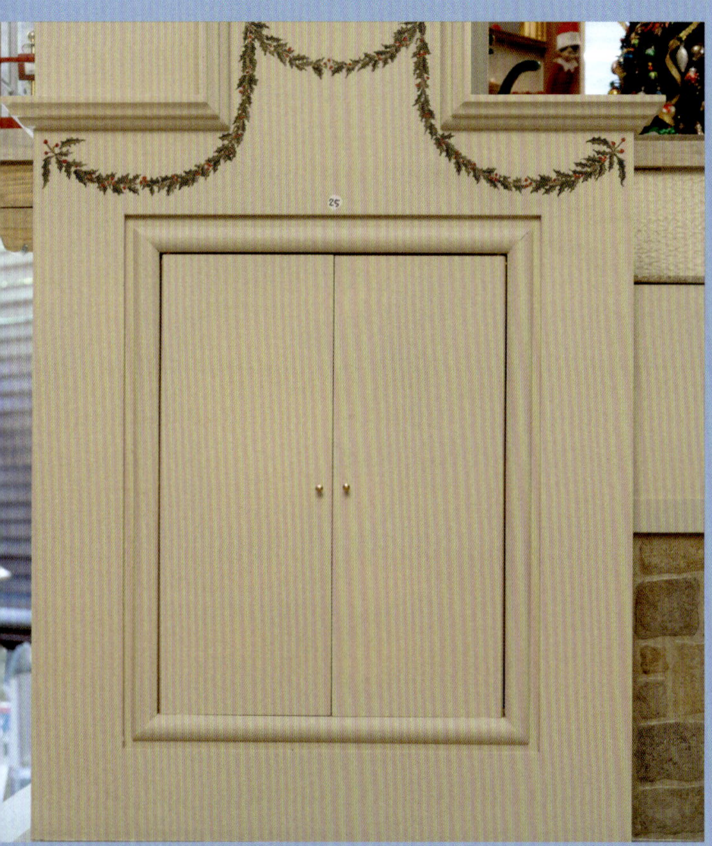

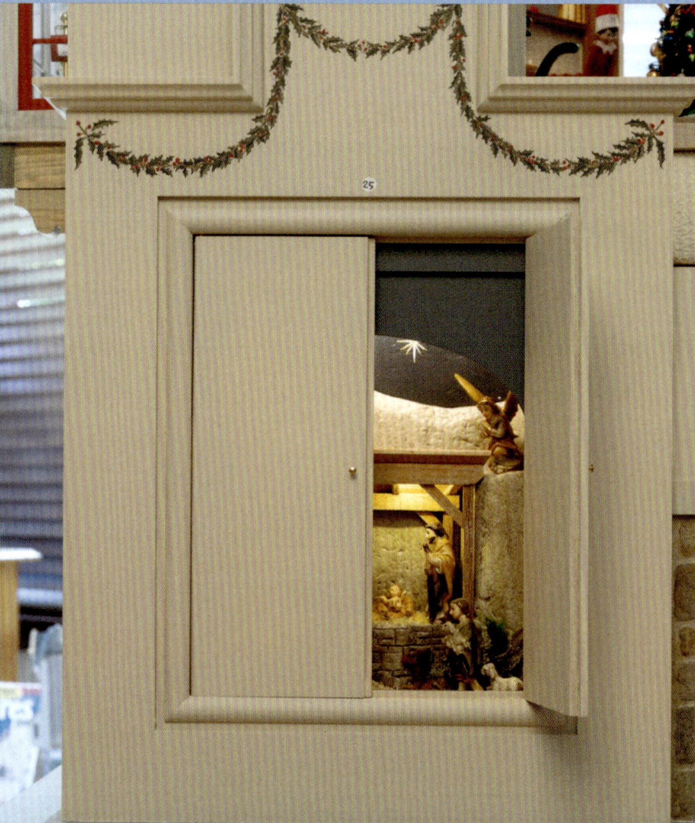

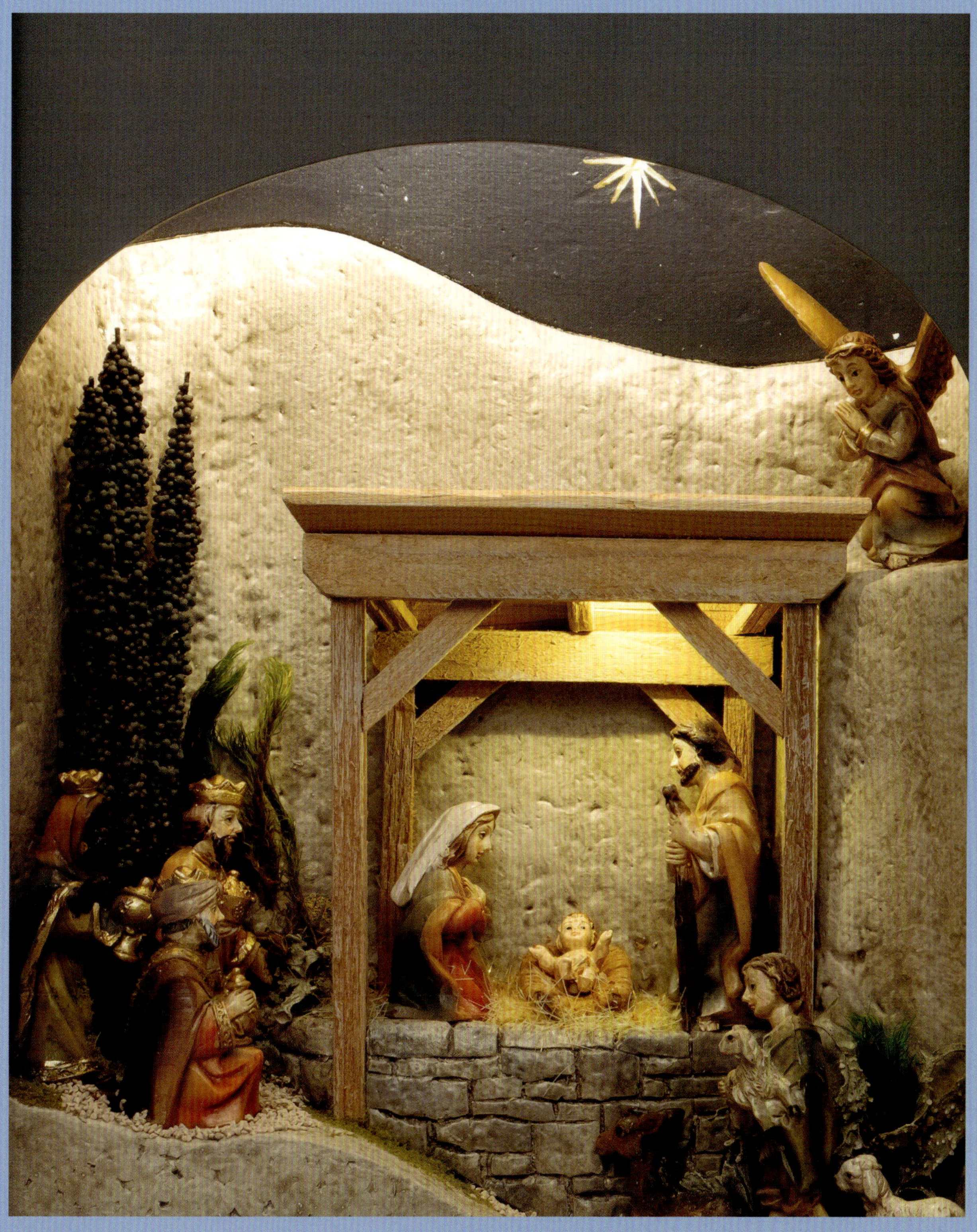

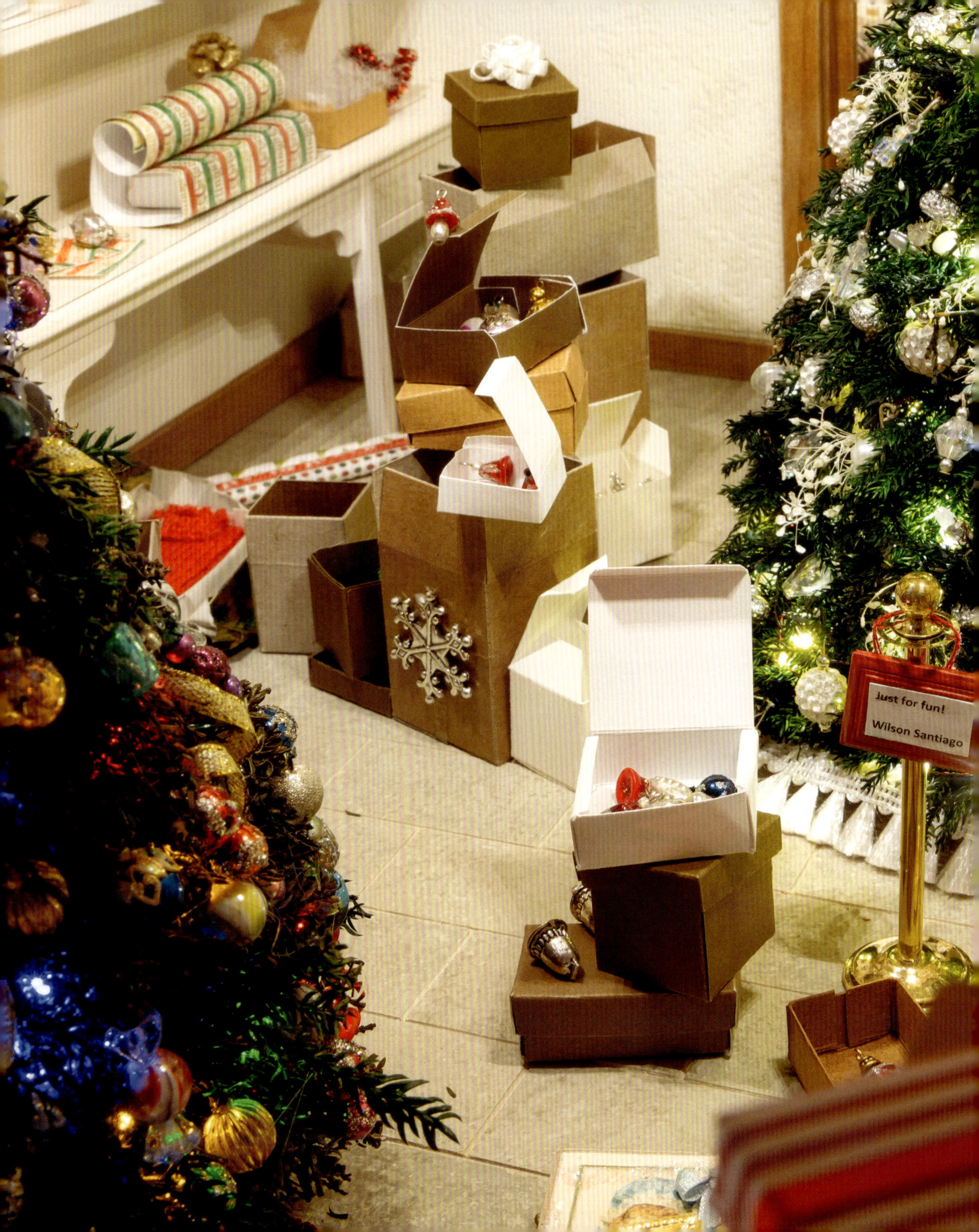

Just for fun!
Wilson Santiago

Santa's Workshop & Office

The lowest level of the Emporium features
a full workshop and office. The office is filled with
wrapping, boxes, supplies, and packages . . . and,
of course, two trees. Here are elves and ornaments
as well as toys ready to be wrapped. Wrapping
paper, scissors, and tape sit on the shelves.

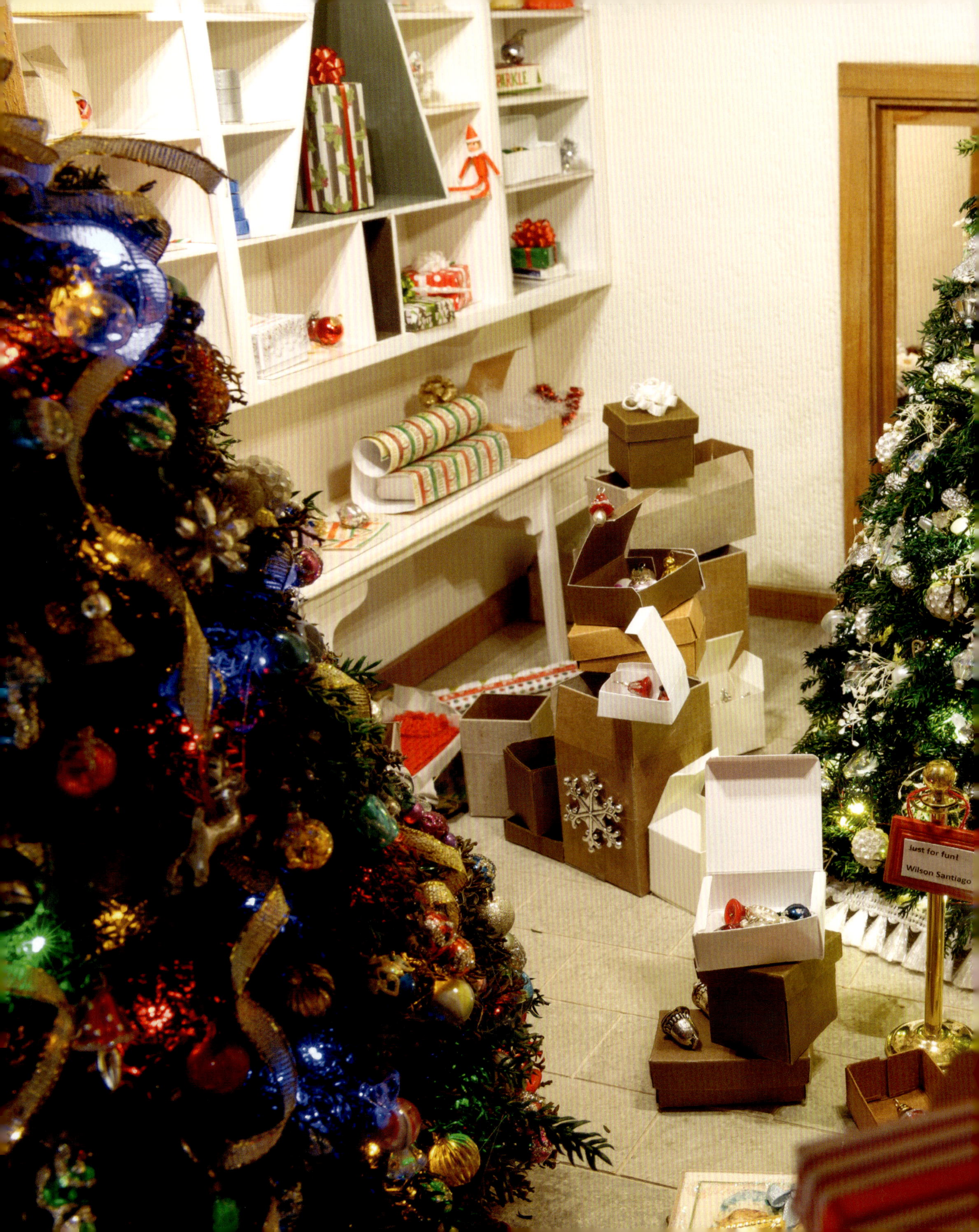

just for fun!
Wilson Santiago

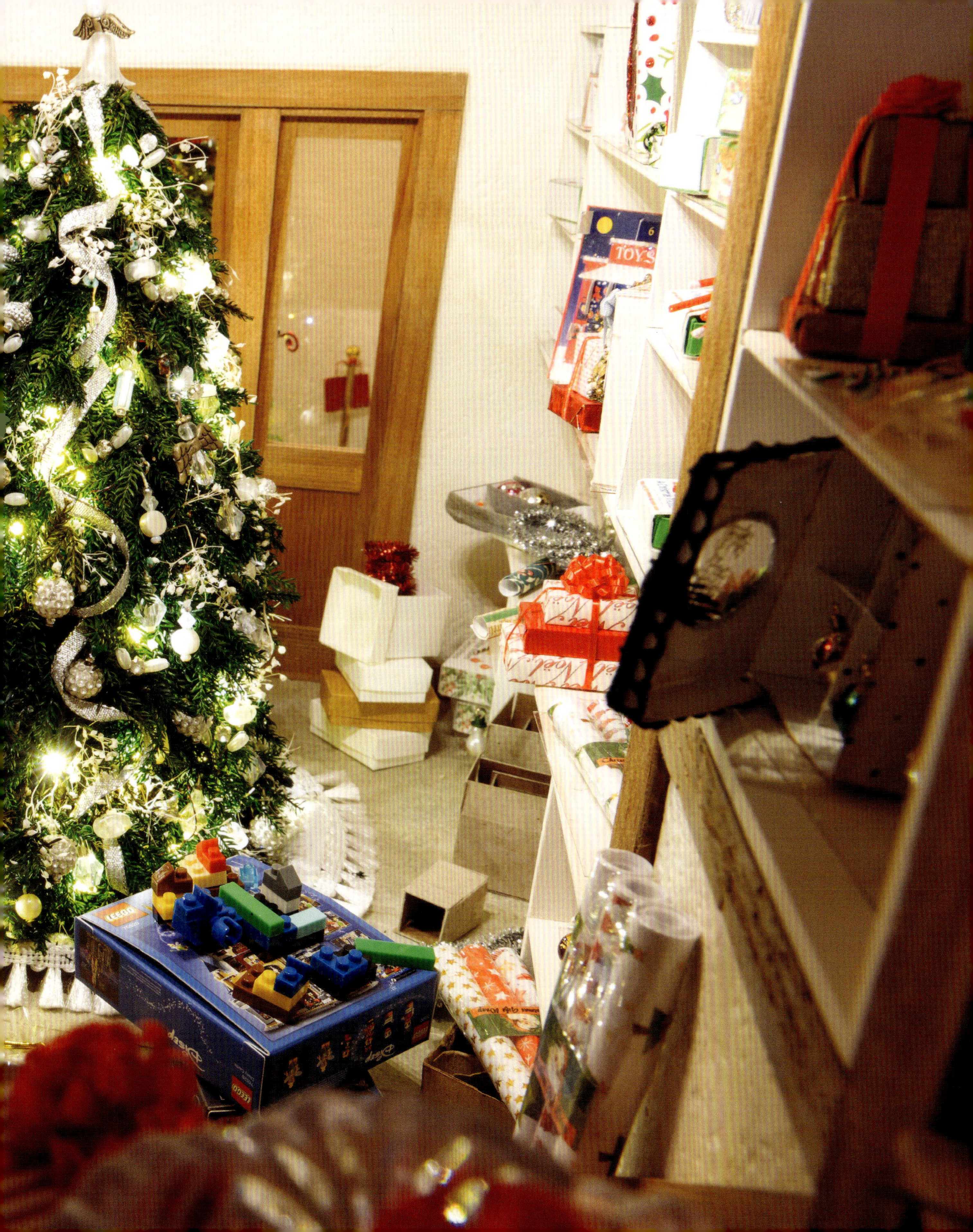

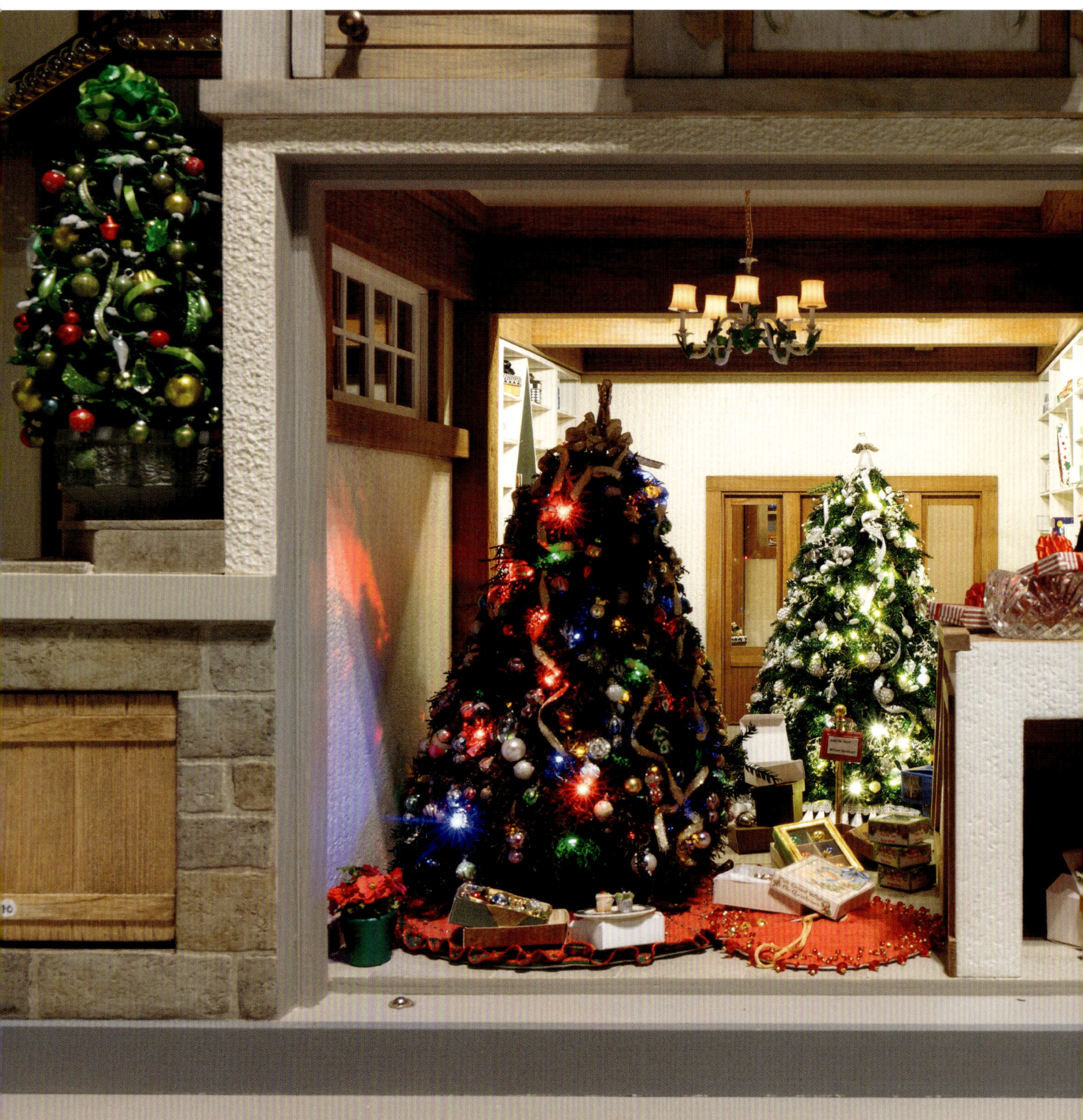

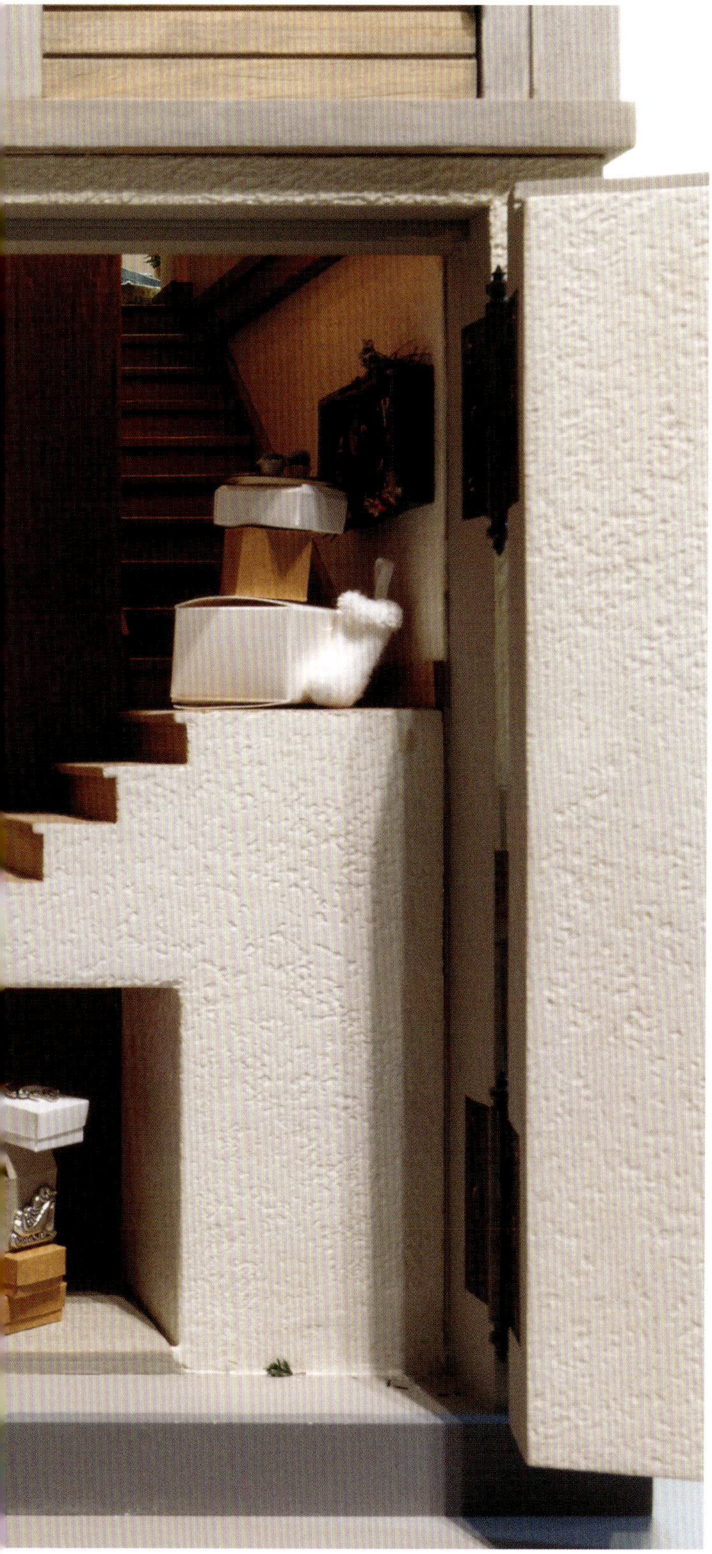

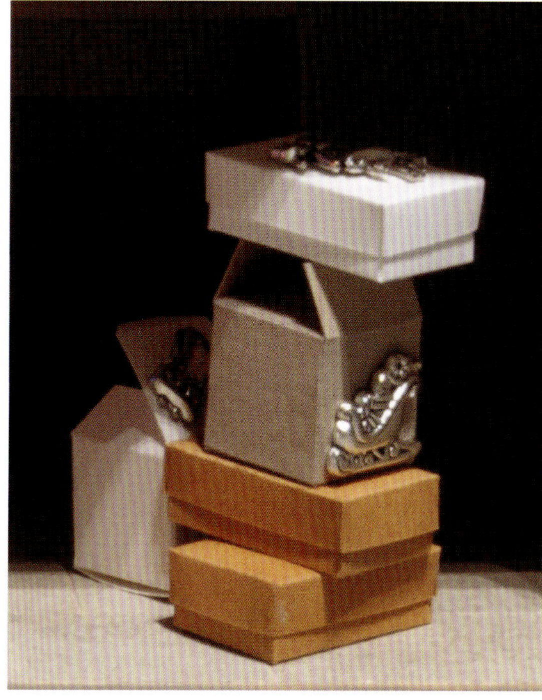

✳ The workshop trees add delightful
clutter to the workroom. Boxes ready
to ship and boxes to be packed are
on and under the stairwells. There
are approximately six hundred
ornaments on each tree in this room.

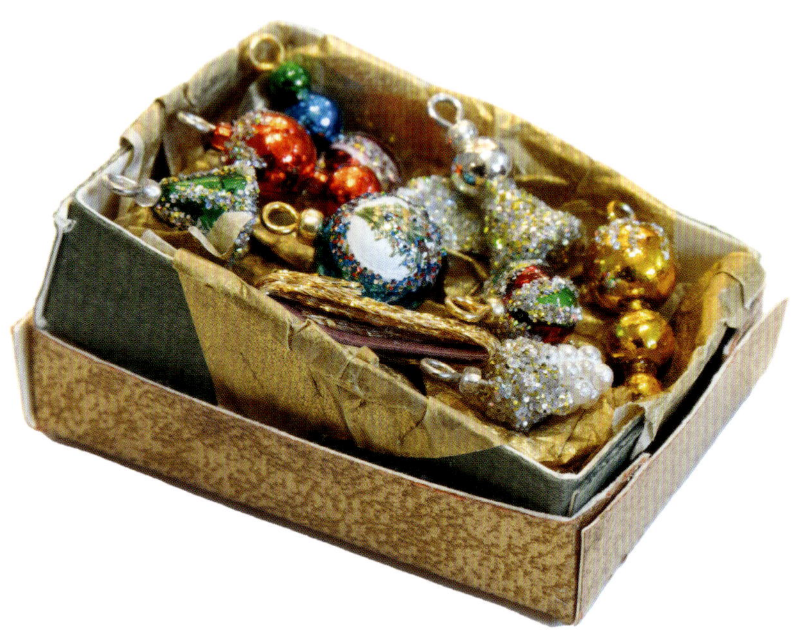

* Trees and boxes of ornaments fill the workshop.
A plate of treats has been set out for the hungry team
of elves, as well.

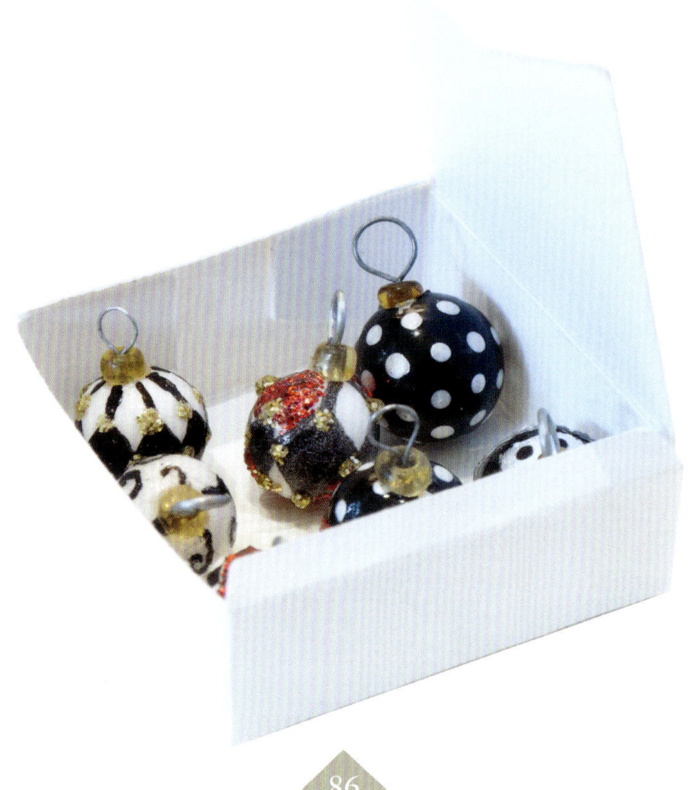

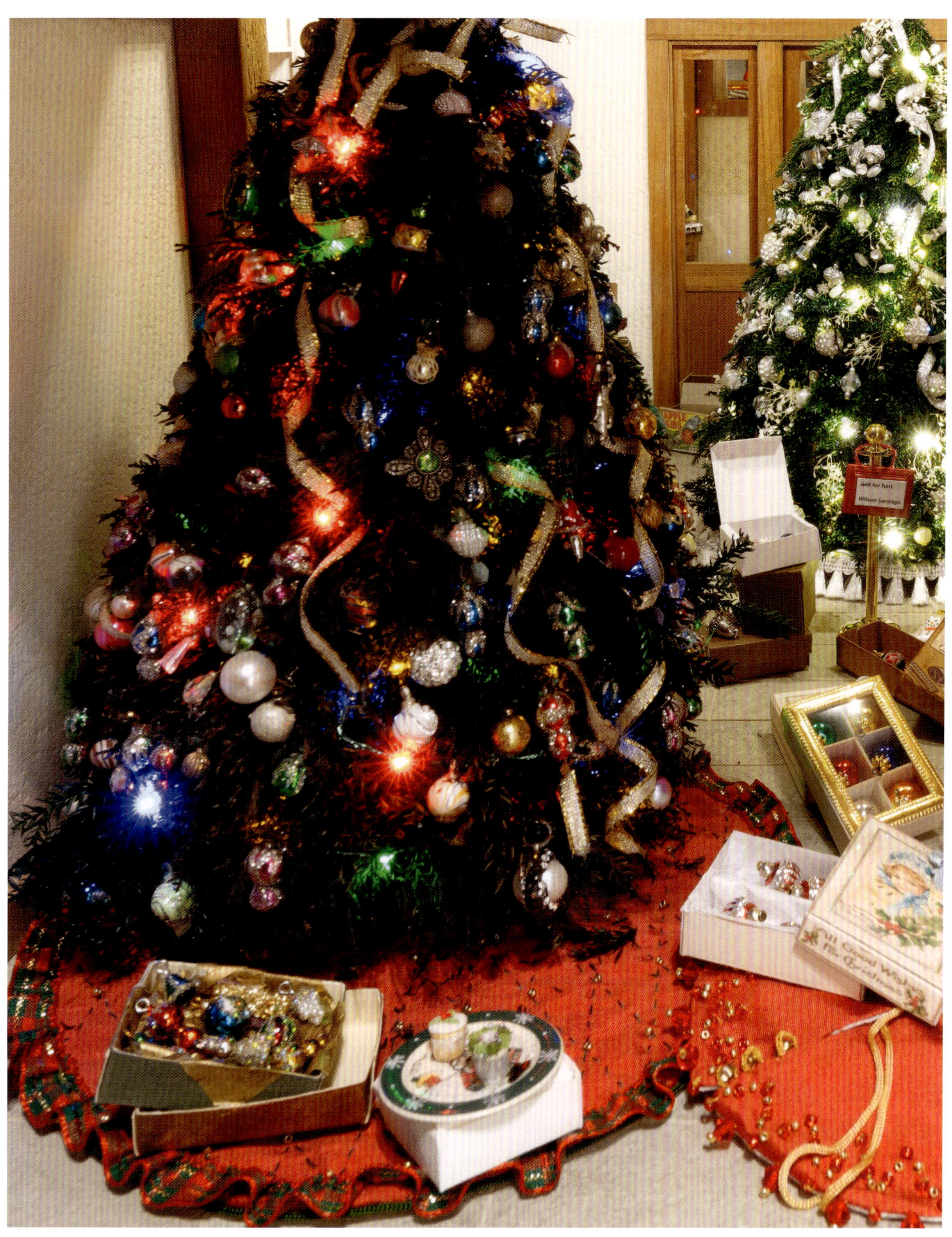

*In Santa's workshop
far away,
ten little elves work
night and day.*

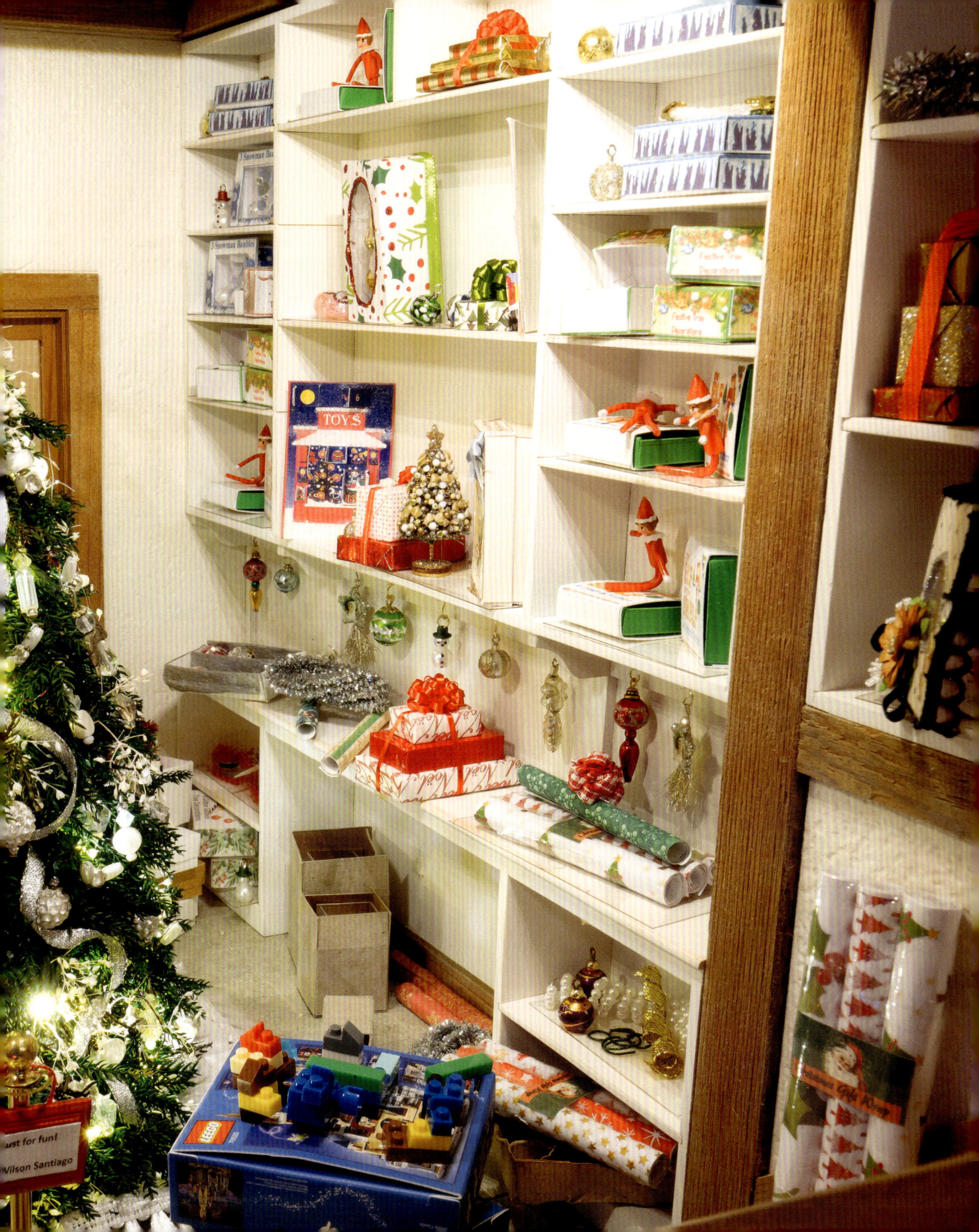
ust for fun!
Wilson Santiago

The office is located on the other side of the workshop. It is filled with coordinated packages, supplies, a Christmas-themed Charlotte Hunt stove, and a whimsical tree.

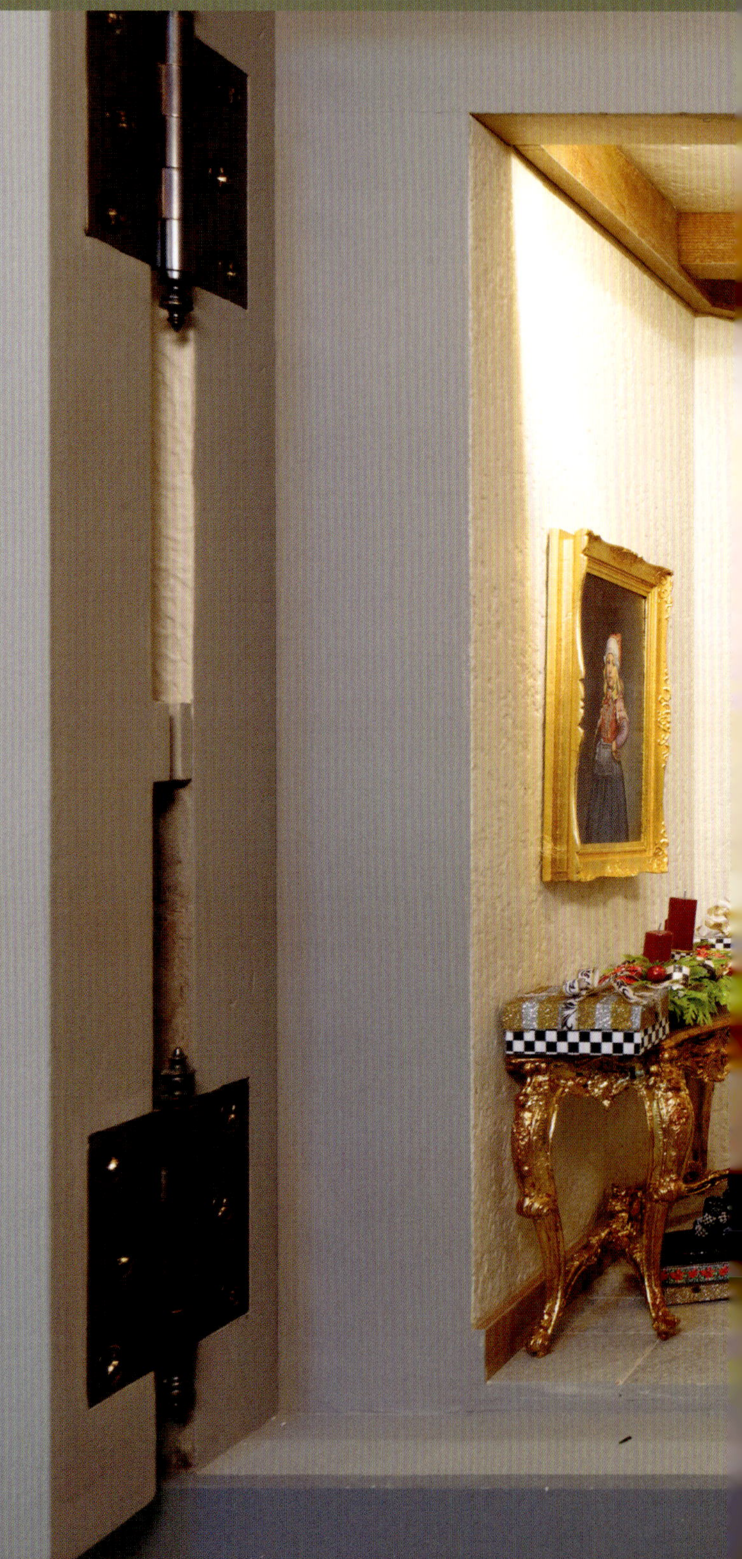

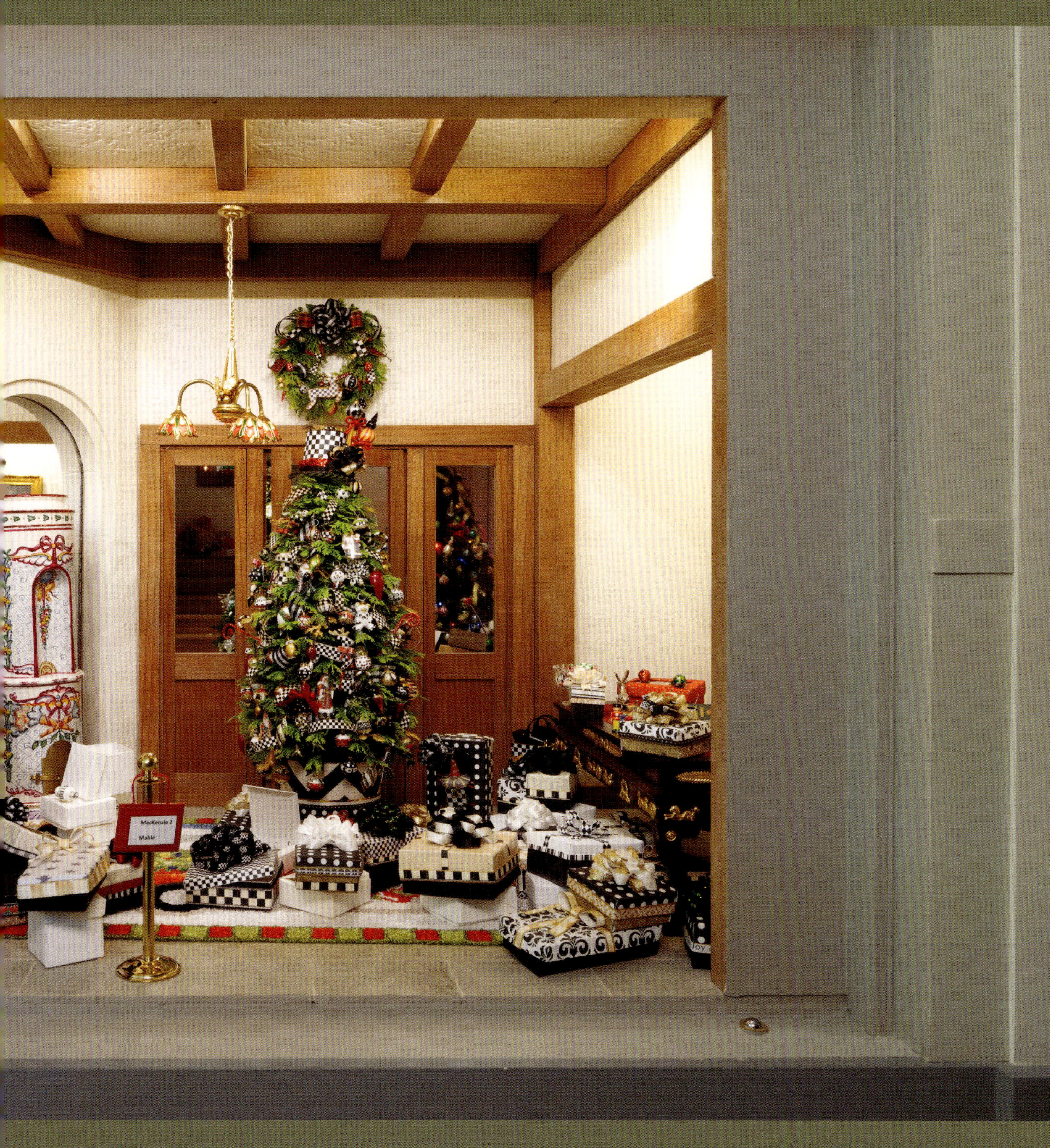

MacKenzie 2
Mable

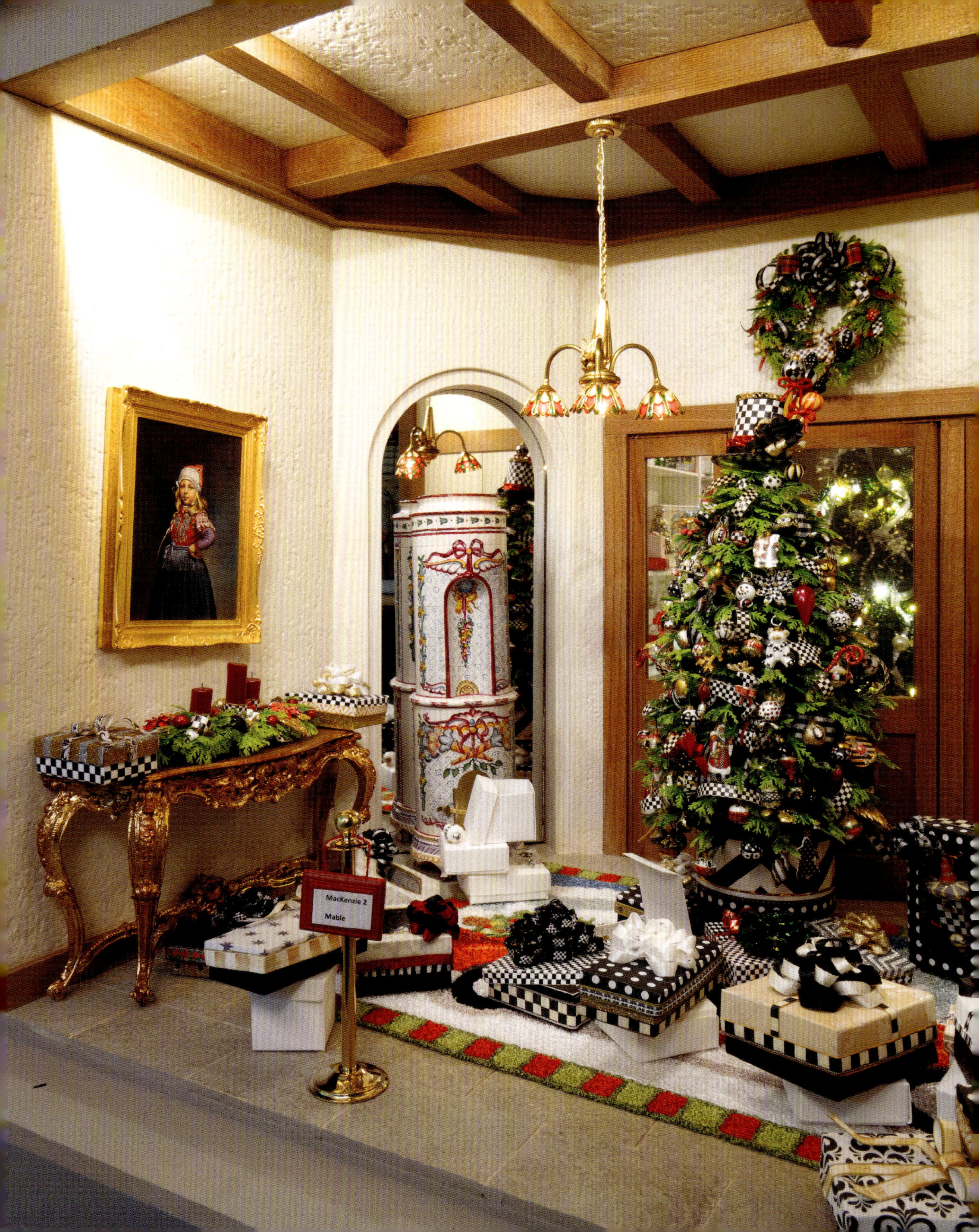

MacKenzie 2
Mable

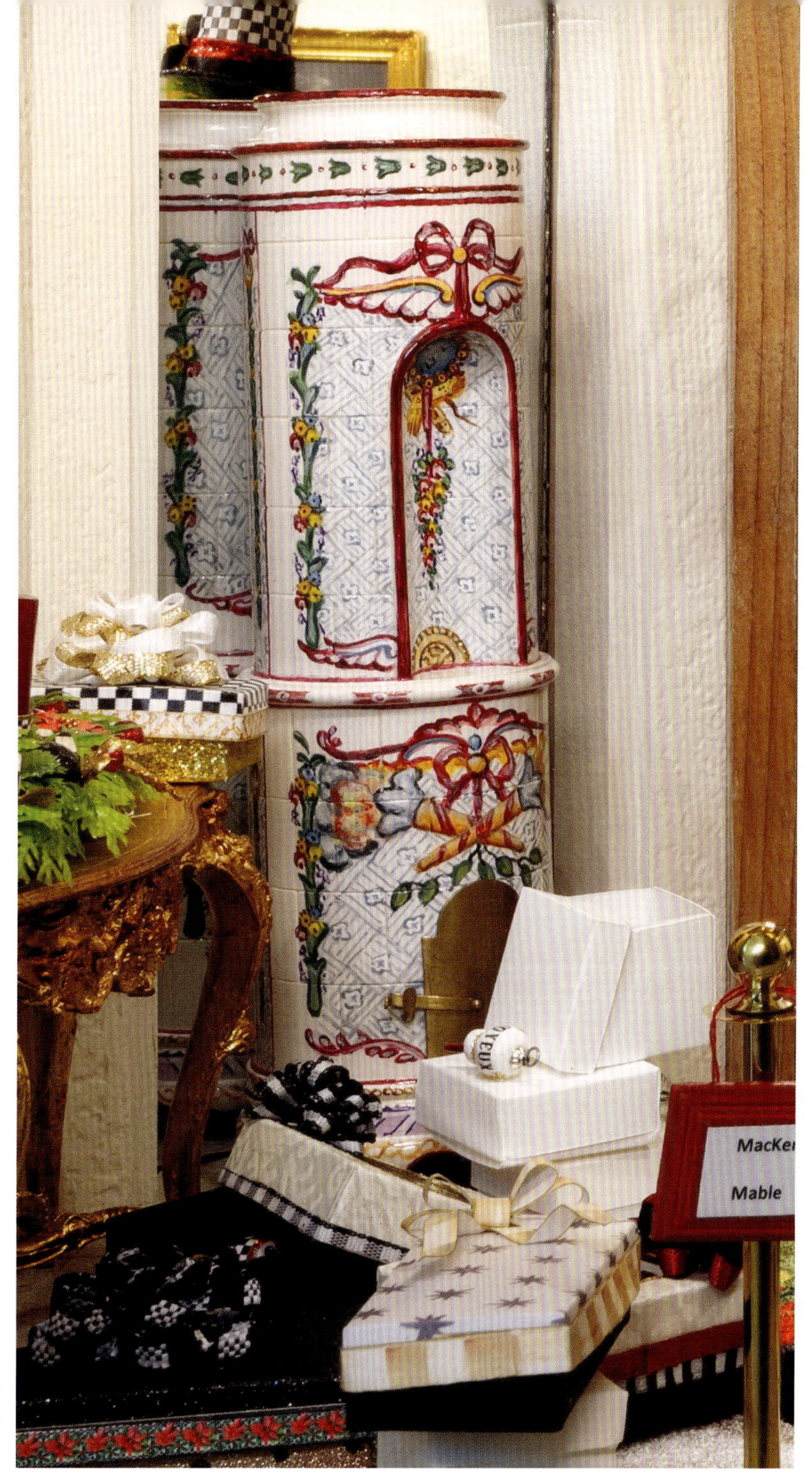

✳The Charlotte Hunt stove is one of a kind. The
packages lay wrapped and unwrapped. Some contain
ornaments and some hold gifts.

*I wish for your
Christmas to be as
merry and charming
as your tree.*

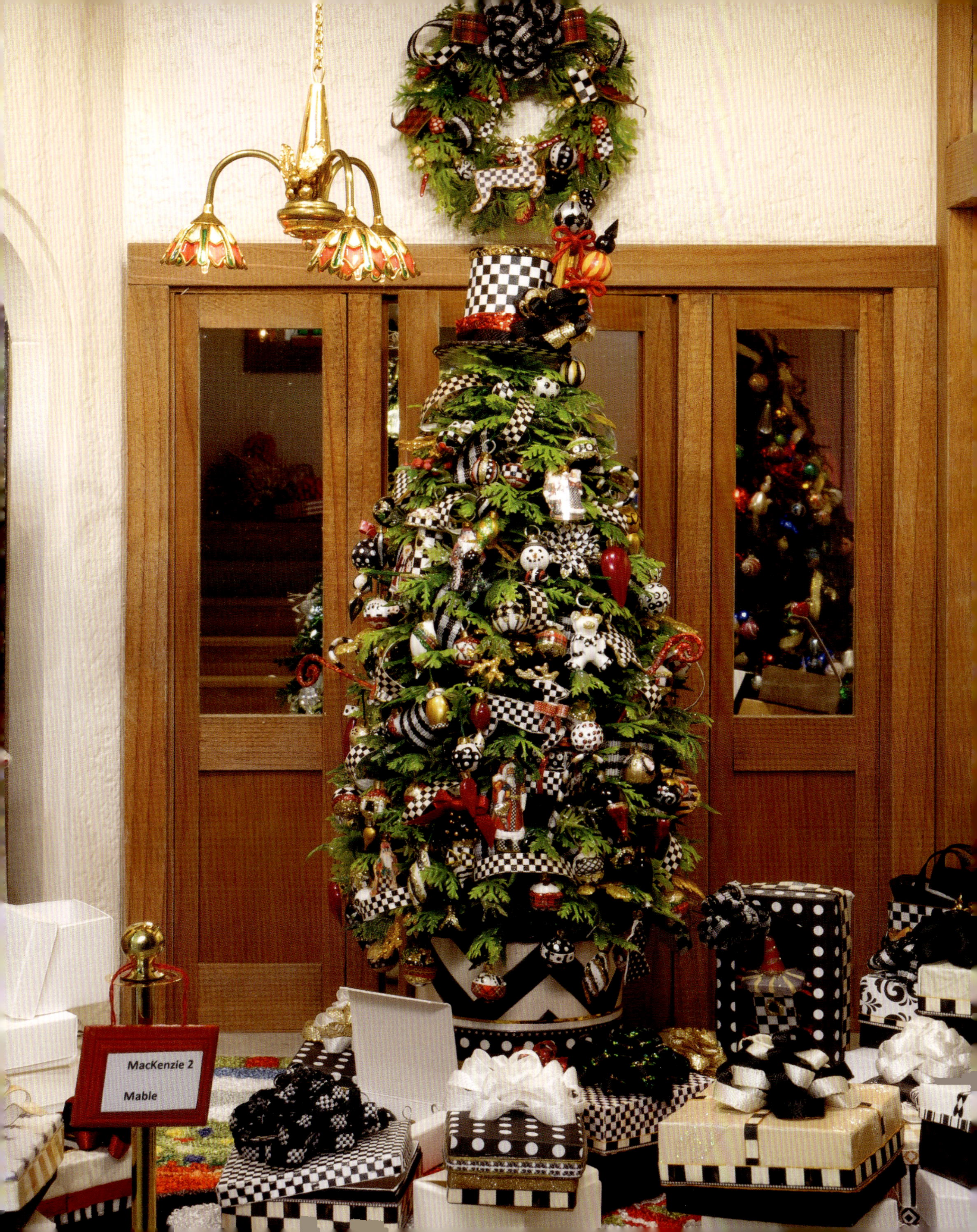

MacKenzie 2
Mable

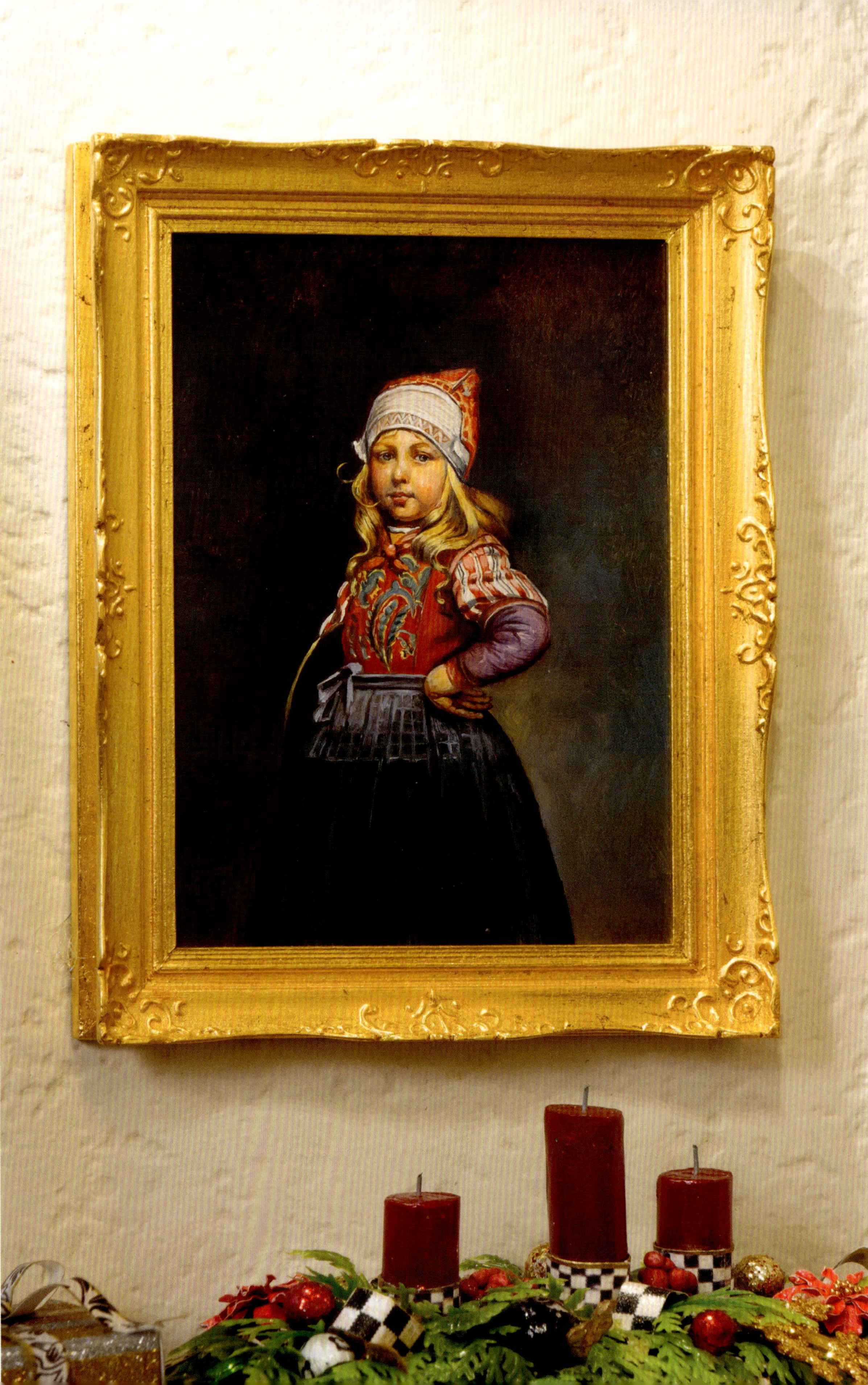

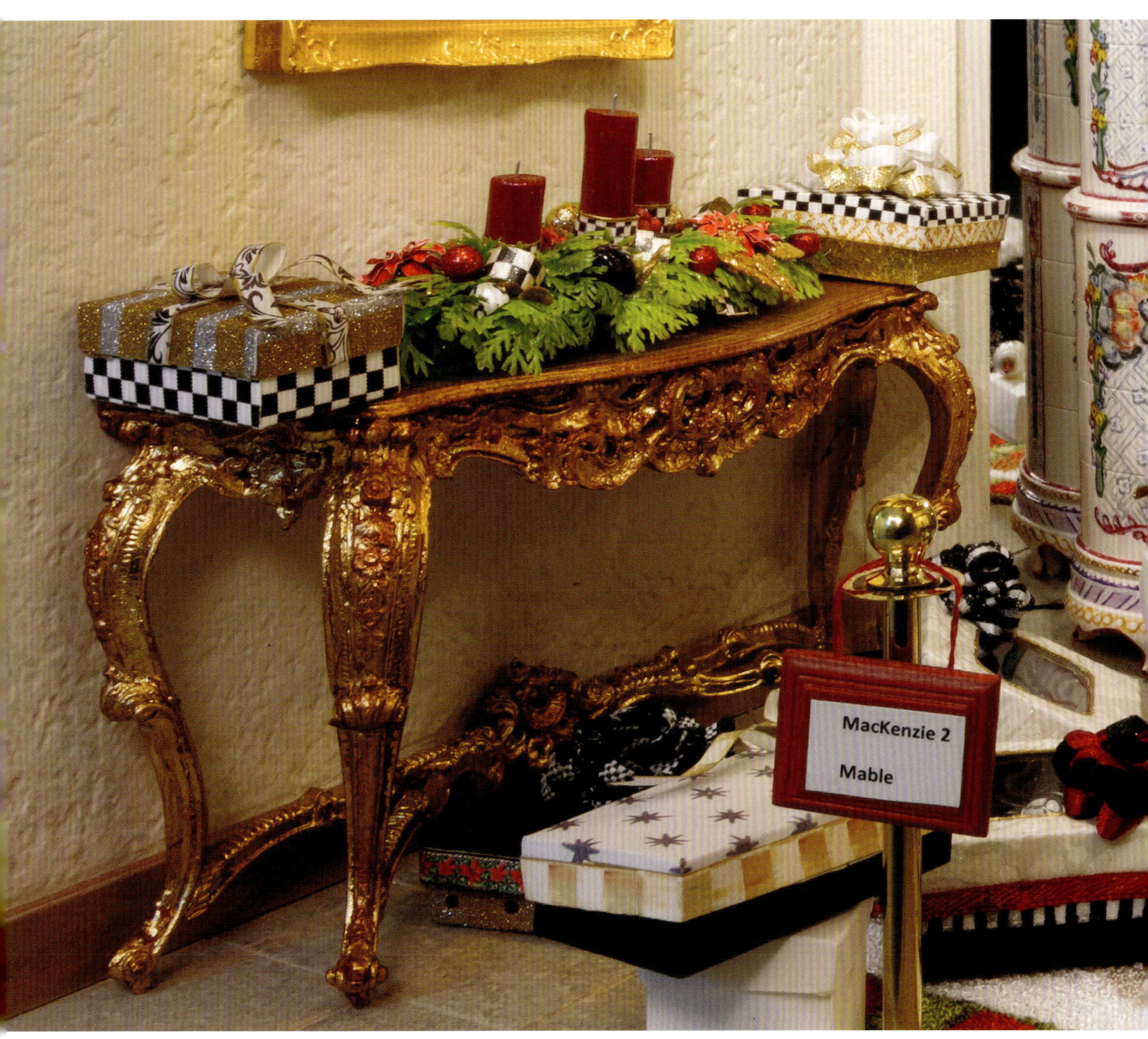

Johannes Landman created all the paintings in the Emporium. Some of them feature Santa, and some of them just suit the holidays.

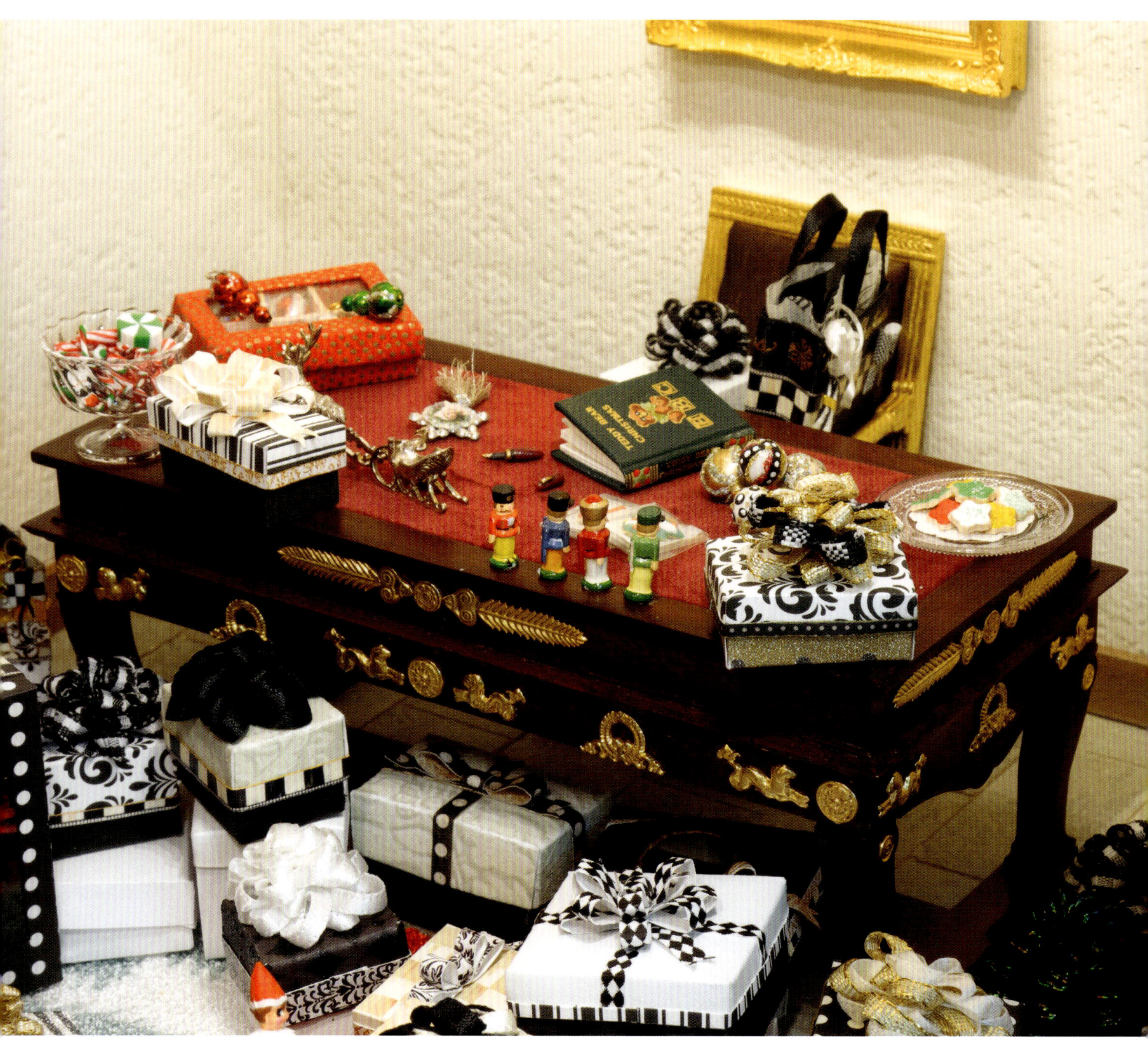

※This desk and chair, created by David Iriarte, is on the far side of the
office. The marvelous Santa was a creation of Johannes Landman.
Candy, cookies, and nutcrackers measuring 3/8 inches tall fill the desk.

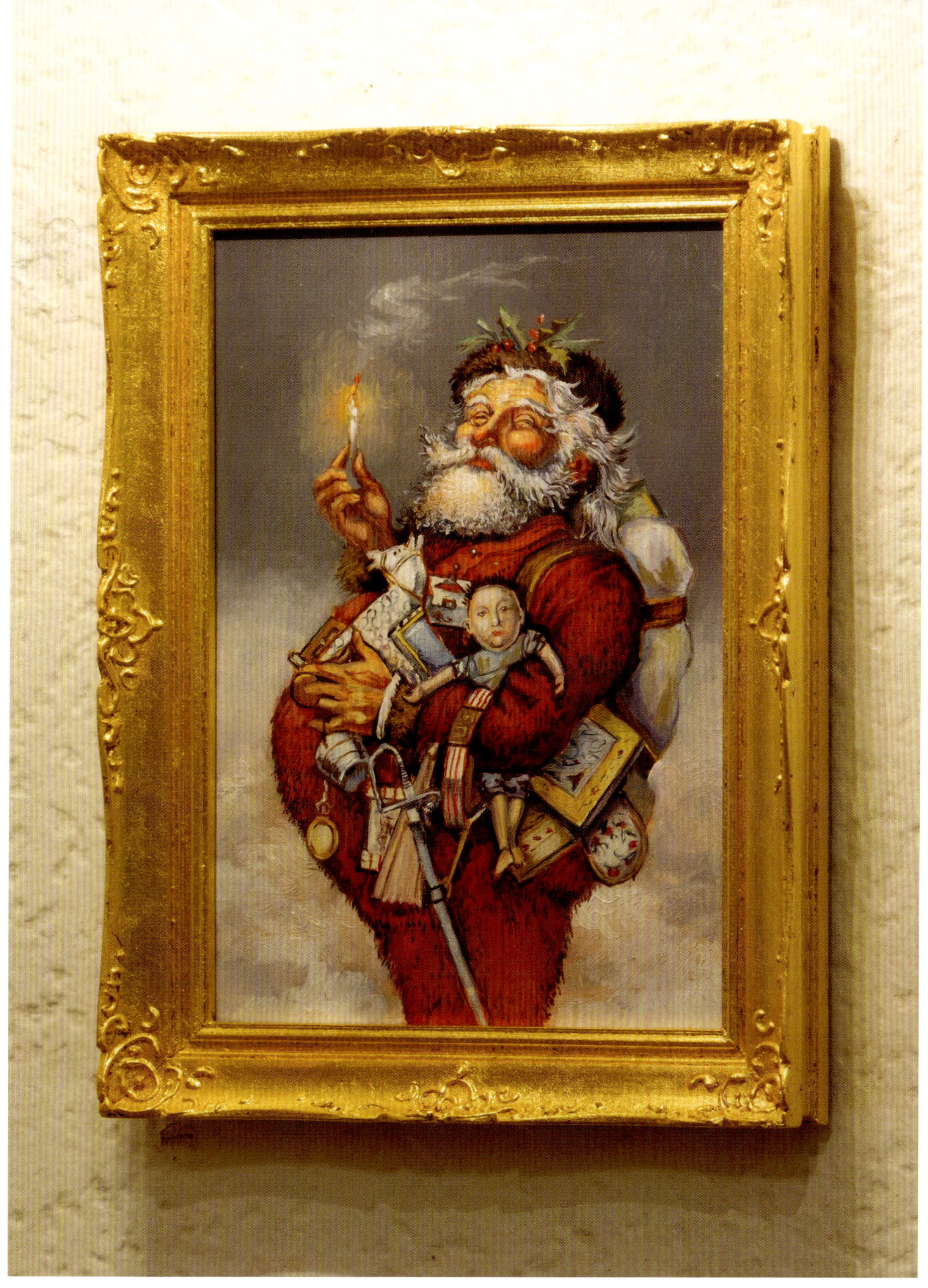

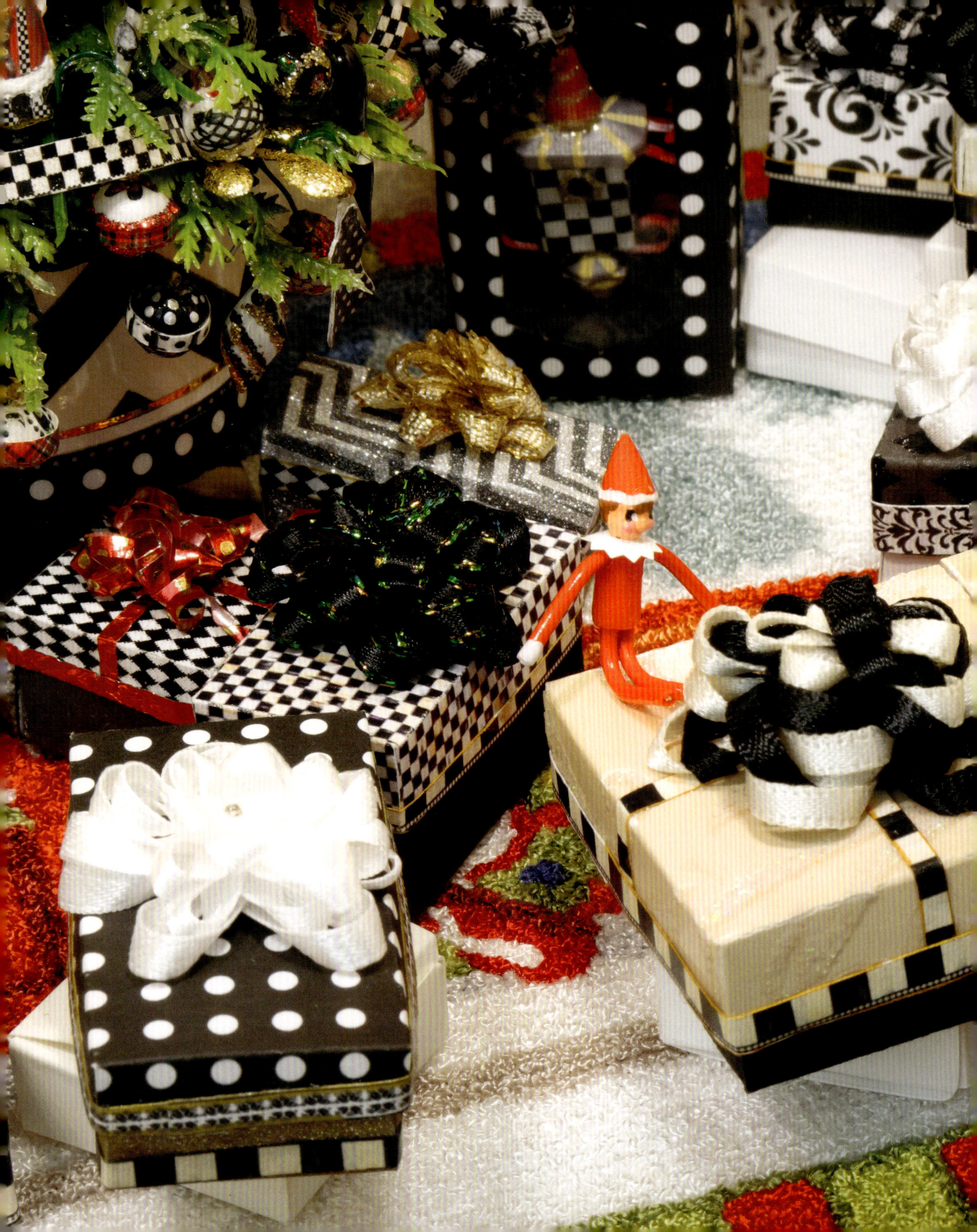

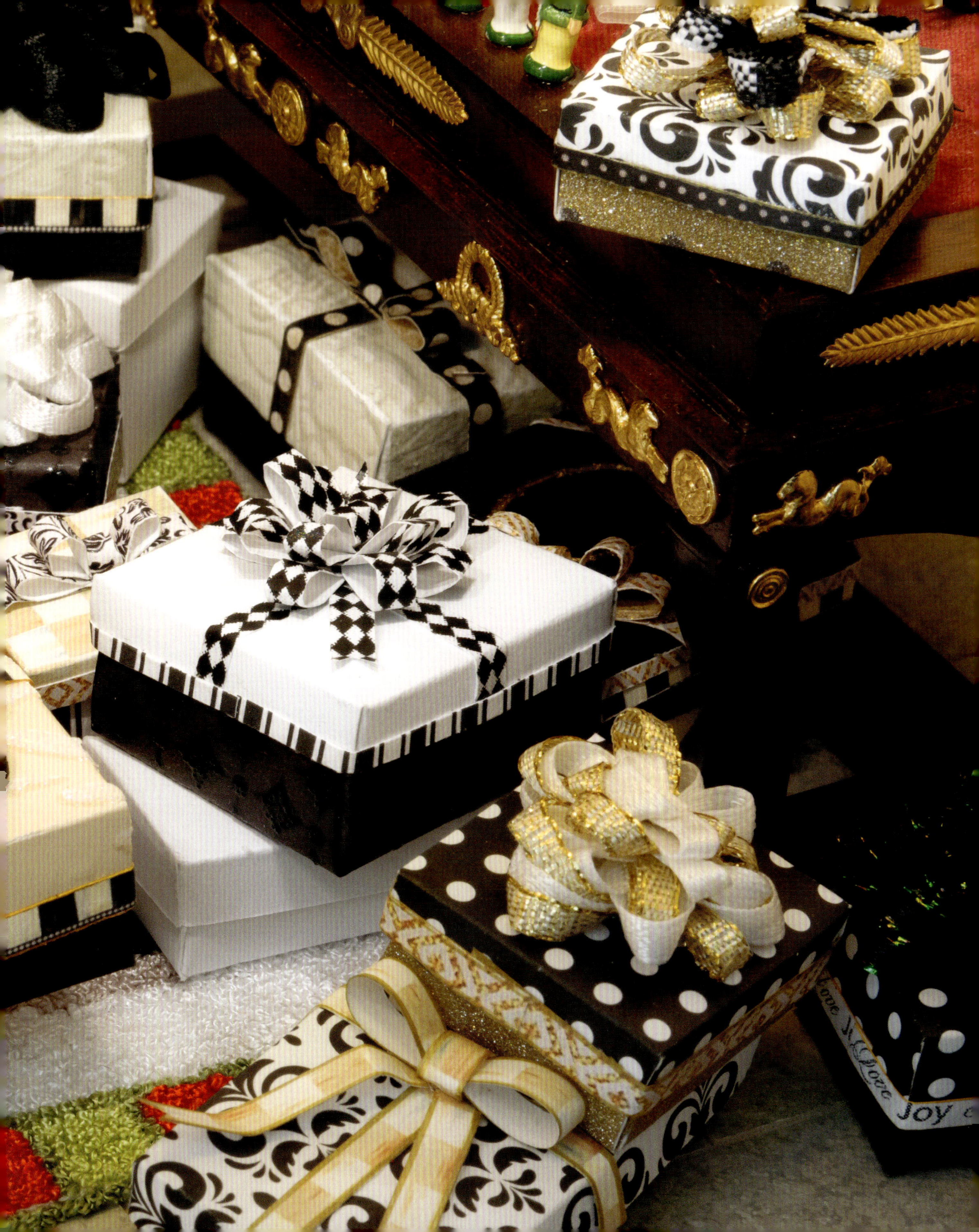

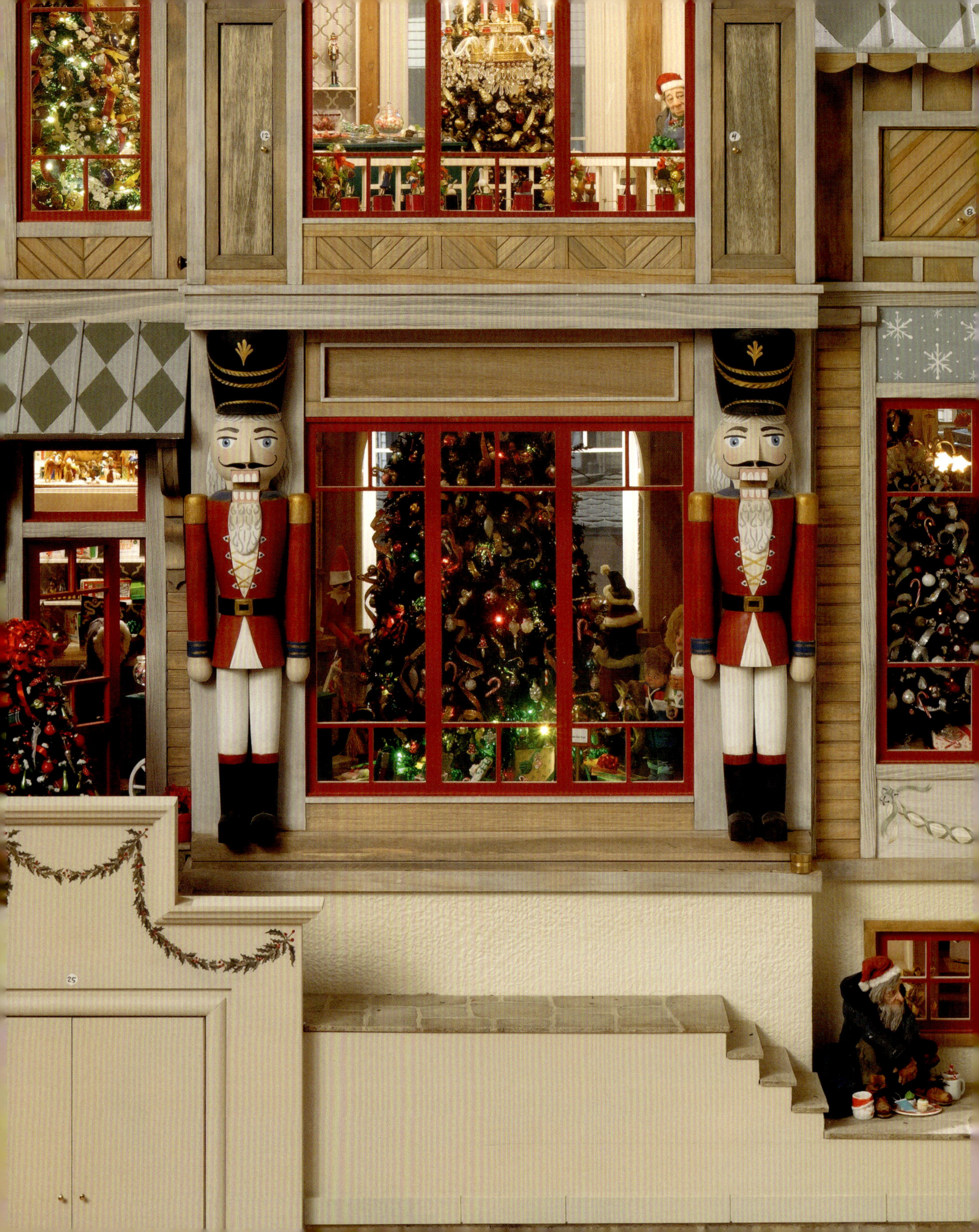

The Emporium

Inside the Emporium there are shoppers
and trees galore. The large tree in the center
holds over one thousand ornaments.
The Emporium is also home to candy canes,
elves, and other treats.

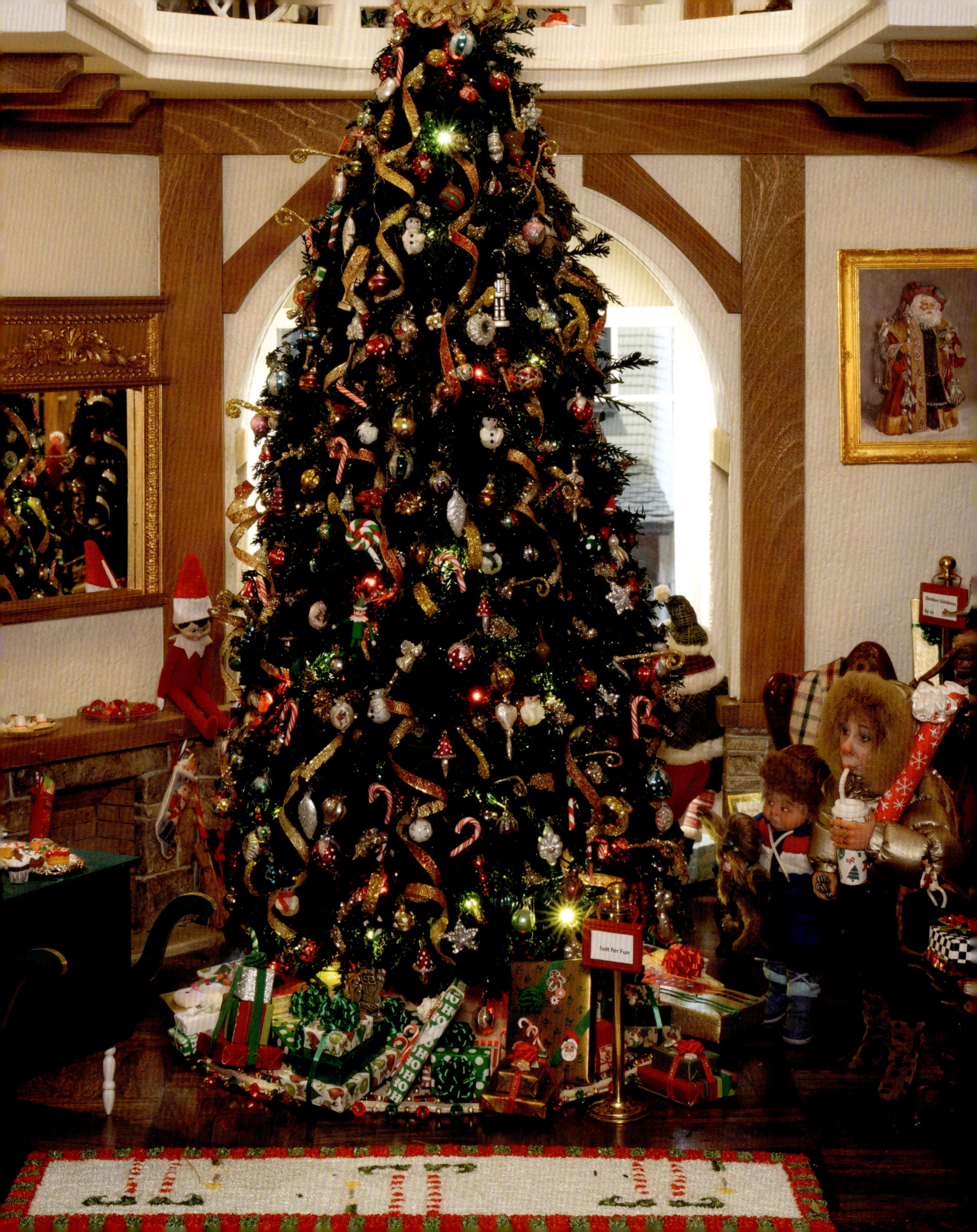

Just for Fun

"T'was the night
before Christmas,

and all through

the house,

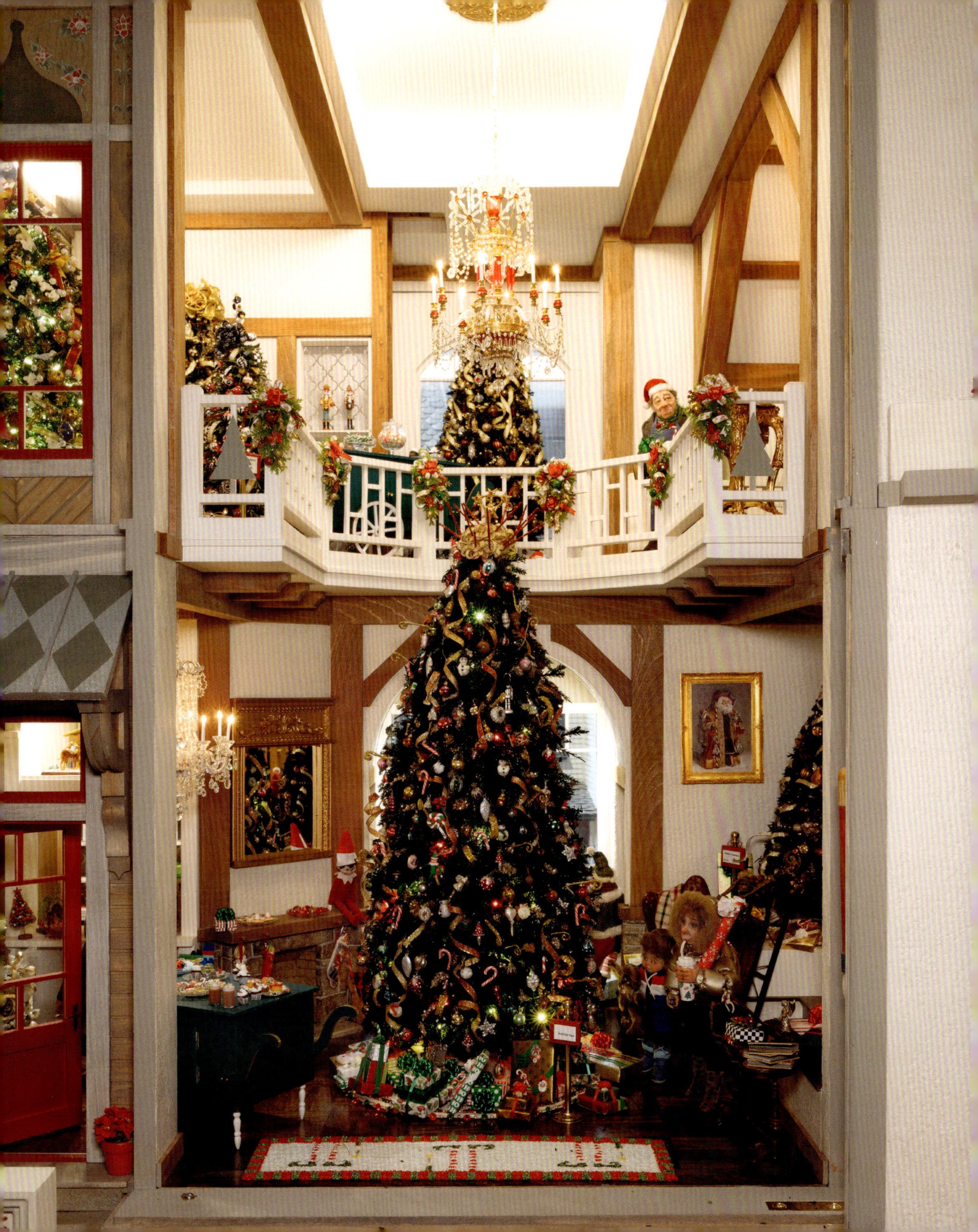

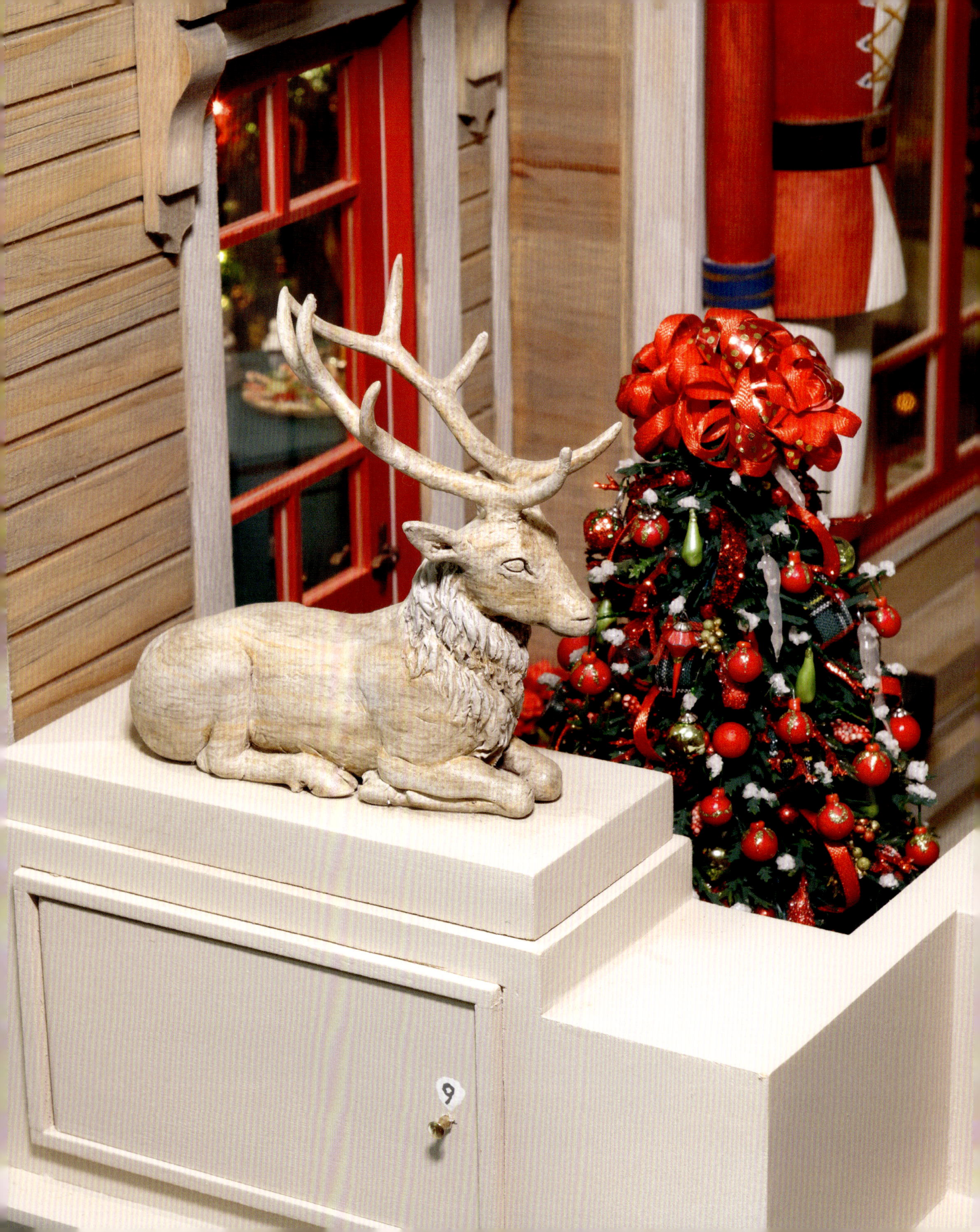

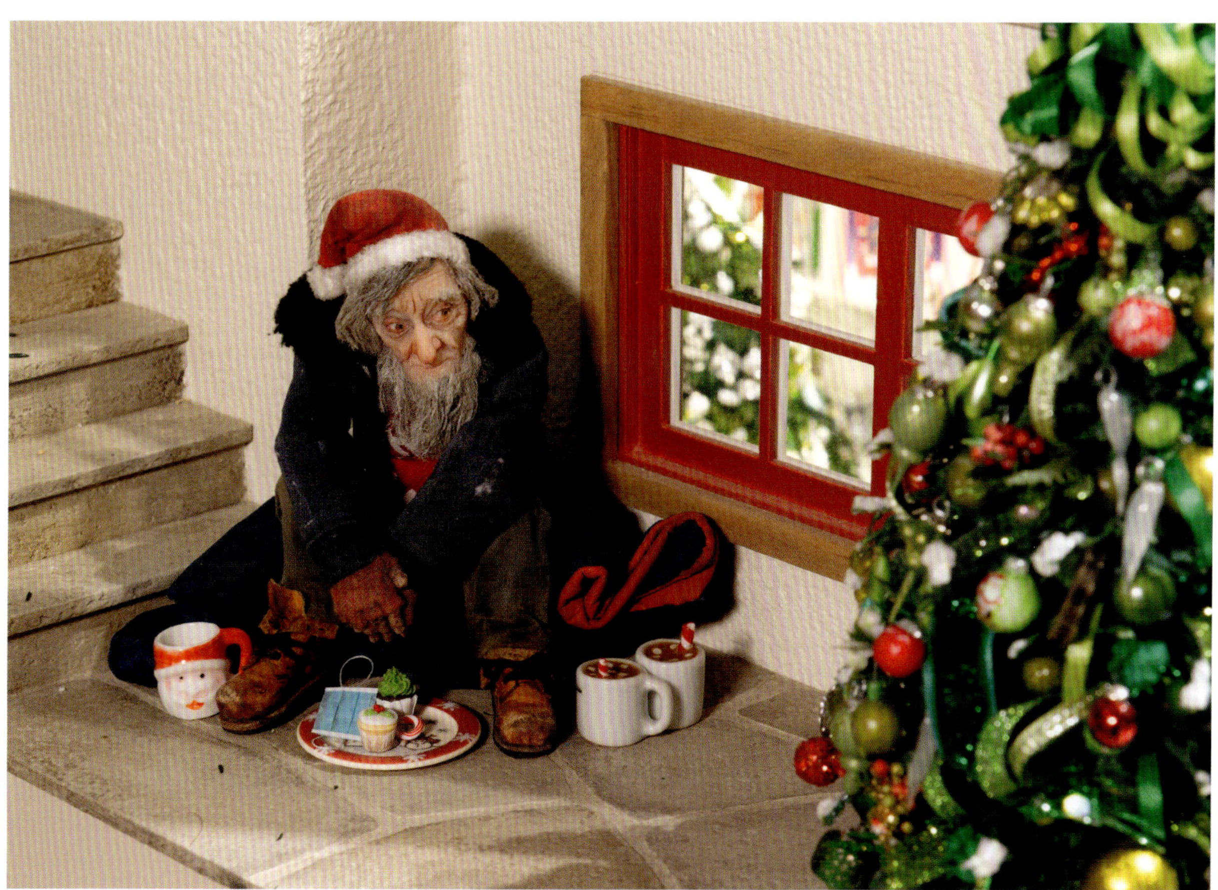

✳ The outside is adorned with a hand carved reindeer and tree by the front door. This homeless Santa reminds us of the many sides of Christmas. The figure speaks for itself. To provide perspective, the disposable surgical mask is ³⁄₈ inch wide.

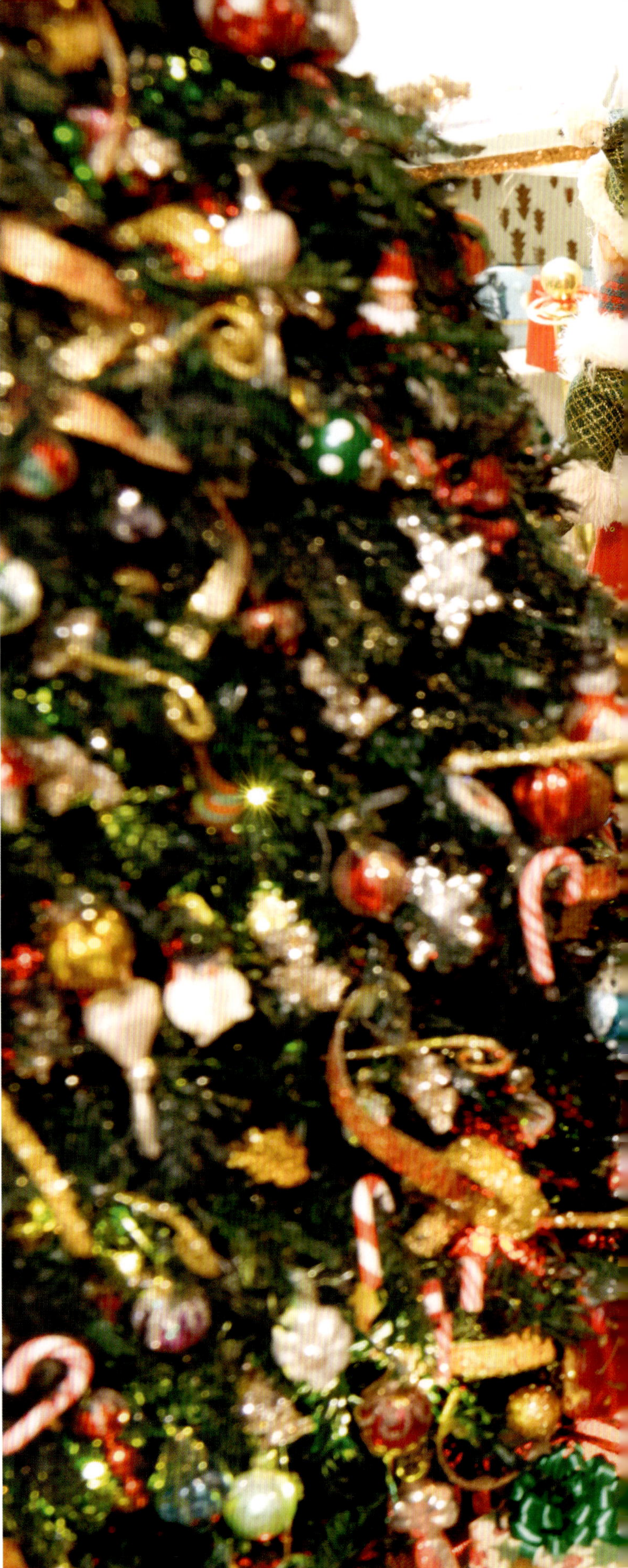

✳ Santa's chair waits for him. The
chair and sleigh were painted by
Maritza Moran.

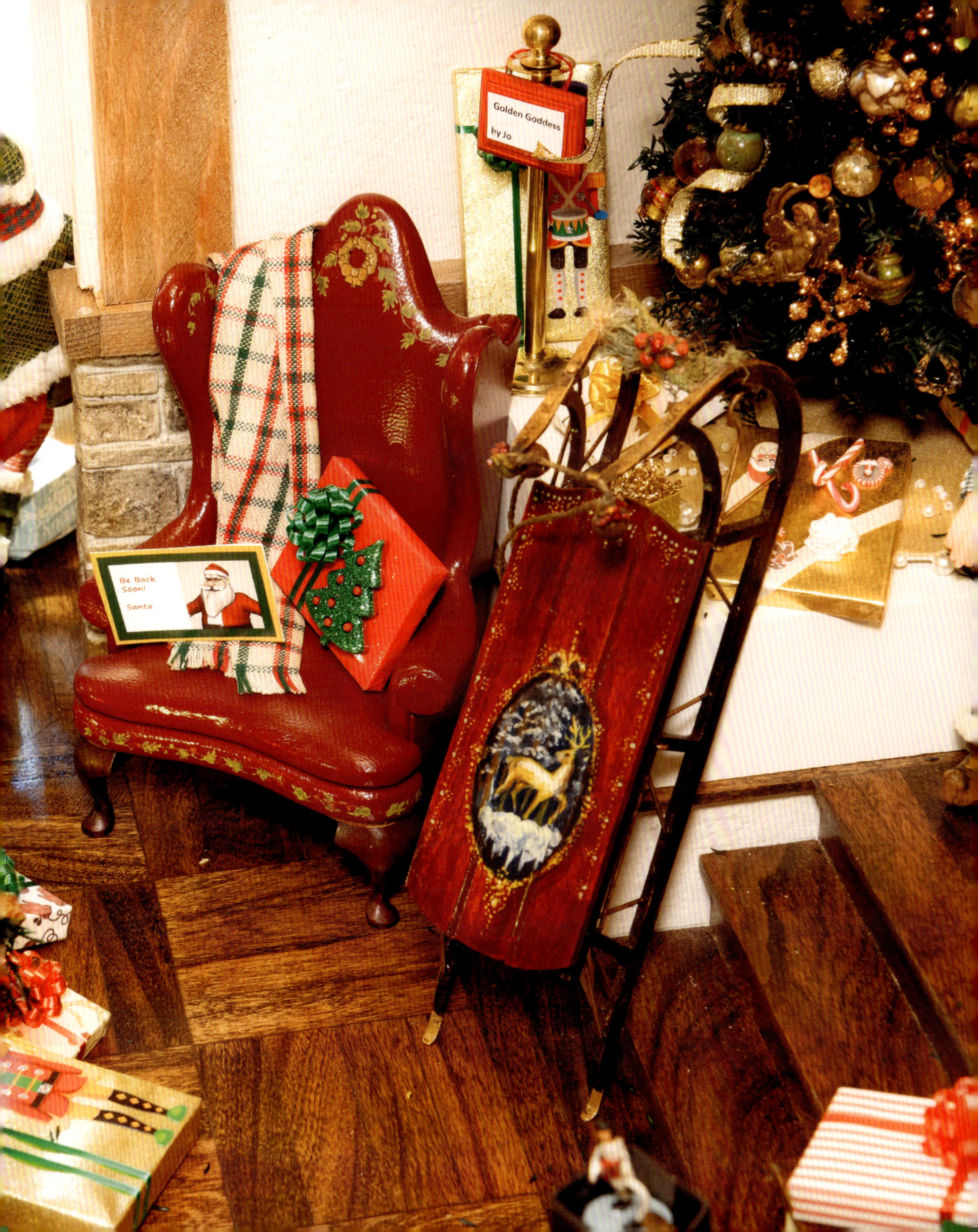
Golden Goddess
by Jo
Be Back
Soon!
Santa

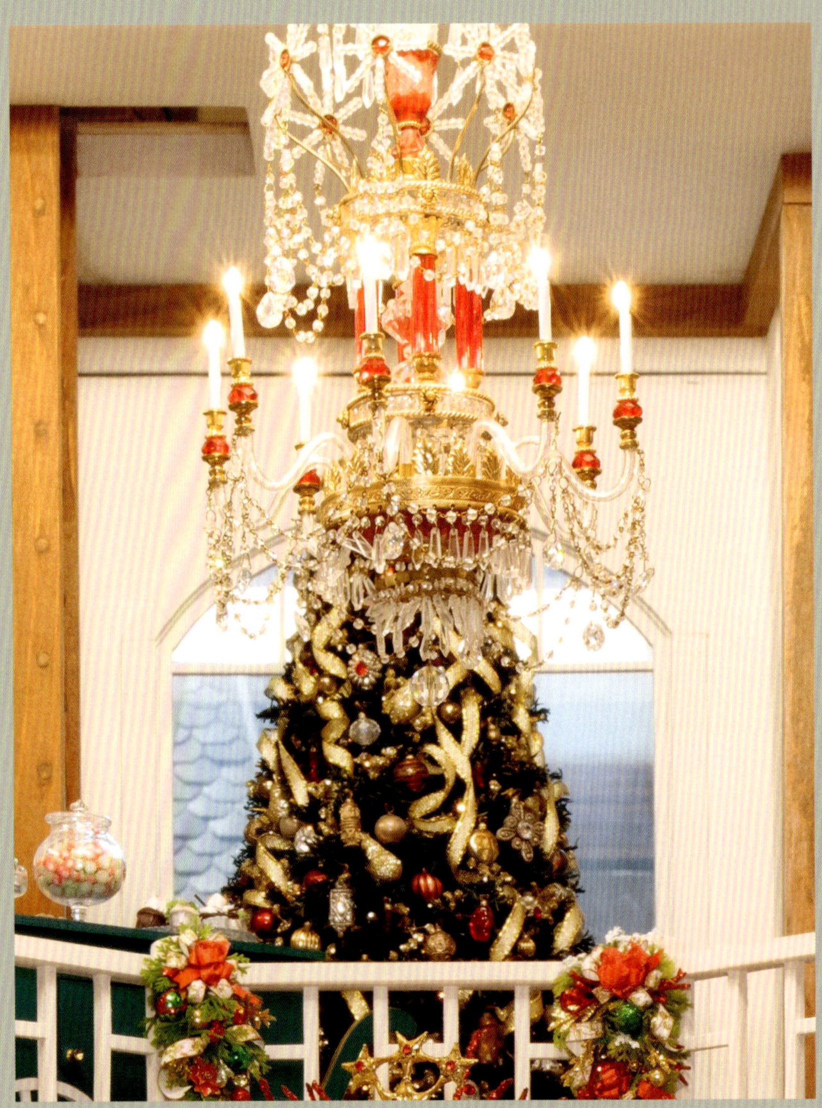

✴This fabulous chandelier hanging directly above the large tree was created by Frank Crescente. Off to the side of the large tree is the Golden Goddess Tree with presents (of course) and an elf sitting guard.

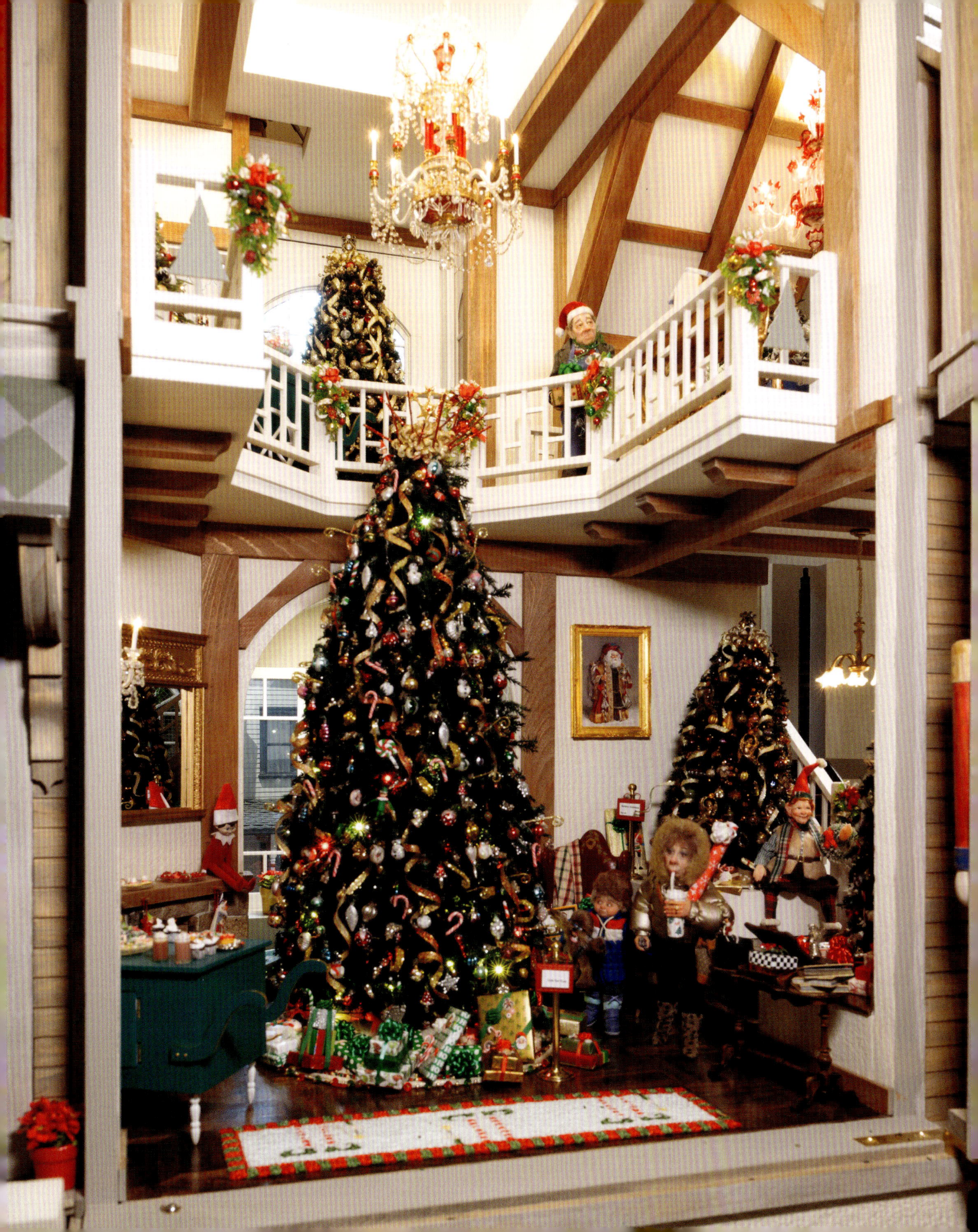

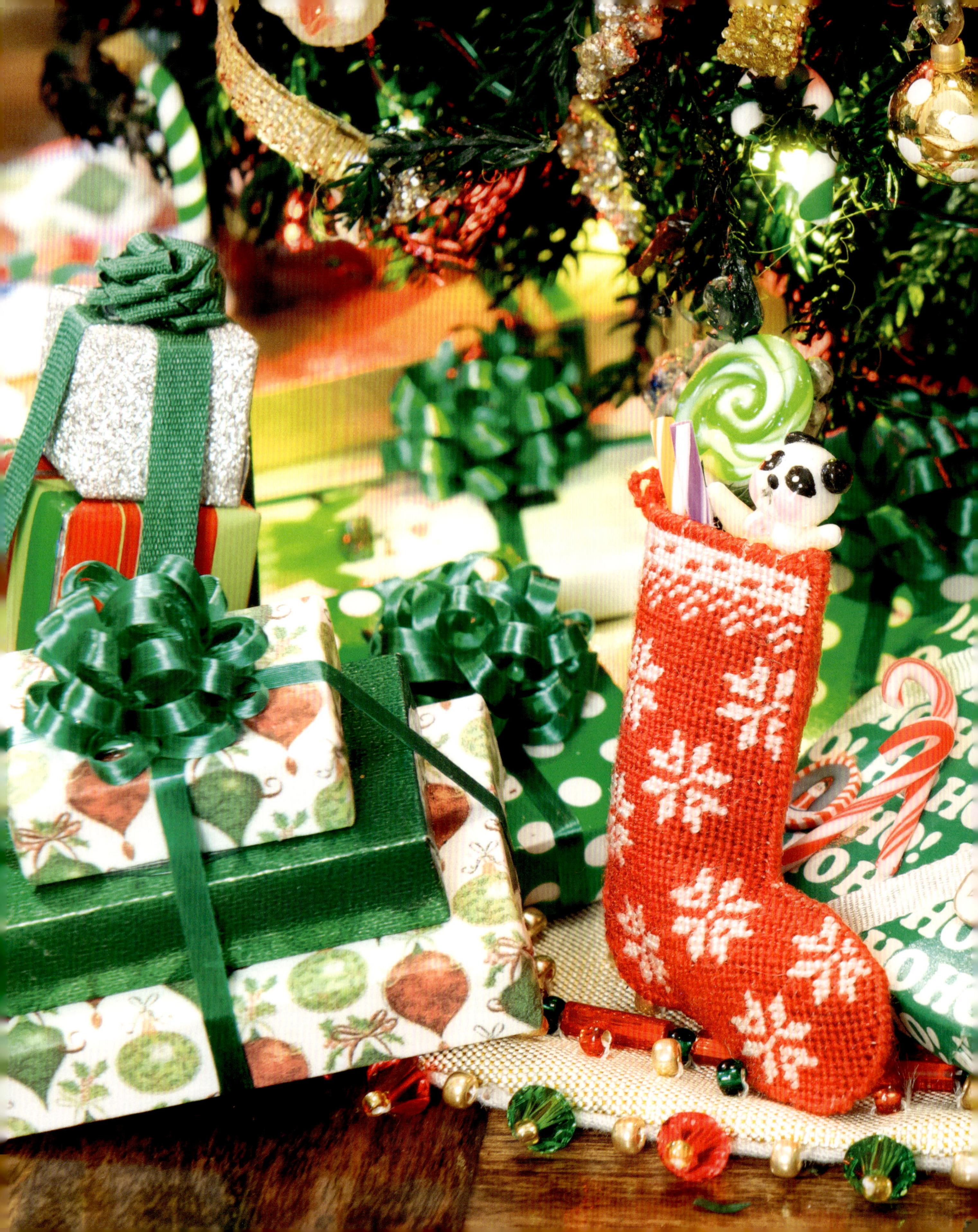

O Christmas Tree!
O Christmas Tree!
Thy candles shine so brightly.

From base to summit,
gay and bright,
There's only splendor for
the sight.

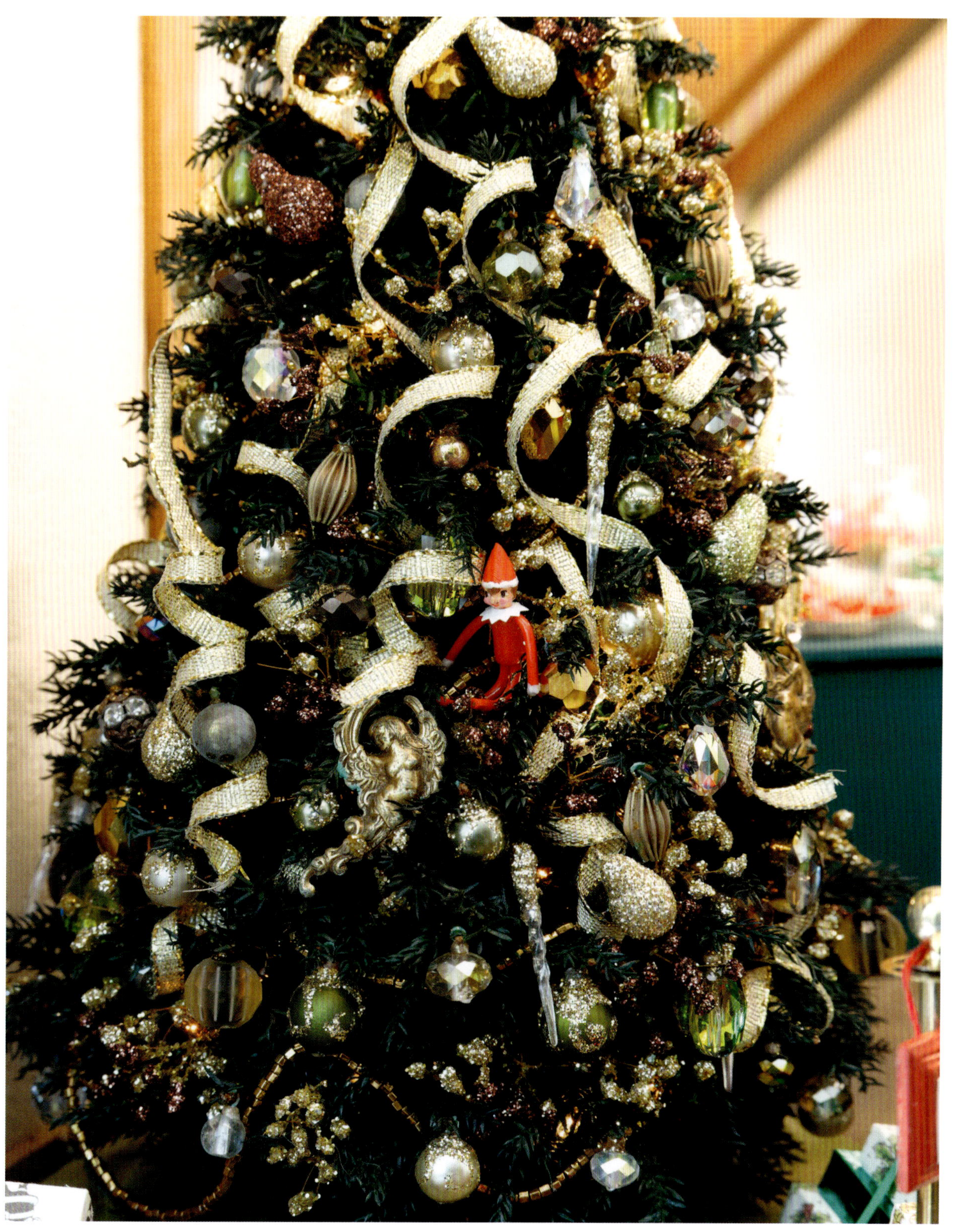

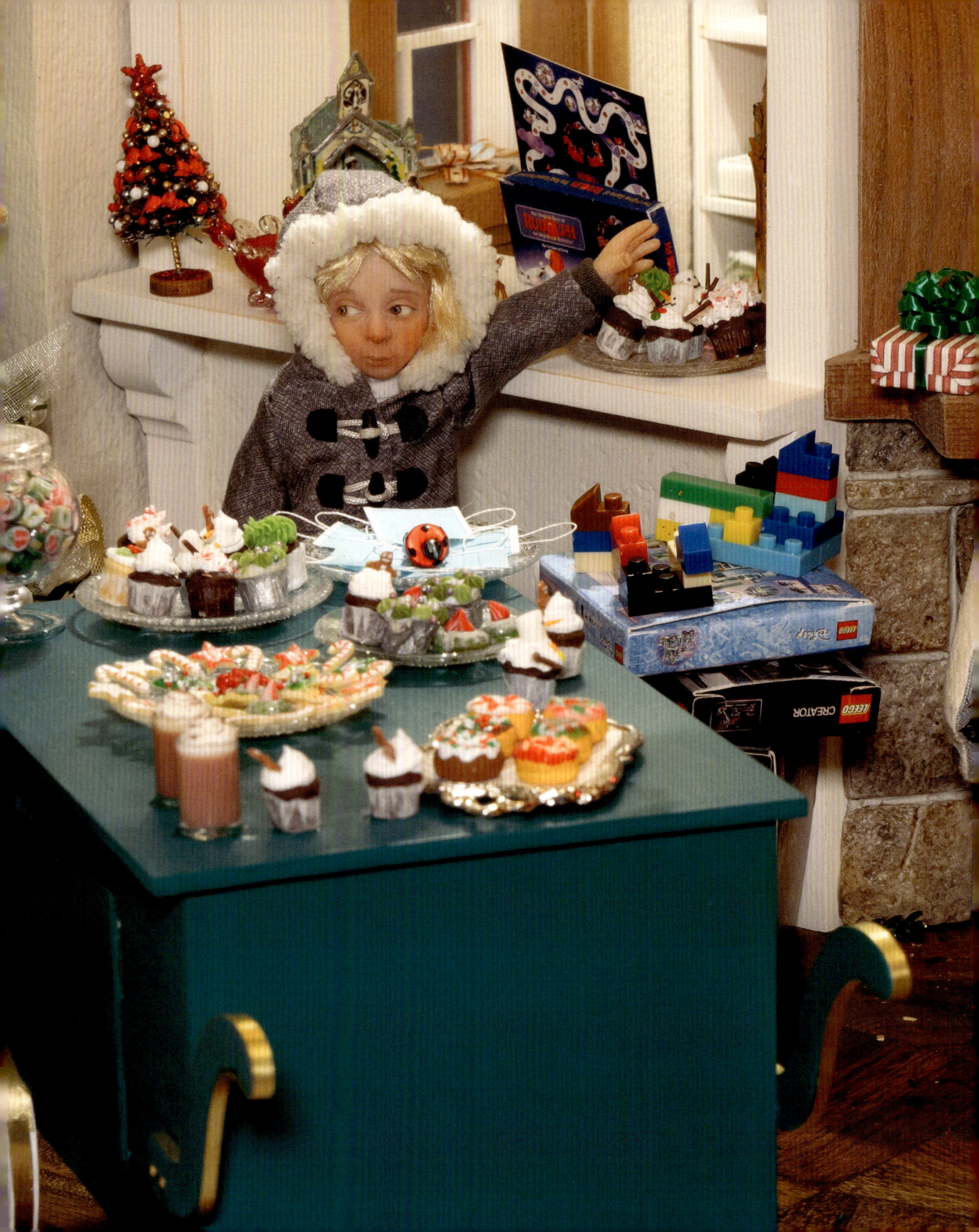

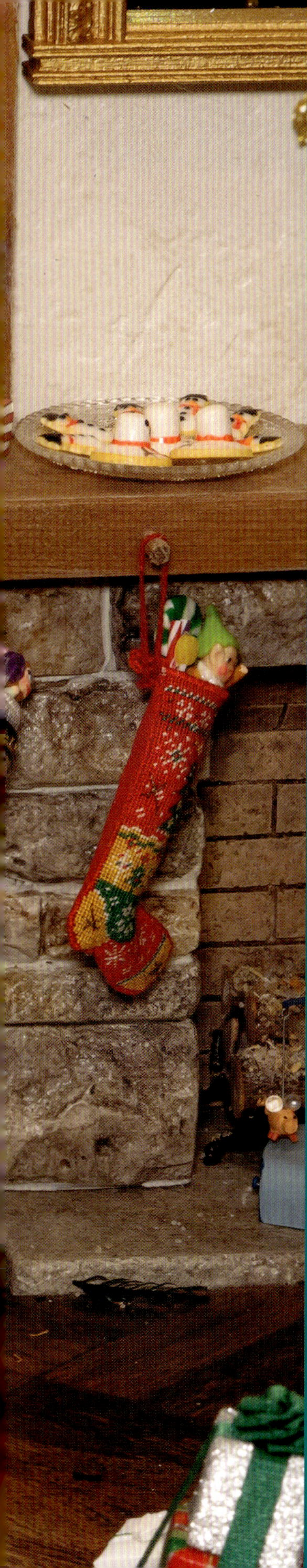

All the stockings you will find
hanging in a row
Mine will be the shortest one
you'll be sure to know …

The Christmas cart has cupcakes, cookies, hot chocolate, and candy—but of course our young shopper wants a cupcake from the counter. The stockings are petit point and filled with treasures.

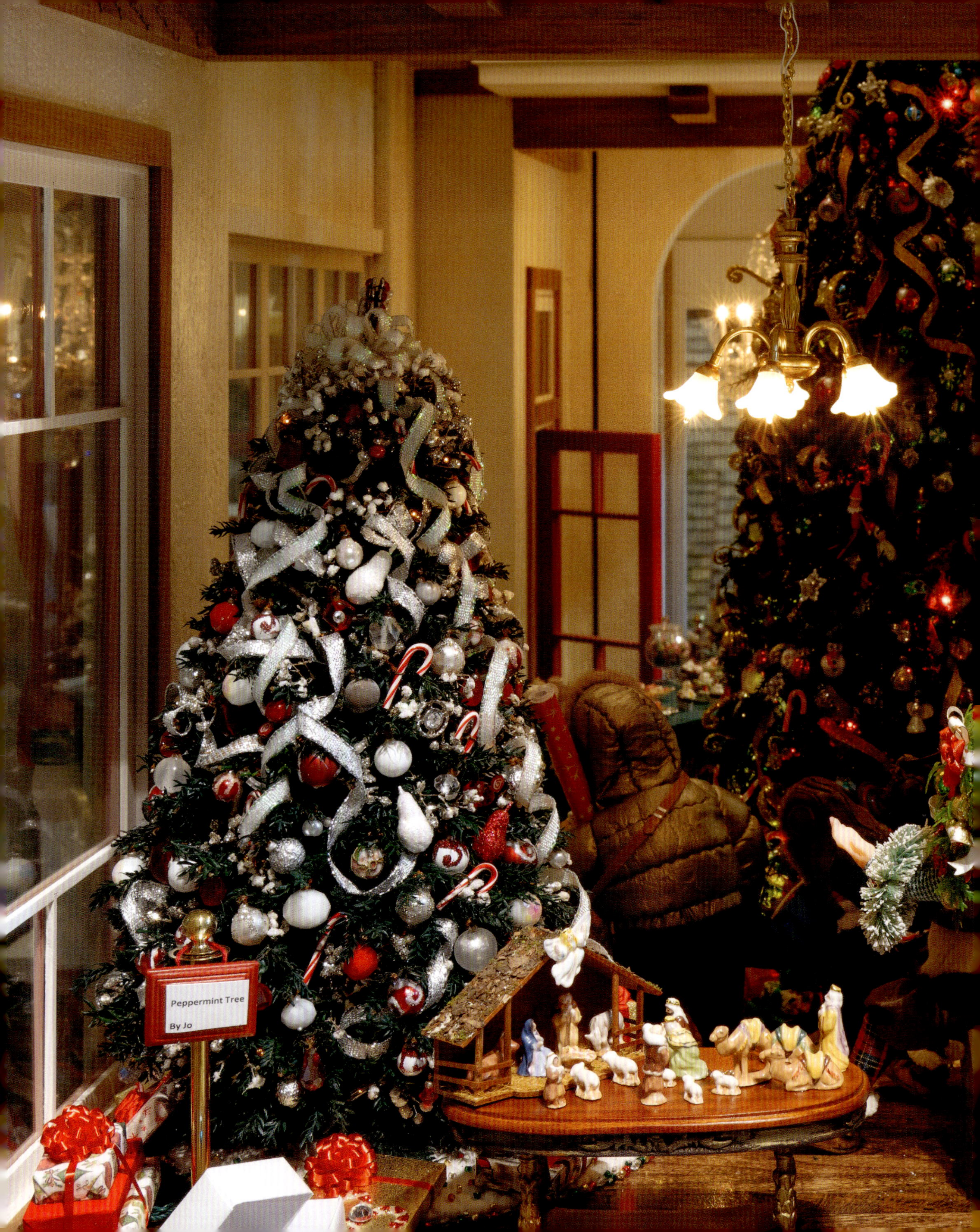
Peppermint Tree
By Jo

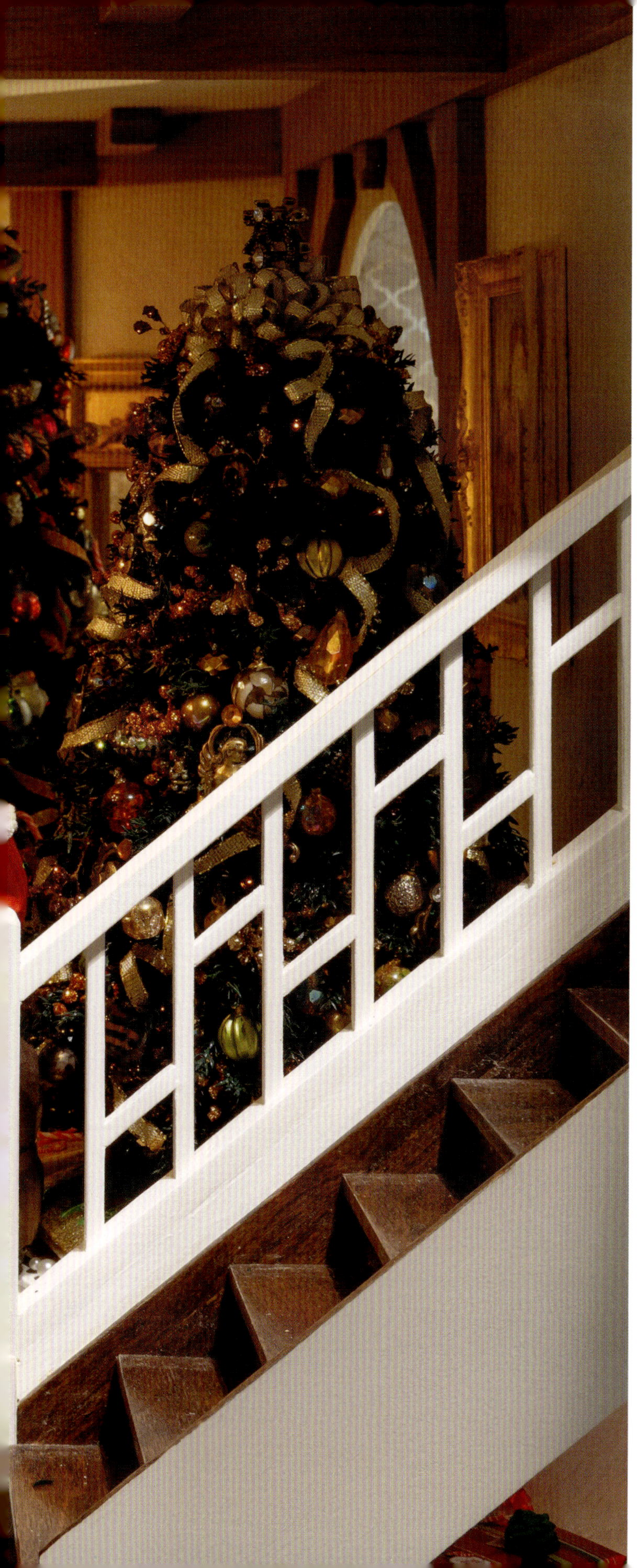

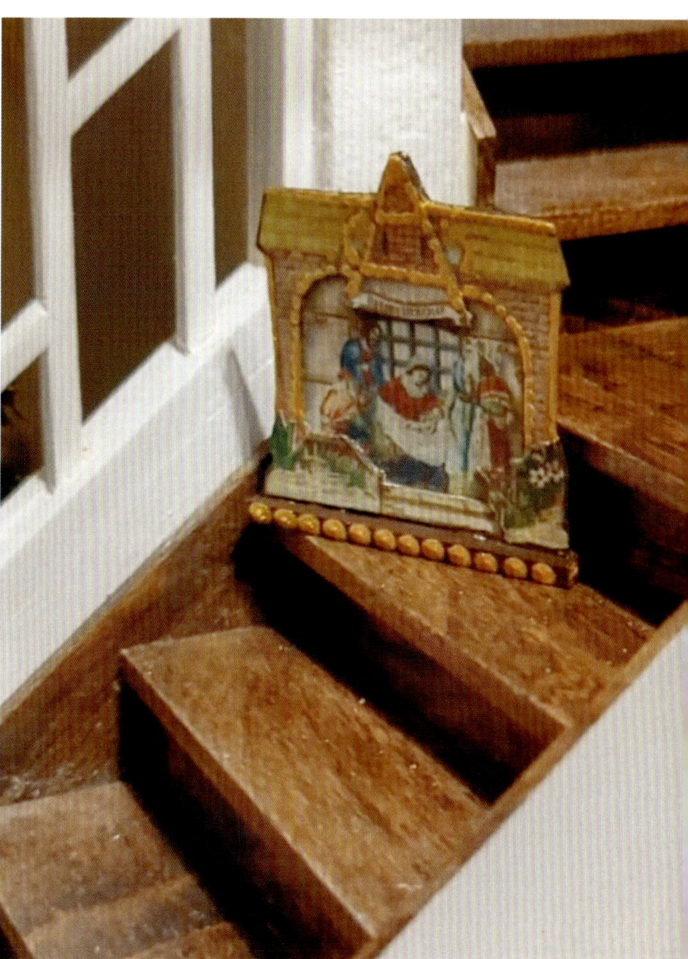

✳ The Peppermint Tree is clearly
visible from the right side of the
building. This view also highlights
the sheer number of ornaments
in the trees.

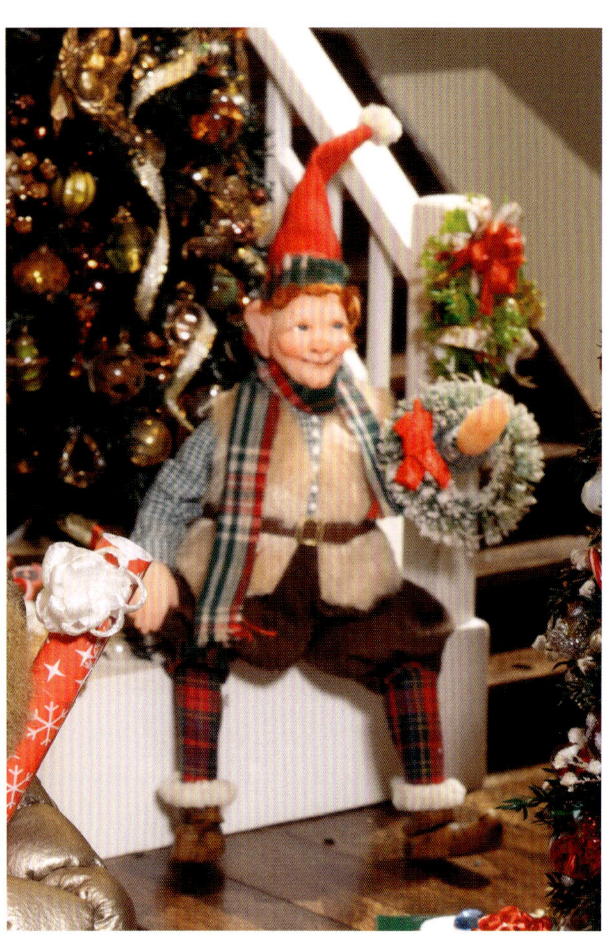

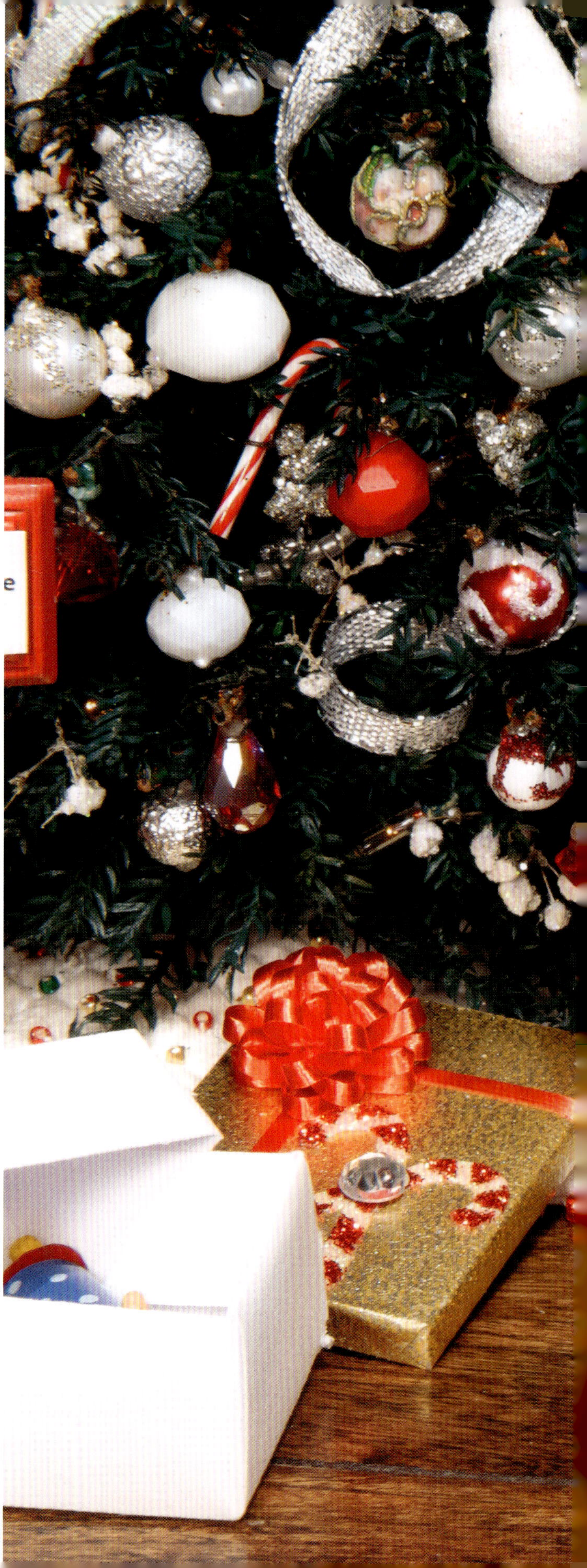

✳ Details . . . details . . . . Although this building is not as large as many others, the number of details is overwhelming. The elf, the nativity set, and the variety of the ornaments all make this a joyful scene.

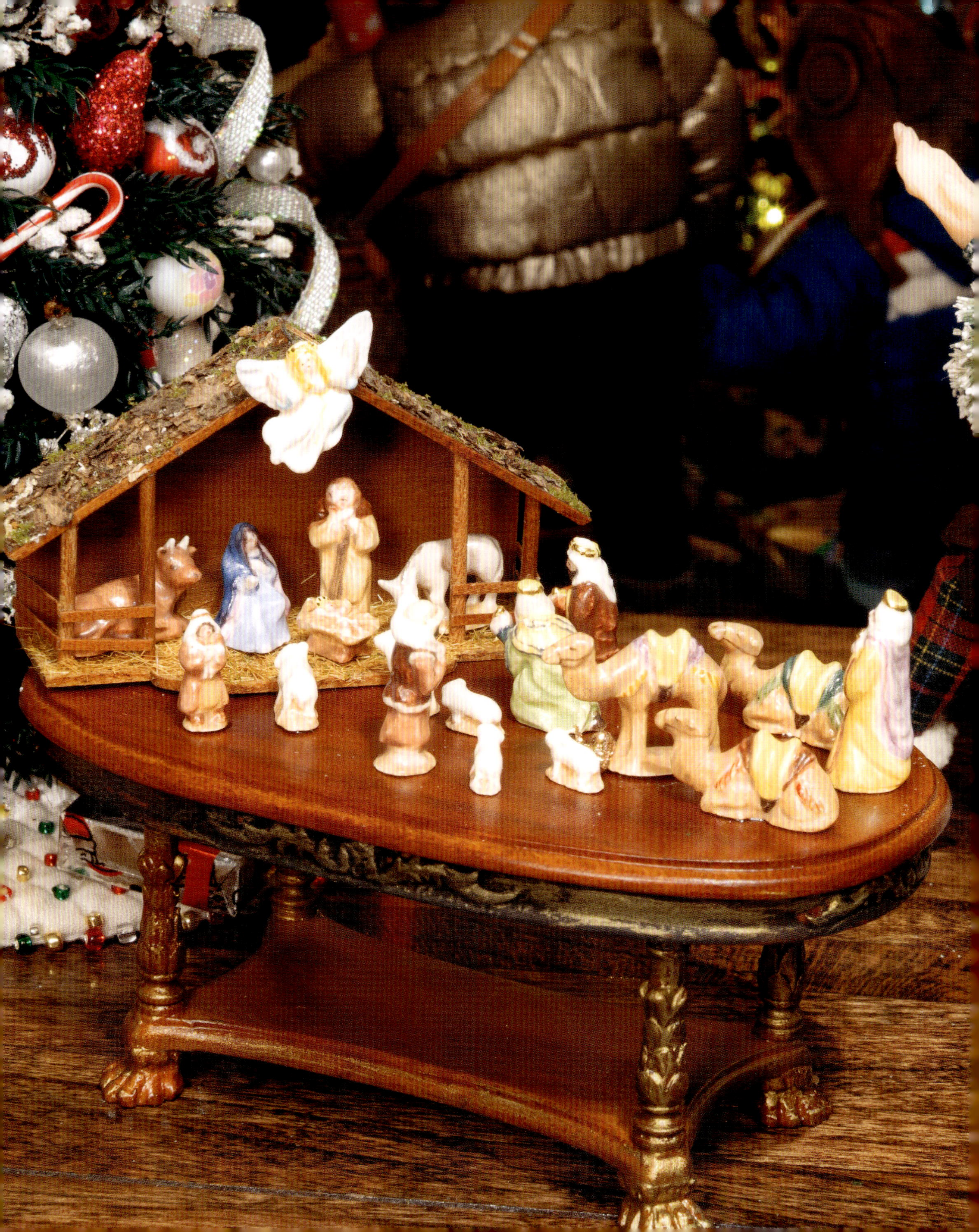

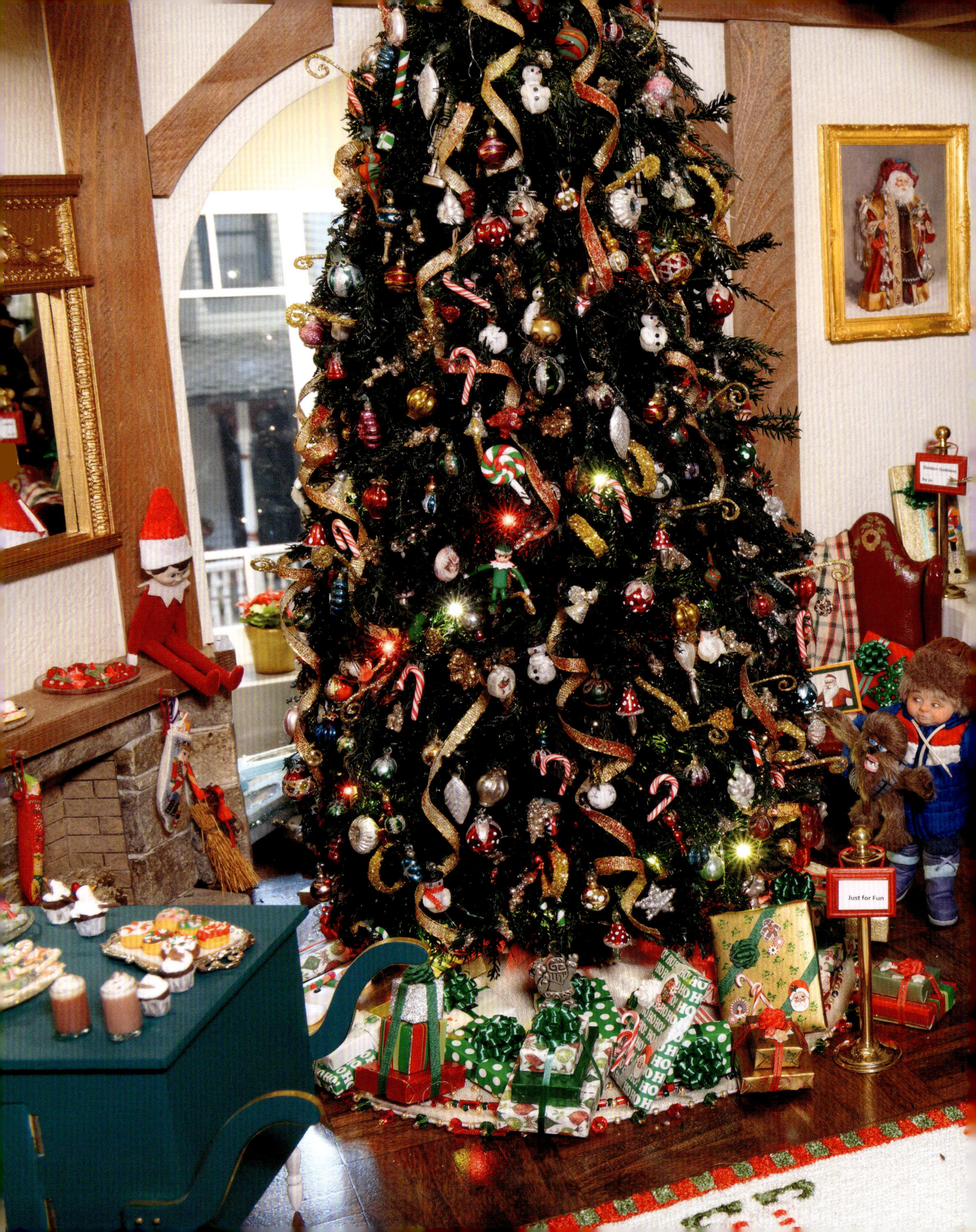
Just for Fun

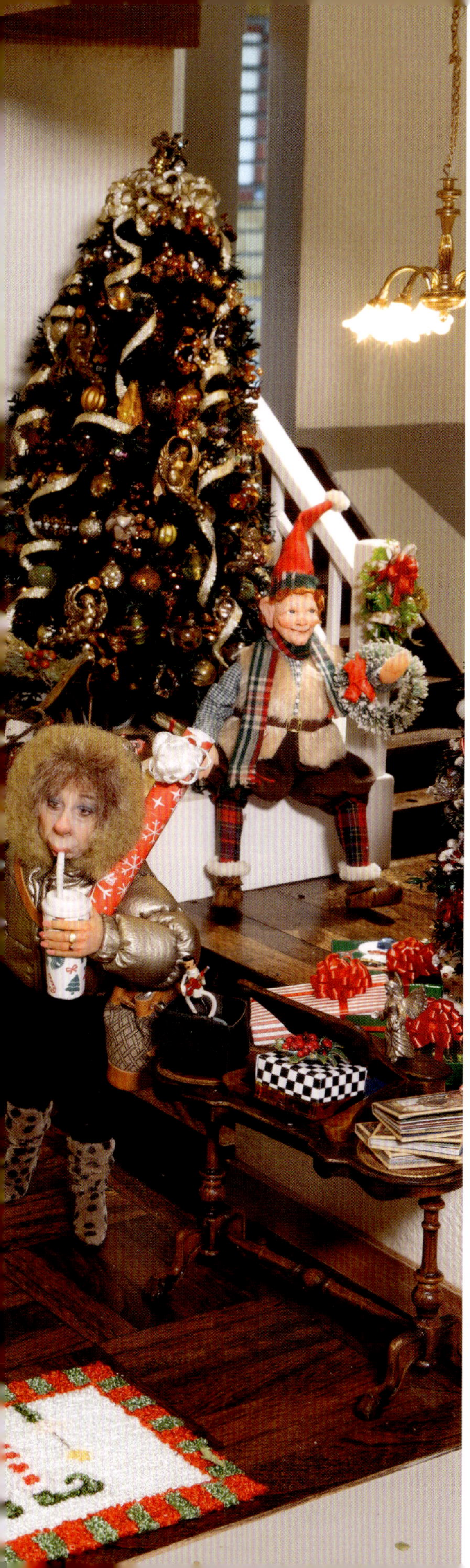

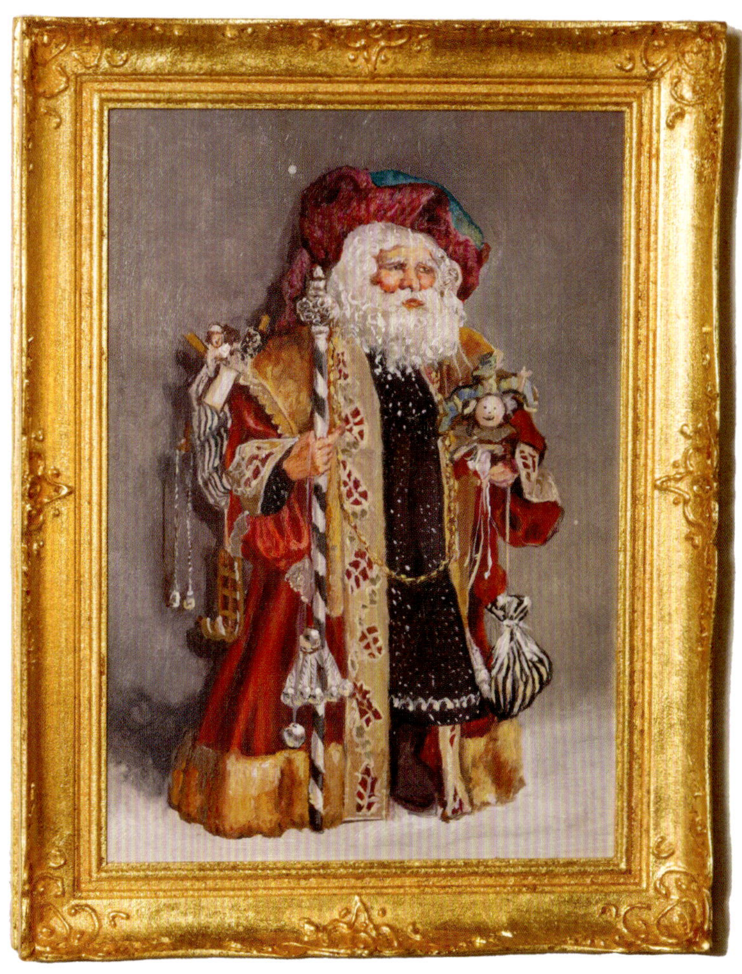

*This fabulous Santa was painted by
Johannes Landman. Mother and son
stop to admire the tree and are
surrounded by every joy of the Emporium.

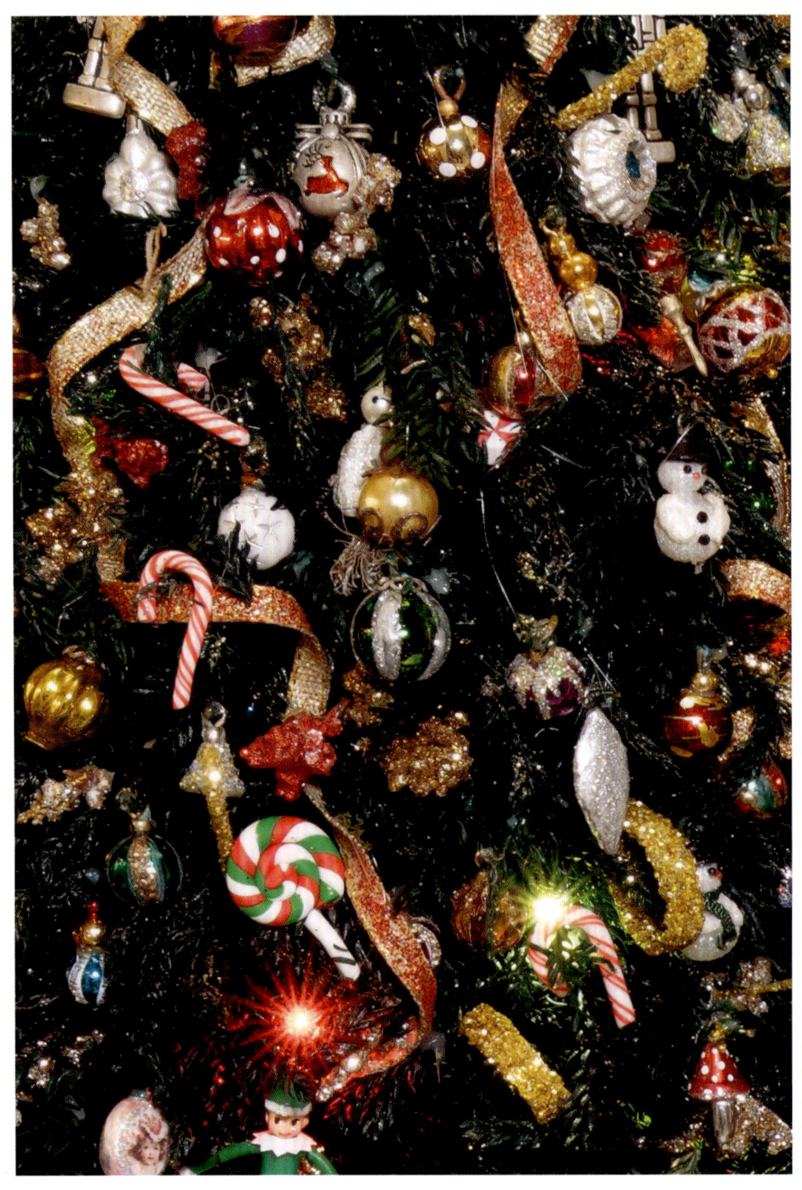

✳ The ornaments are each hand-painted and personally designed by the artists. More packages and toys are visible.

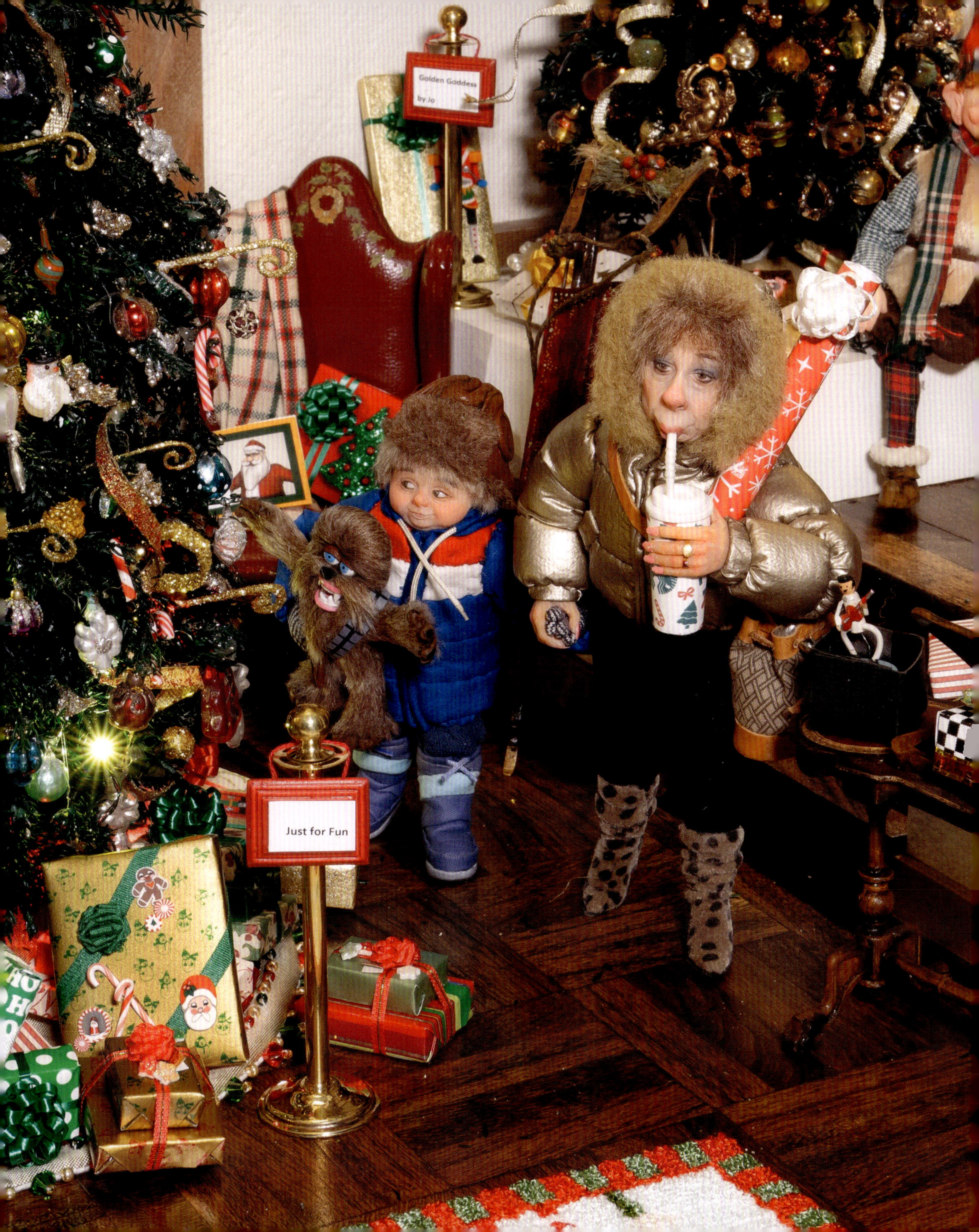

Golden Goddess
by Jo
Just for Fun

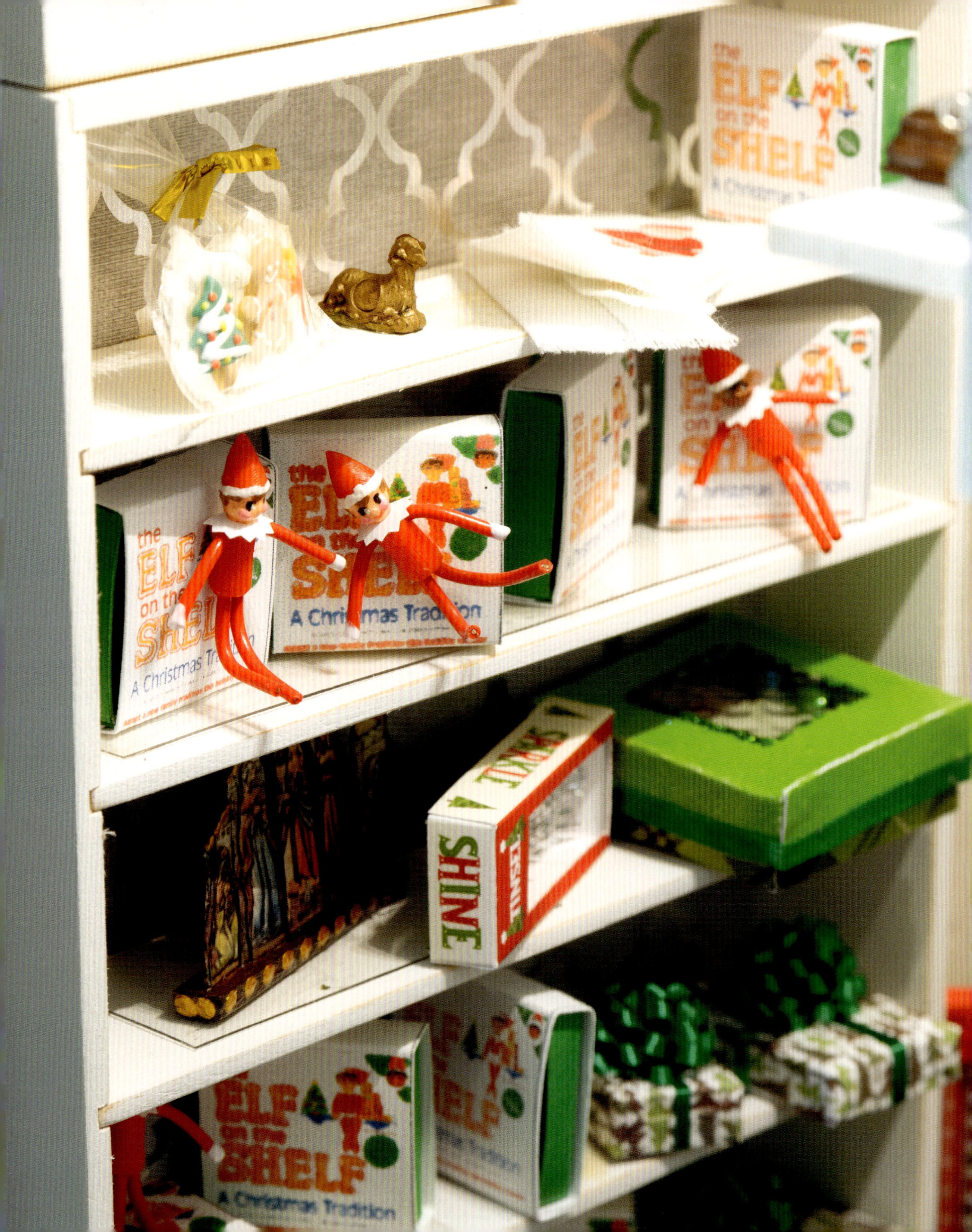

the ELF on the SHELF
A Christmas Tradition
SHINE
TINSEL

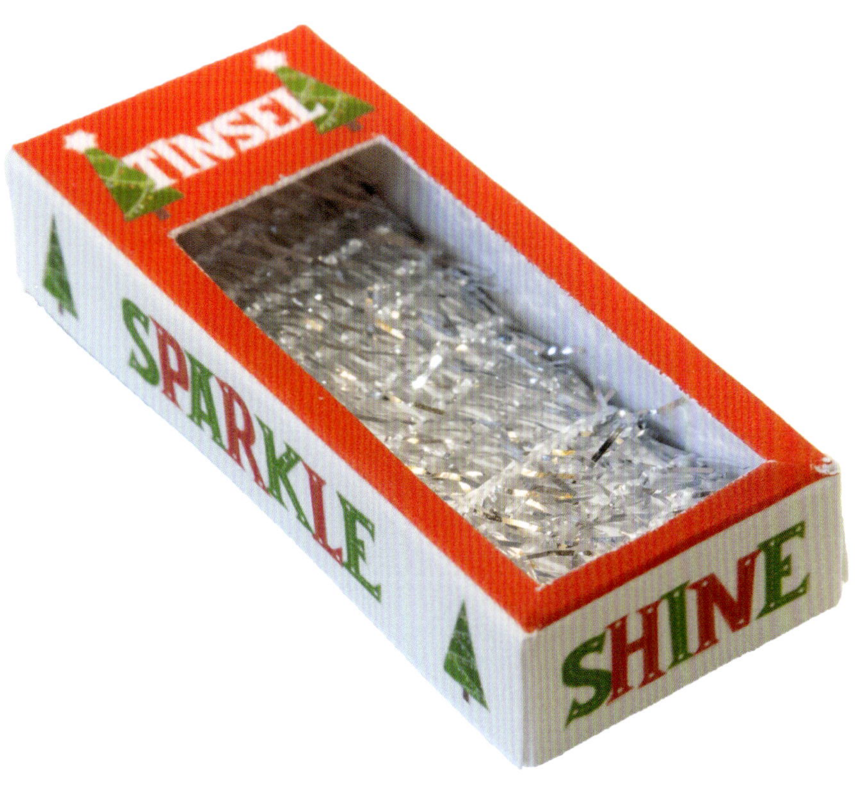

✳ The shelves behind the counter are filled with elves, supplies, packages of tinsel, and treats. The tinsel box is $1/2$ inch by 1 inch.

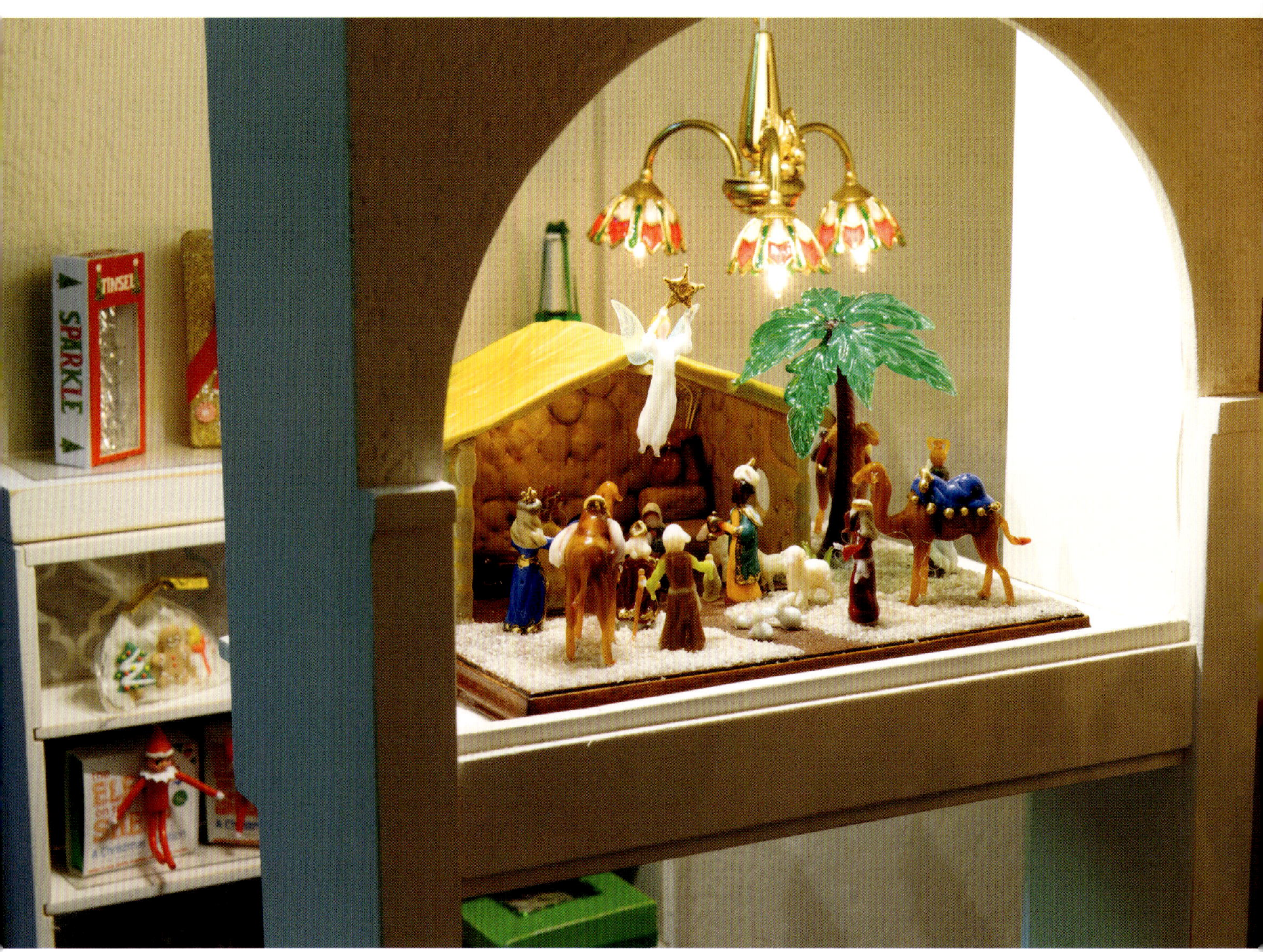

✳Maria and Mario Ramos of Vitreus Ignis created the nativity set that sits above the sales counter. Each piece is hand-blown glass. There is a light in the crest of the manger that highlights all of these details. It is a magnificent piece.

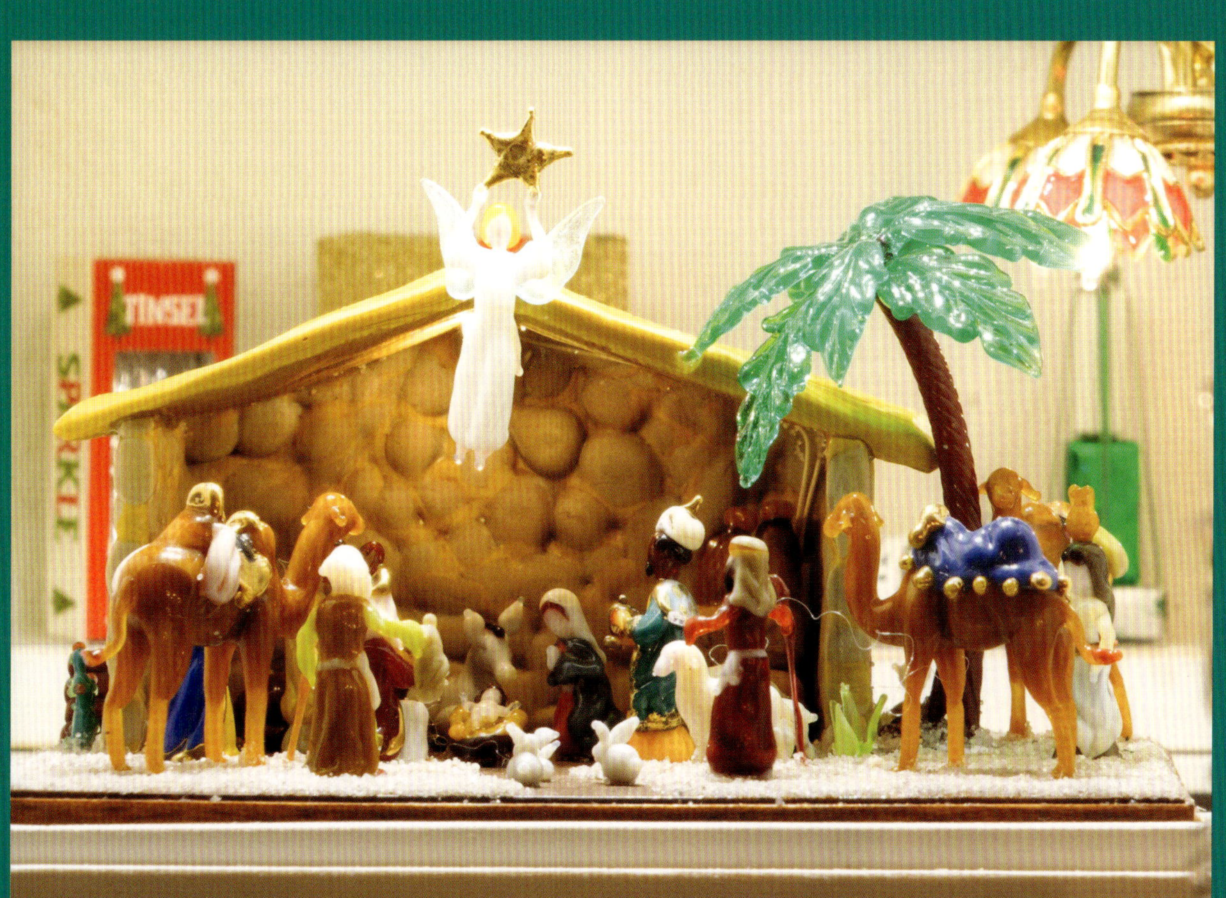

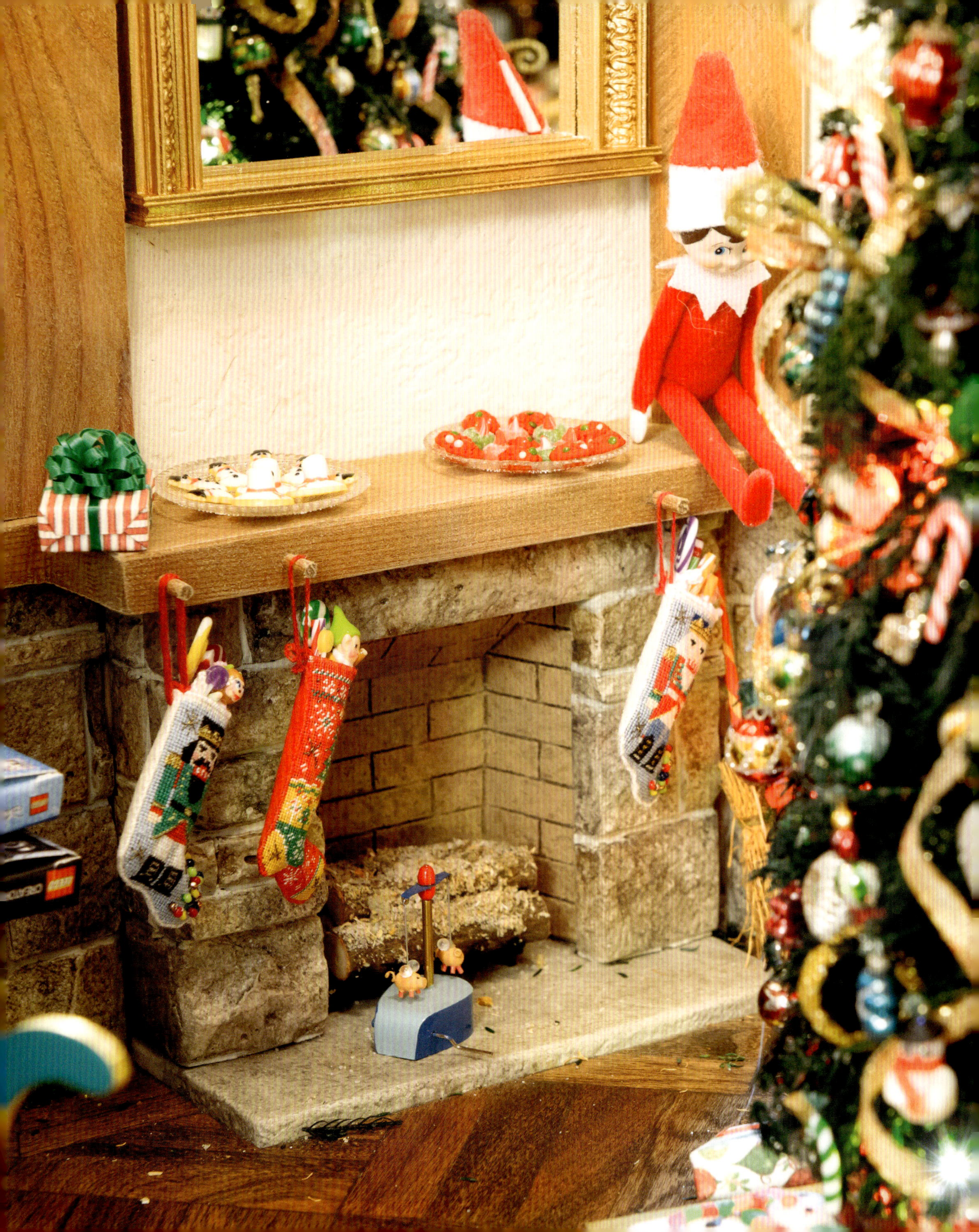

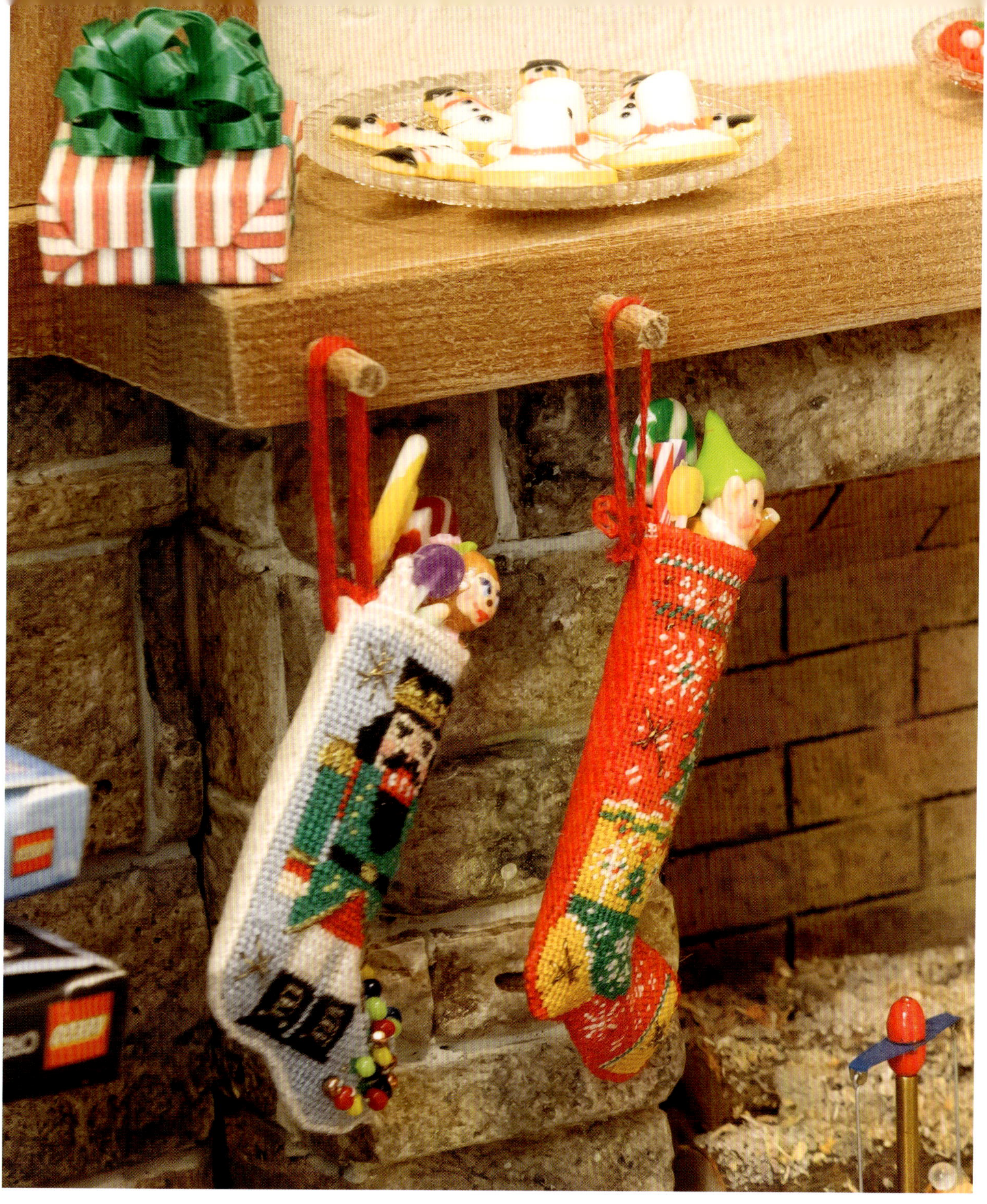

✳ The petit point stockings by Natalie Frank hold
treats and an elf and hang on the fireplace mantel. A
St. Leger working toy sits at the base of the fireplace.

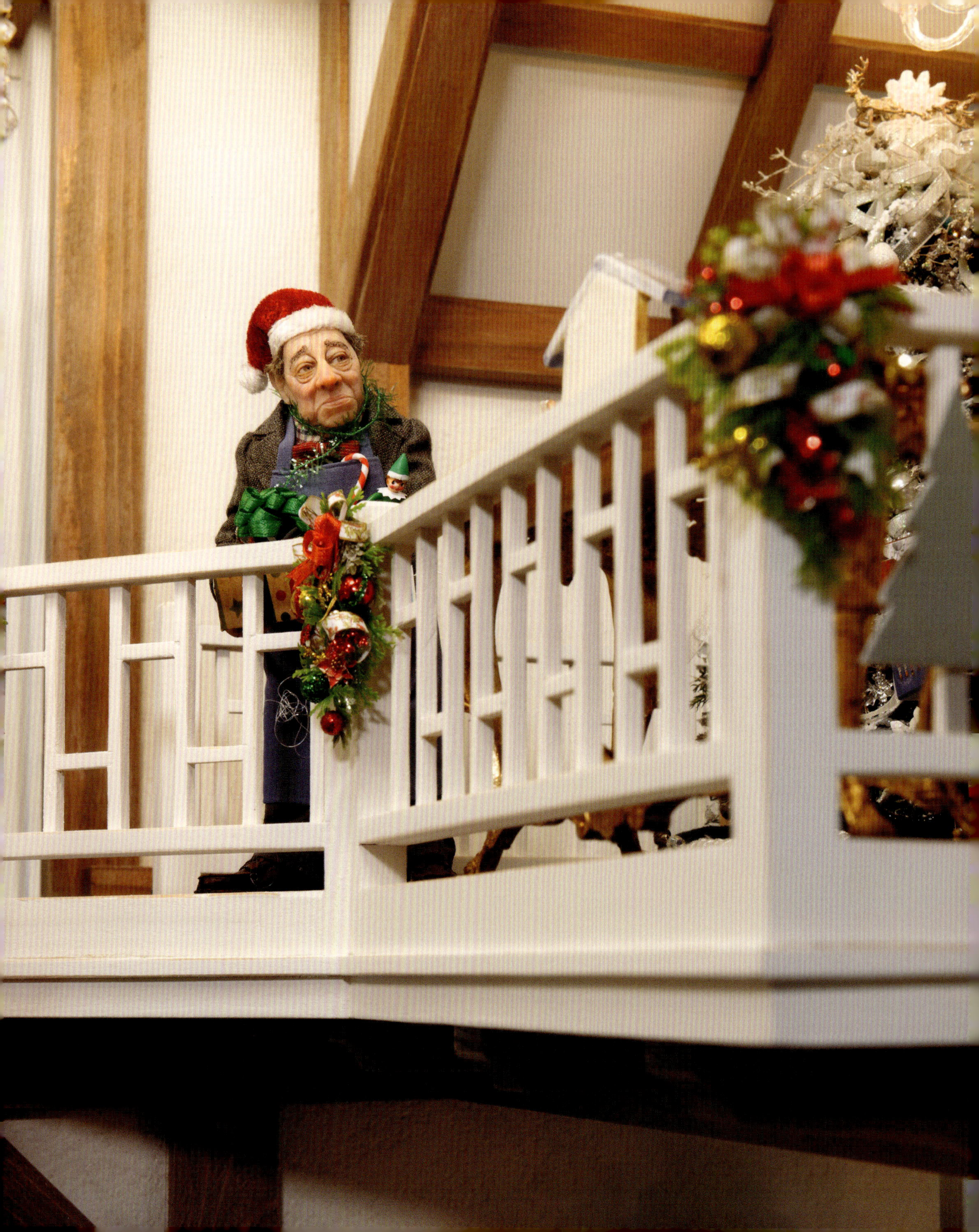

The Balcony
& Attic

The balcony allows space for yet more trees—
six, in fact. It also holds a beautiful nativity set
by Jack Cashmere and detailed ornament swags
throughout . . . . The attic is carefully hidden.
To reach it, one has to go around the back
and carefully open a closed door. But there is
much to be seen in it.

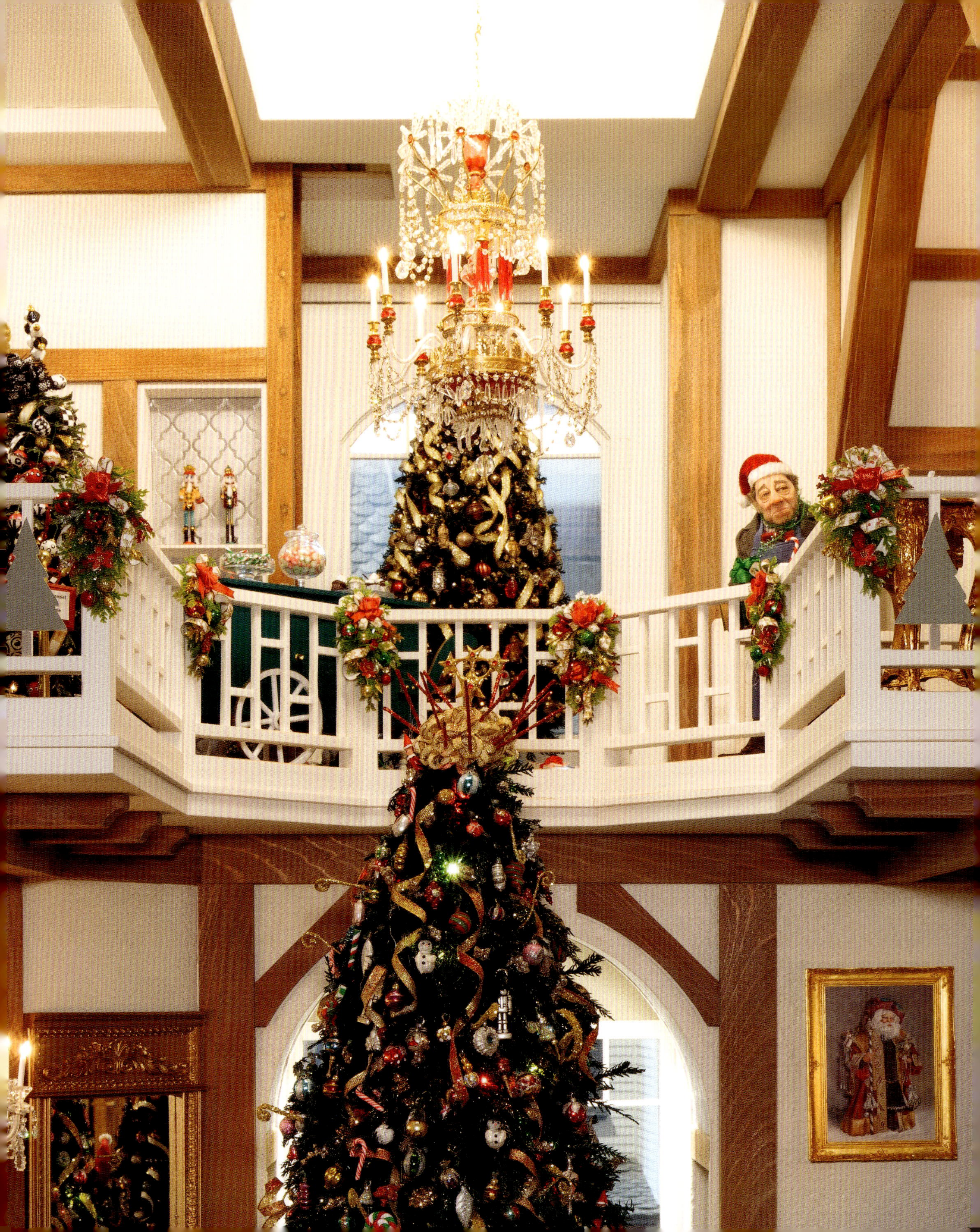

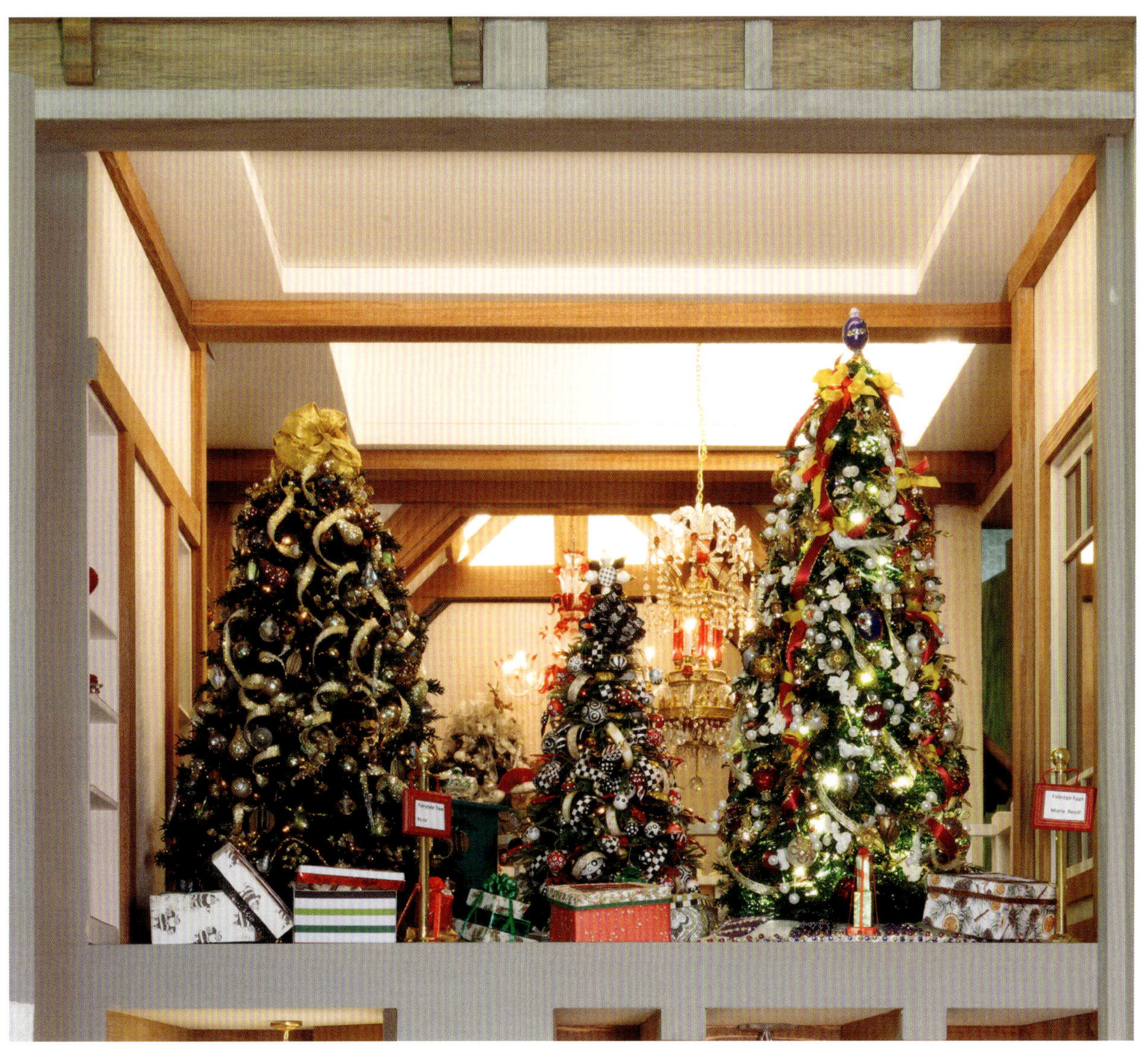

✳The three trees above were each created by skilled artisans. On the right Maria Bevill created the Fabergé Egg Tree and Marcia McClain hand-beaded the skirt to accompany it. Mable Mobley created a character tree, which sits in the center, and on the left is a tree by Jo Bevilacqua. Jo's tree has close to one thousand ornaments and an obviously gold theme. Hand-blown nutcrackers, another tree, and another candy cart completely fill the balcony.

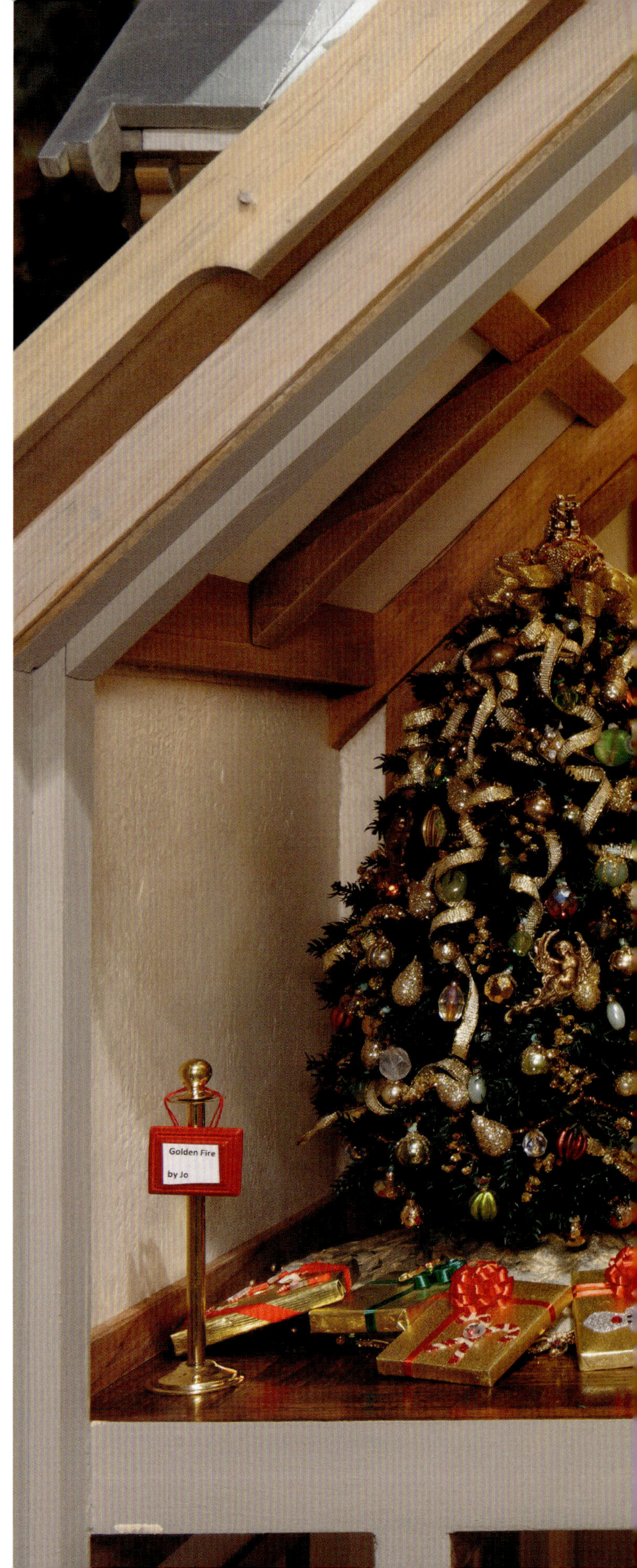

✳ Trees, toys, and packages fill this side of the balcony. But of most special note is the chandelier, which is handblown glass by Maria and Mario Ramos of Vitreus Ignis. From this view, which is the open right side of the Emporium, the view clearly shows all of the trees, two magnificient chandeliers, a ceramic nativity set by Jack Cashmere, and of course, more presents.

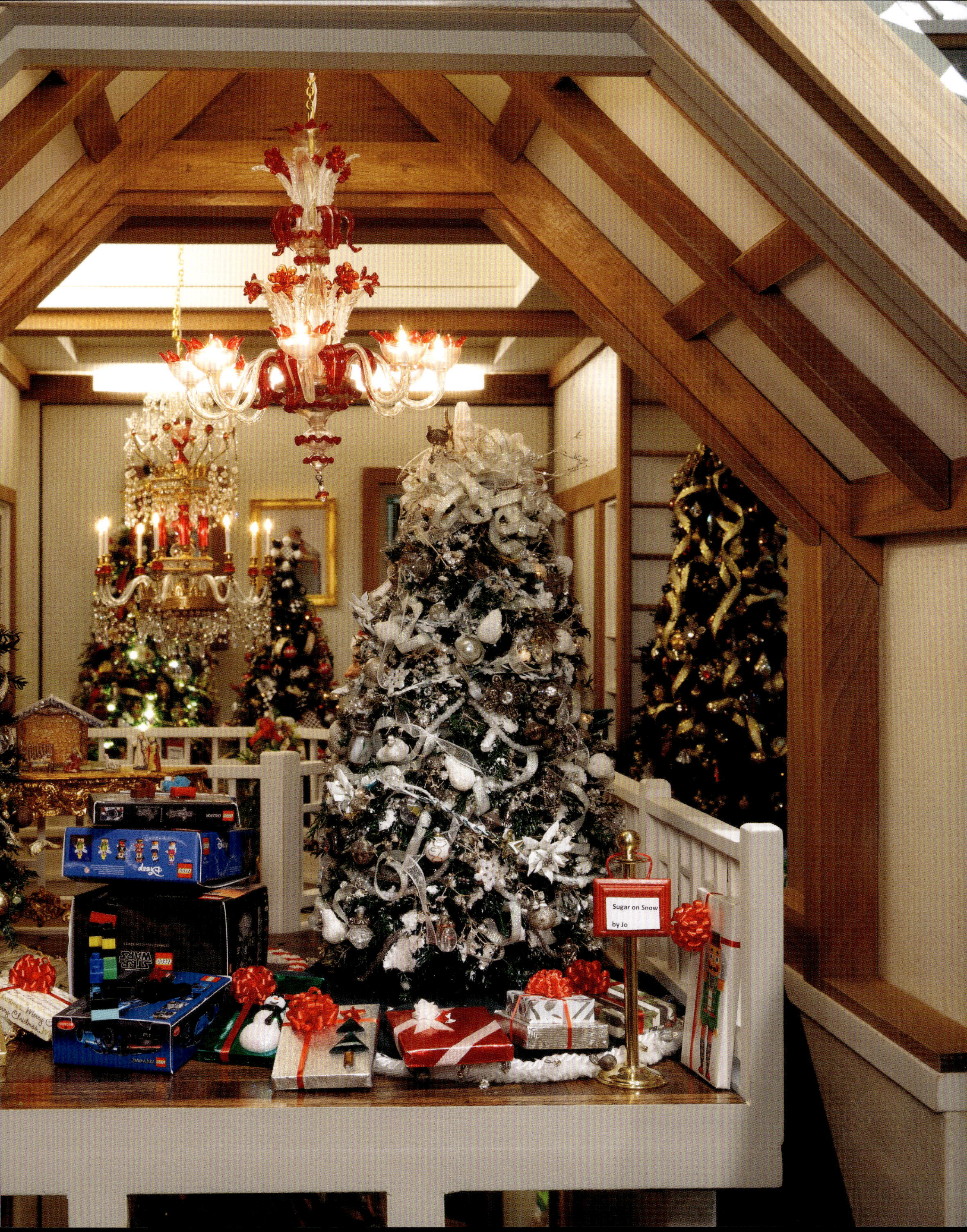

Sugar on Snow
by Jo

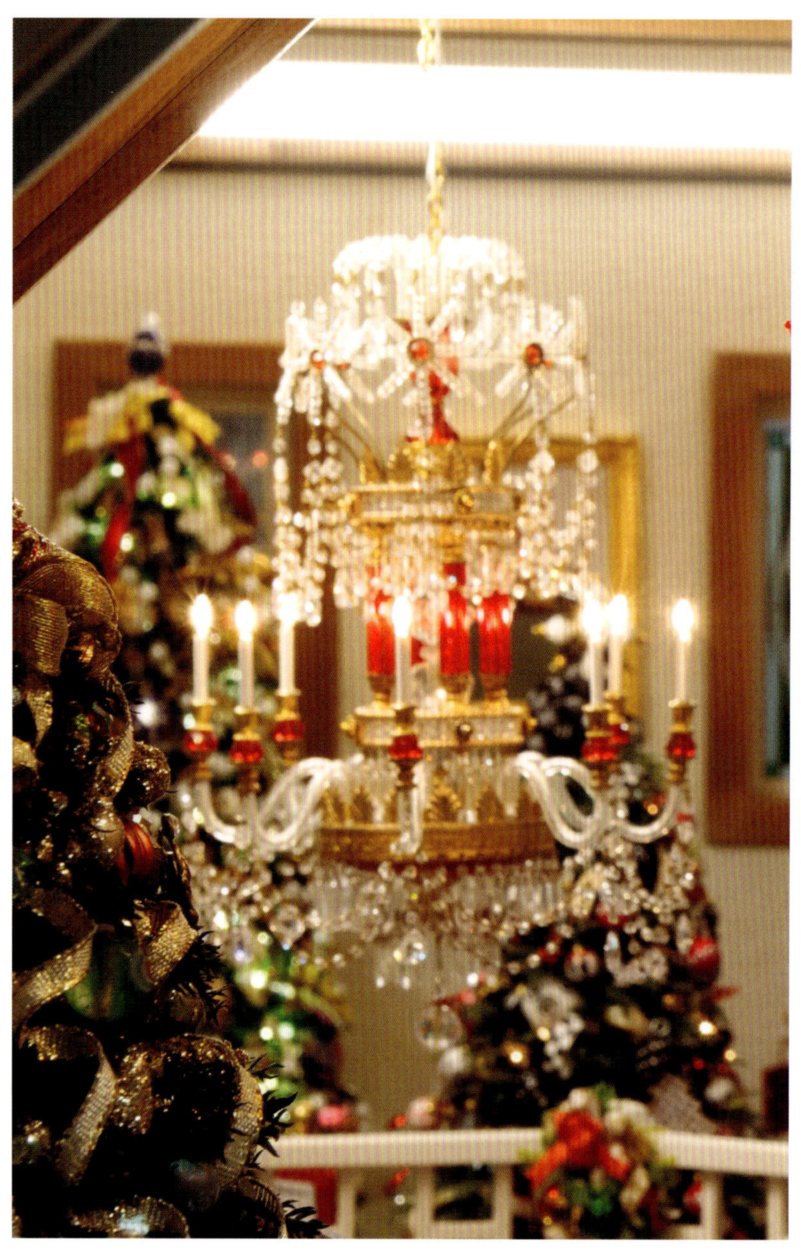

The chandelier on the left is by Frank Crescente and the one on the right is by Maria and Mario Ramos. Both artisans do remarkable and unparalleled work. These chandeliers make the entire Emporium sparkle with delight.

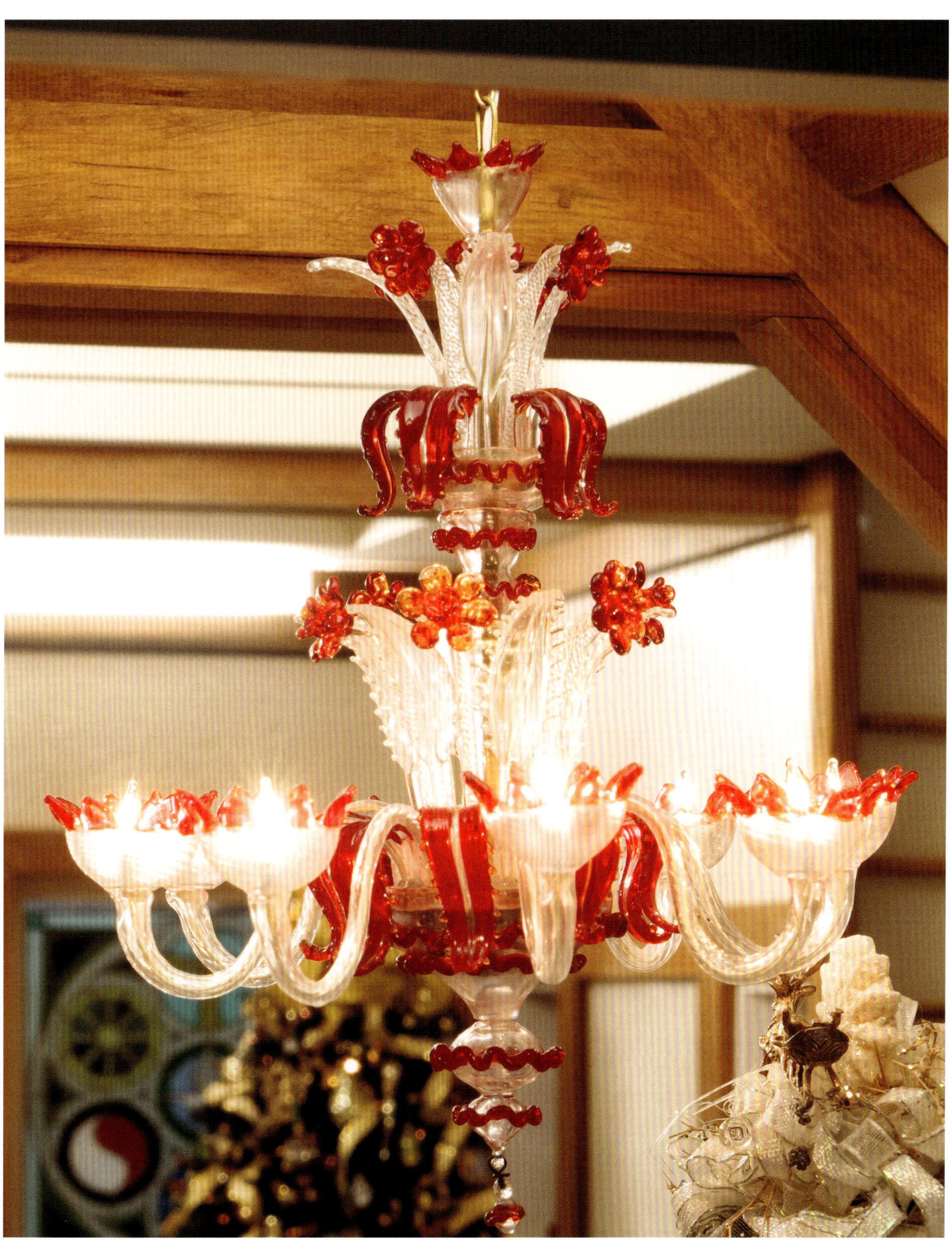

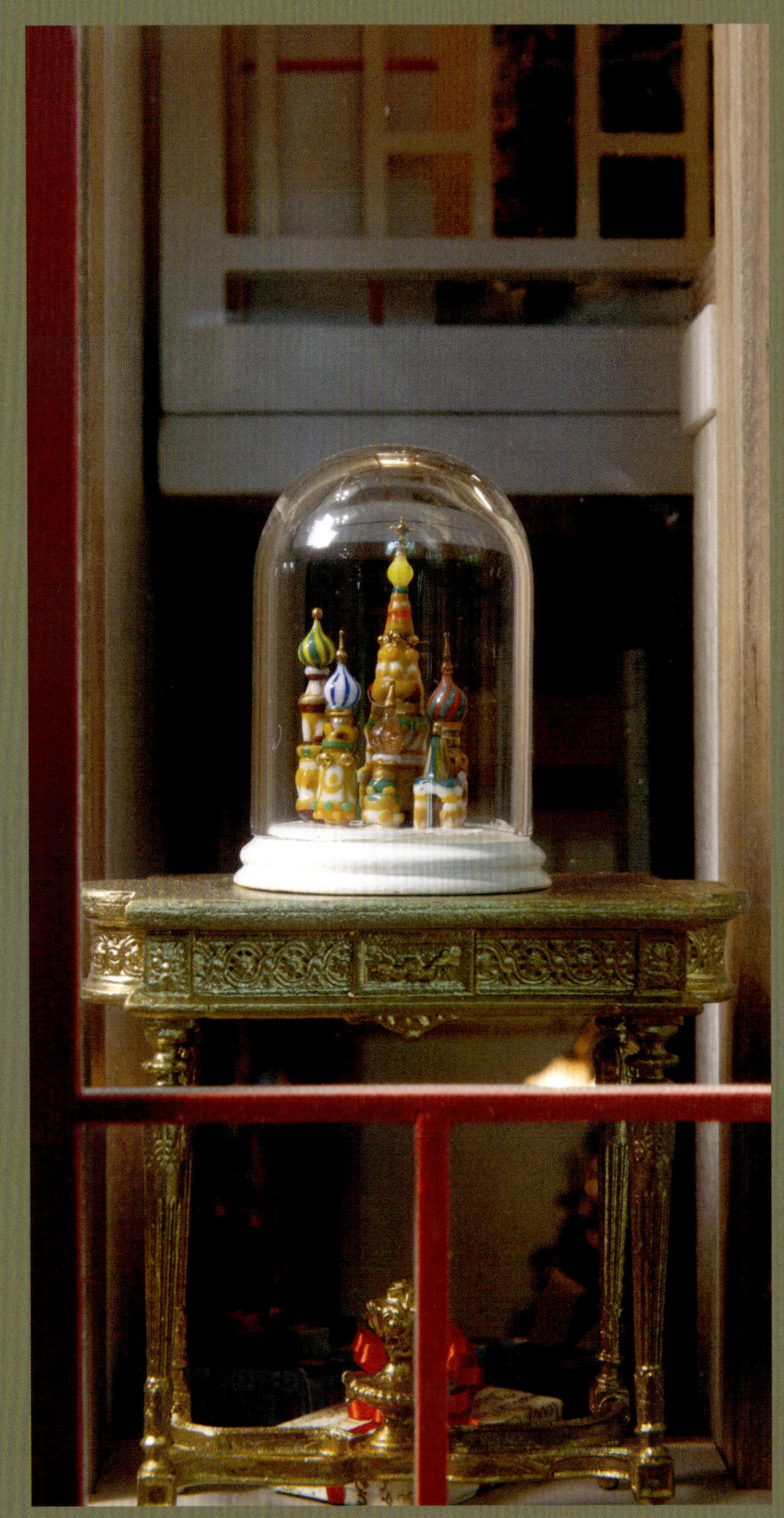

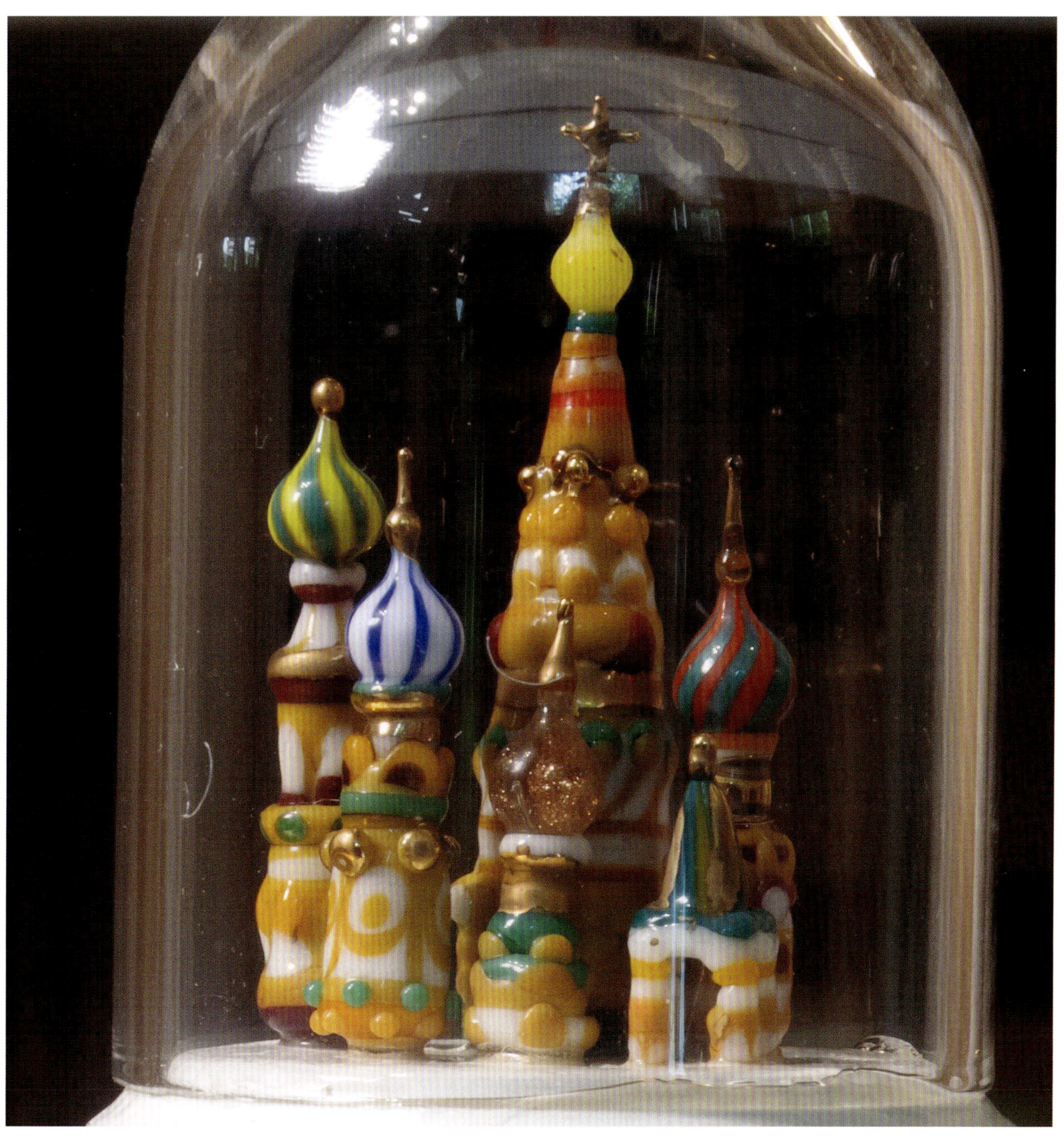

✳This domed glass is displayed in a window. The blown glass is only 2 inches tall at its highest point. It is an incredible piece by Maria and Mario Ramos, displaying Russia's important Orthodox church, Saint Basil's Cathedral. This blown glass is so fragile that it cannot be removed from the dome.

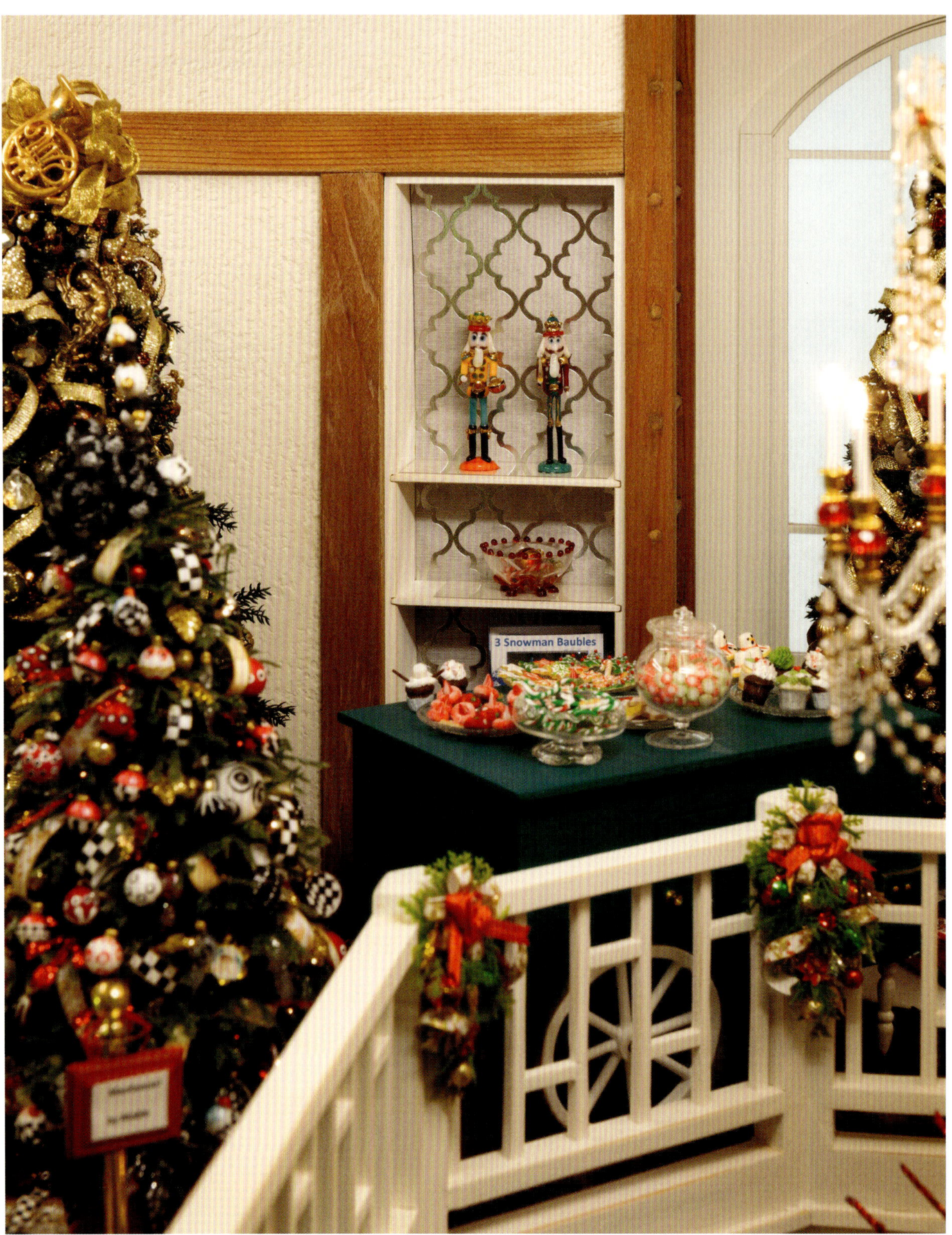
3 Snowman Baubles

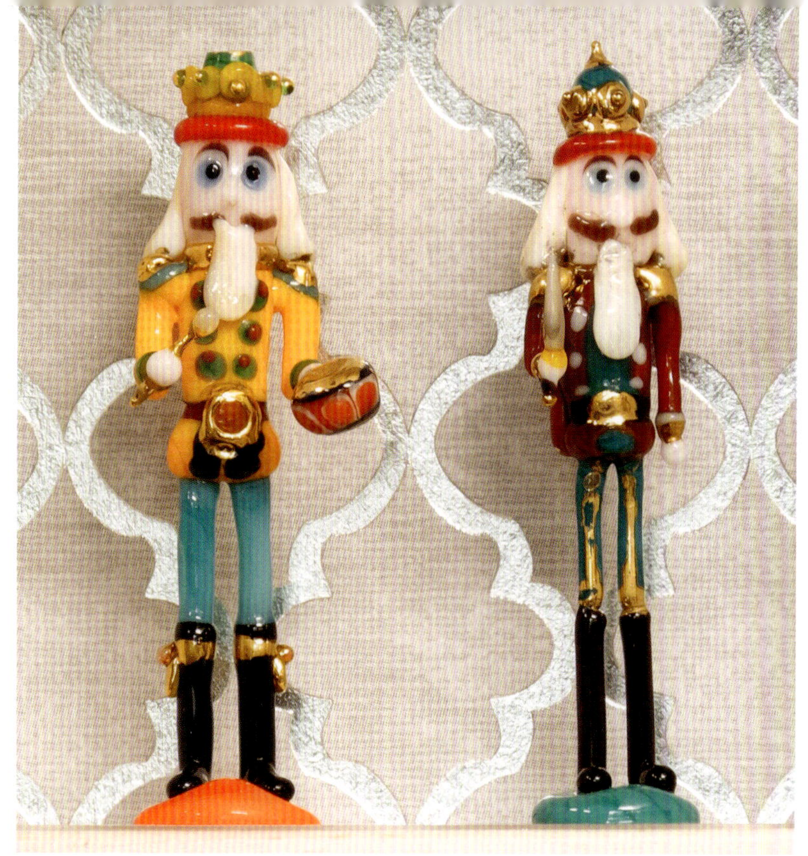

✳ The small details on the shelves and set about the Emporium complete its authenticity. The two nutcrackers above are actually two of four that were, once again, created by Maria and Mario Ramos. The blown glass is magnificent in its detail. These are a little more than 1 inch tall. The candy in the candy dish and all the treats on the cart were created by Orsolga Skulteti. Hundreds of individual treats fill the cart.

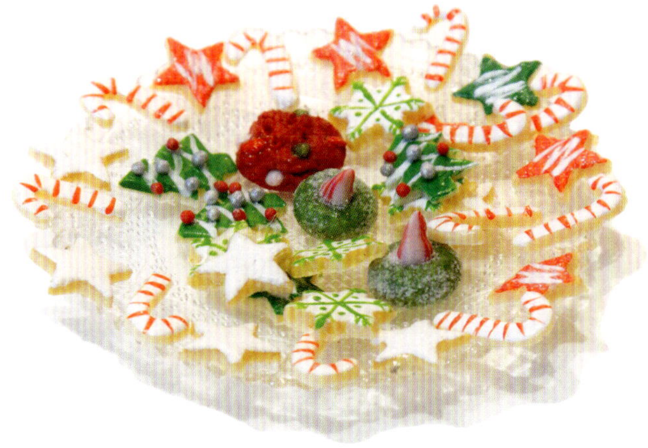

Here we come

a-caroling among the

leaves so green.

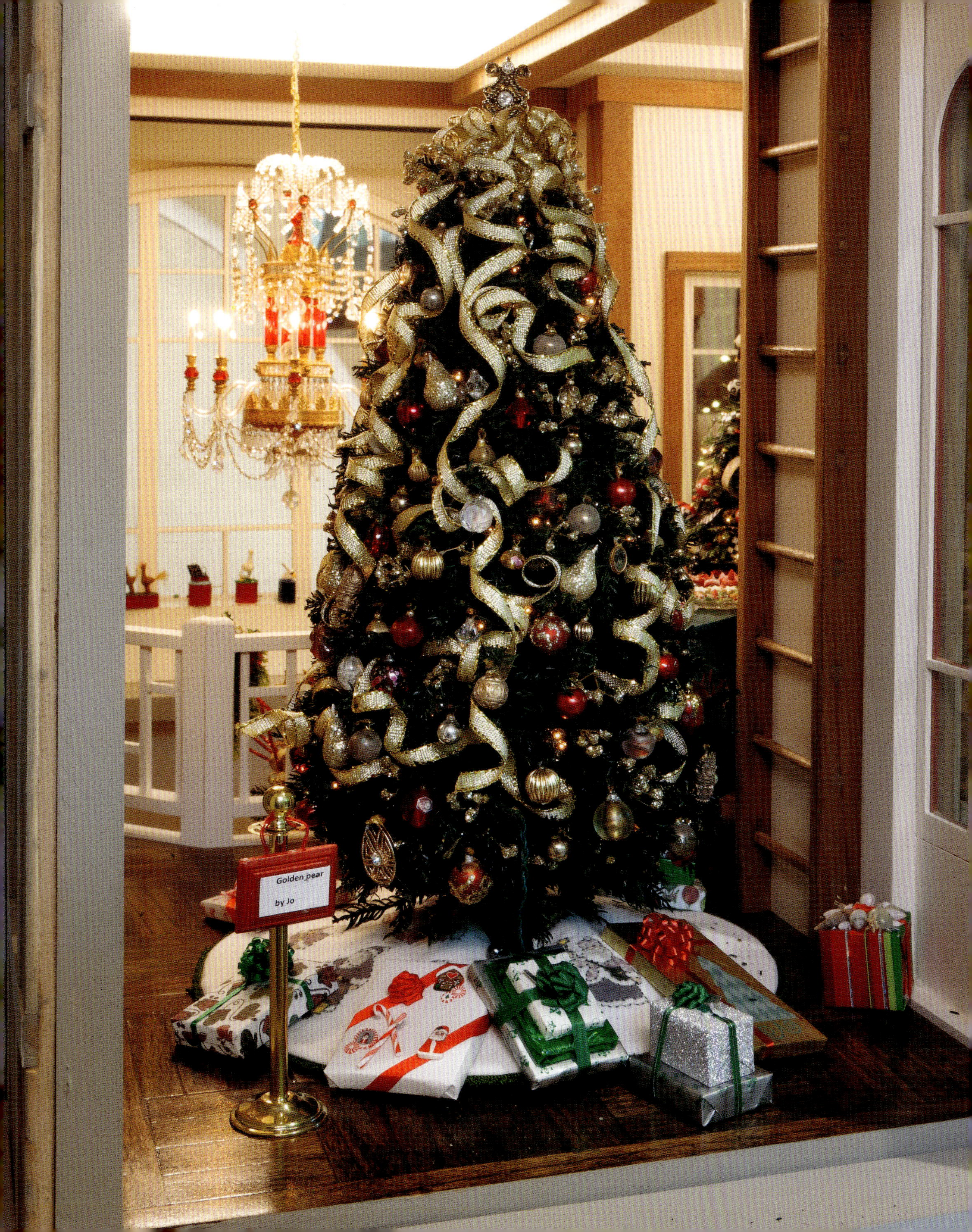
Golden pear
by Jo

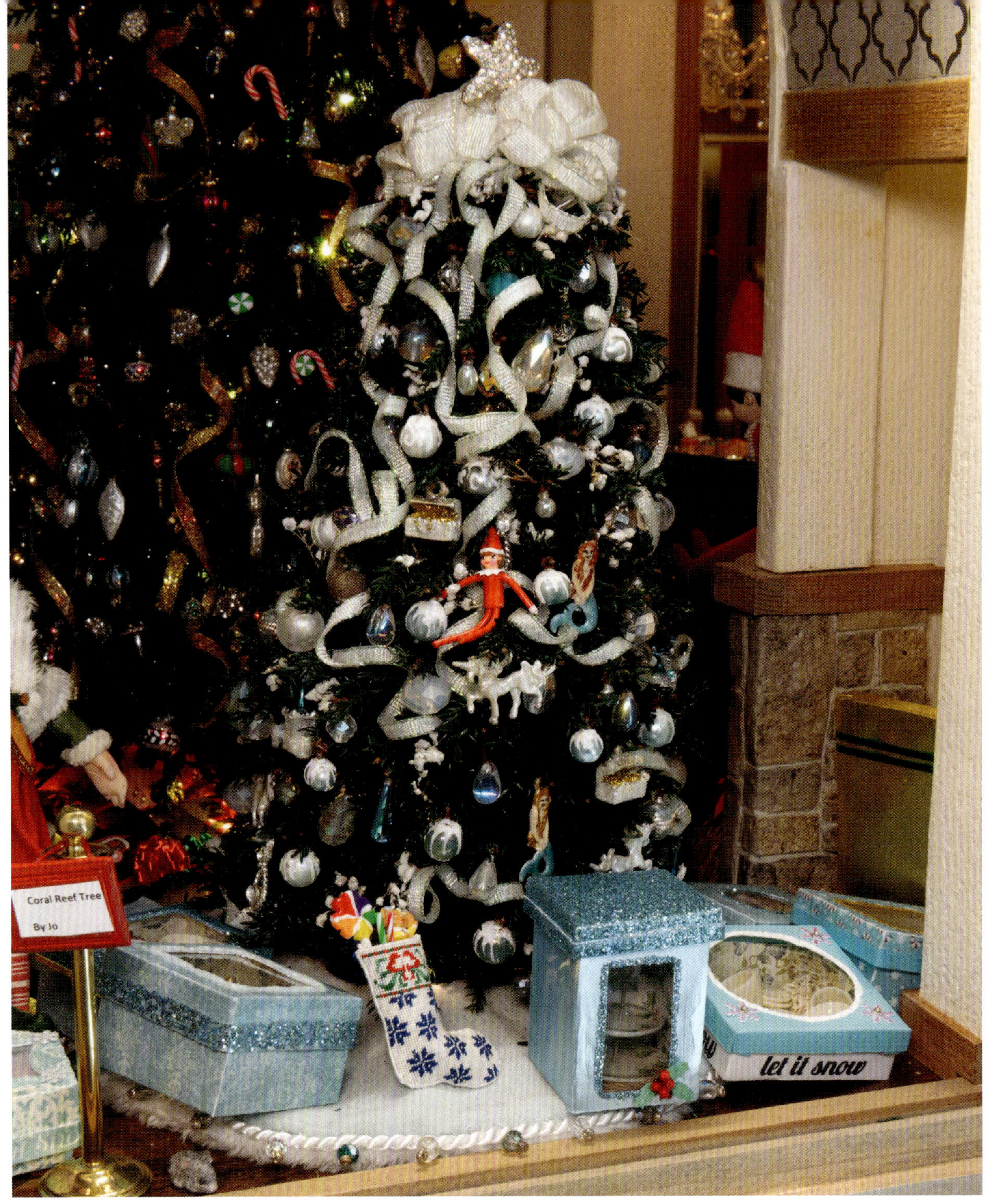

*Behold the Coral Reef Tree with all the details. Jo Bevilacqua created this tree and included almost a thousand ornaments. The aqua-colored boxes (to match the tree) contain Christmas plates and cups.

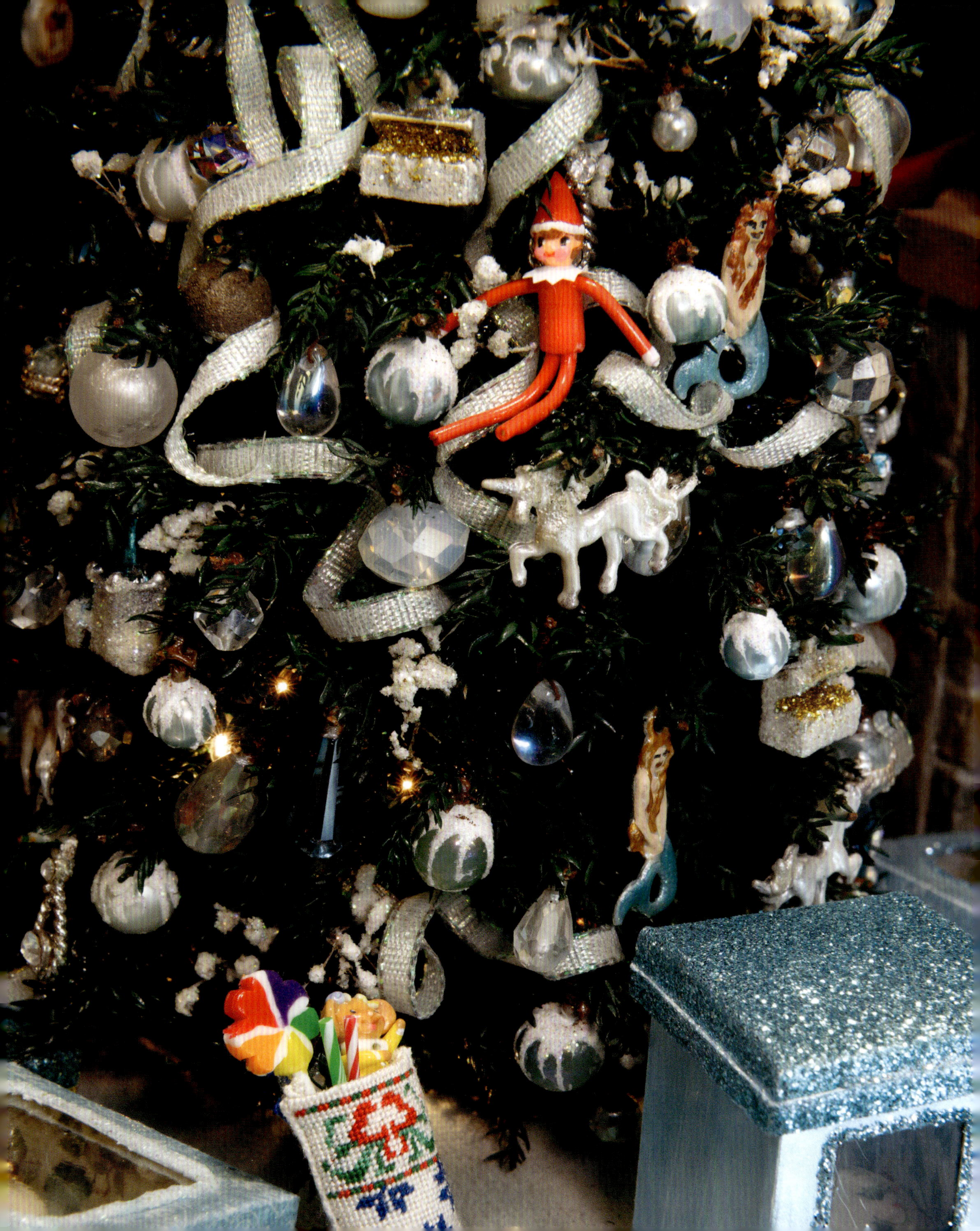

And then in a
twinkling I heard
on the roof...

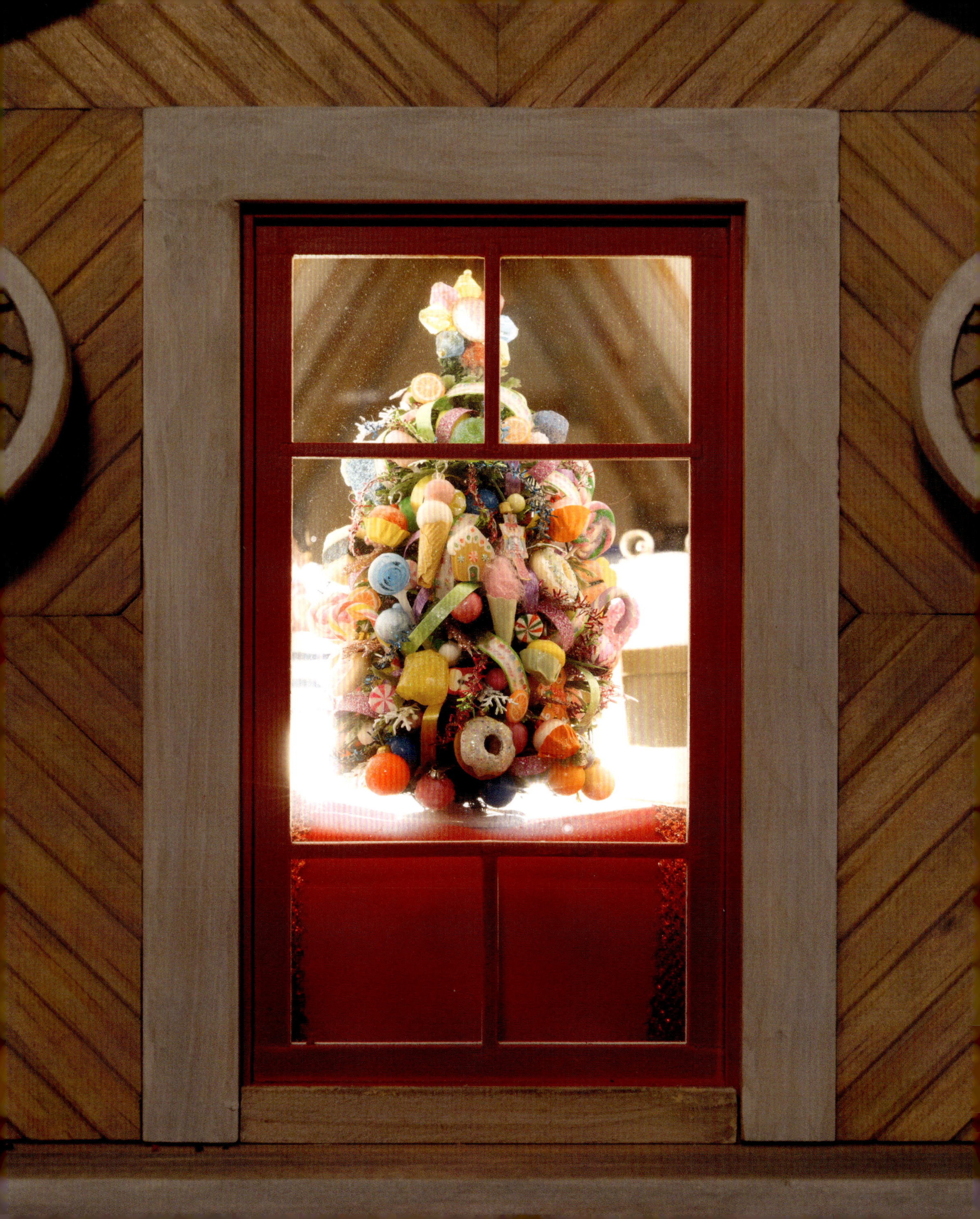

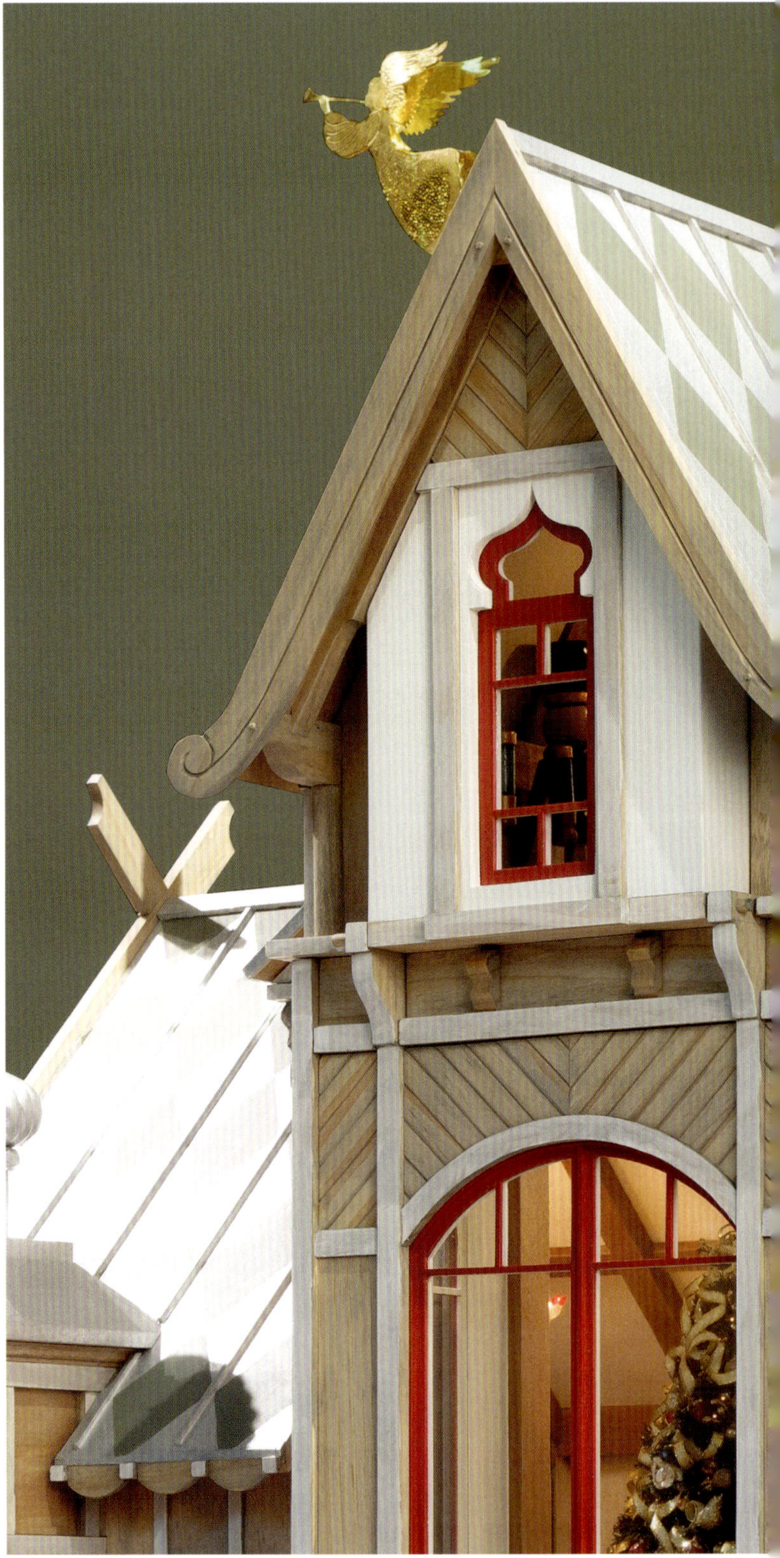

A view of the very top—complete with Santa's sleigh, the small door to the attic, and Advent door number 1 open to see the twinkling light inside.

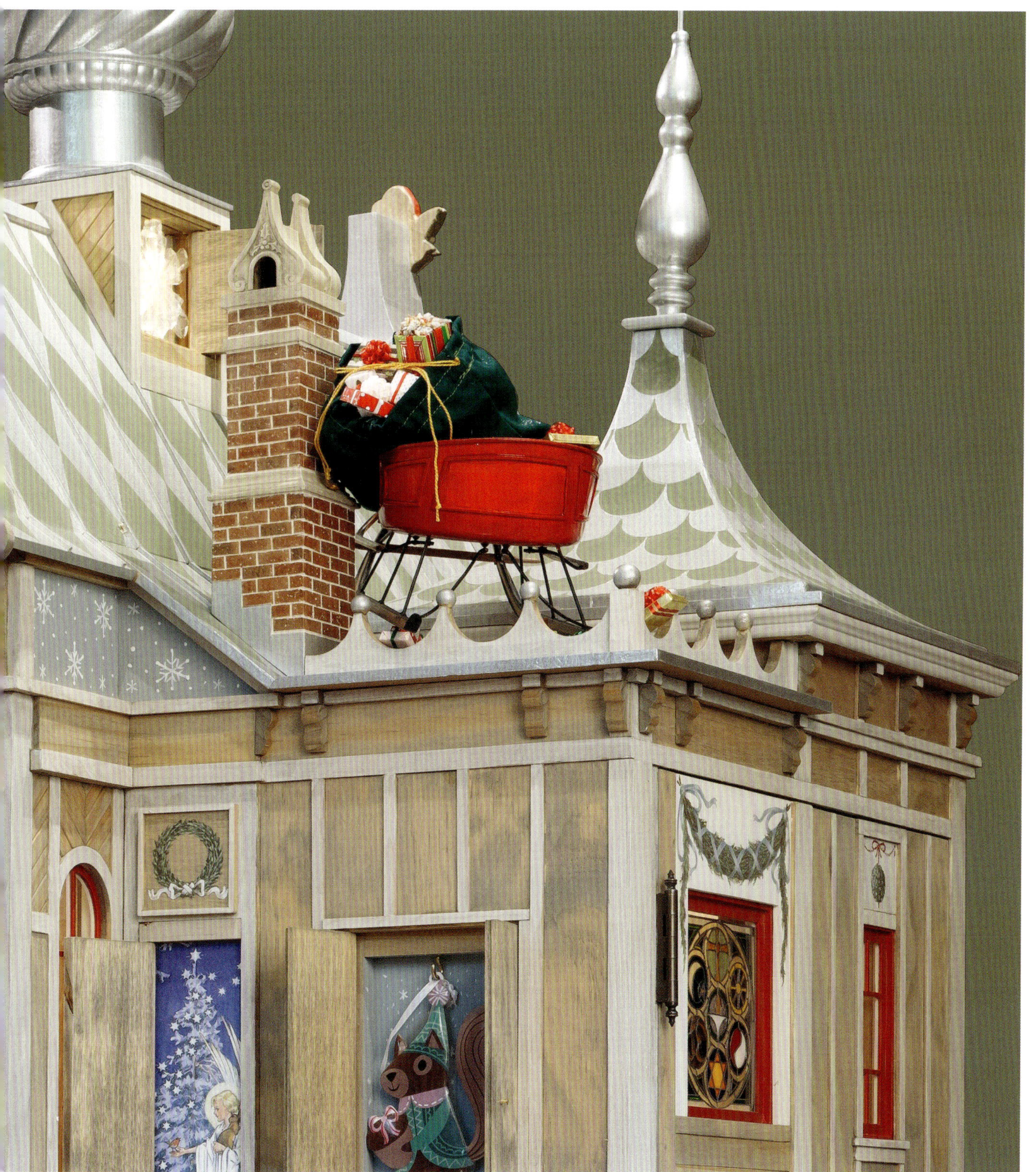

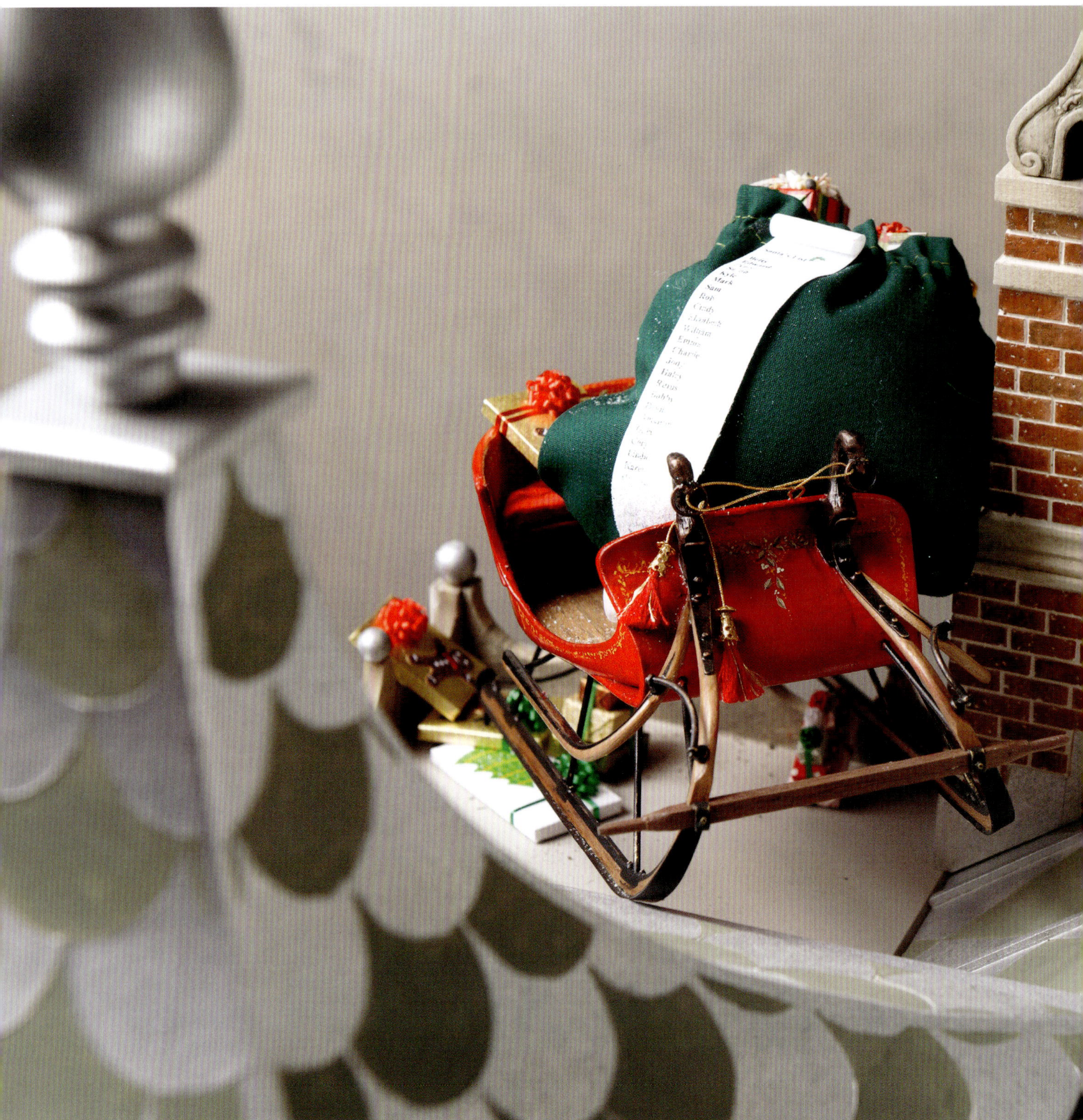

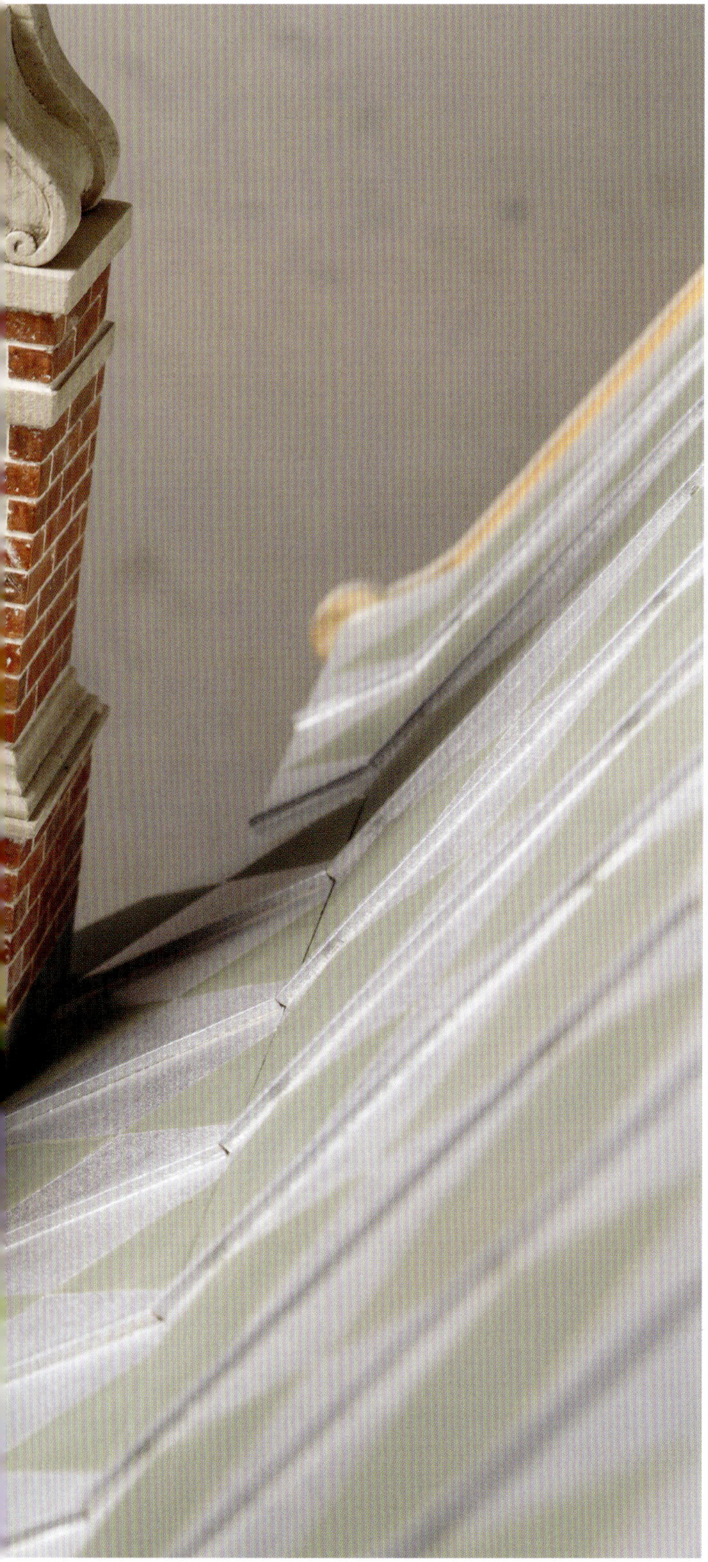

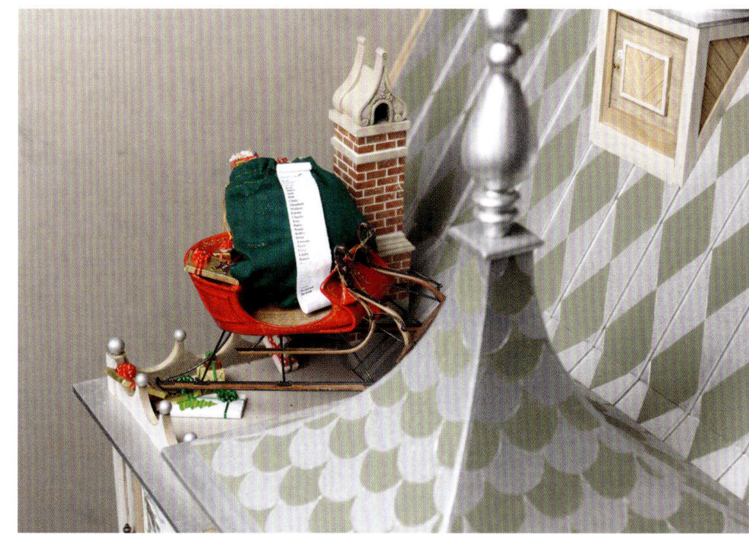

✳The sleigh was created by Jim Larson and painted by Maritza Moran. Of course it carries presents.

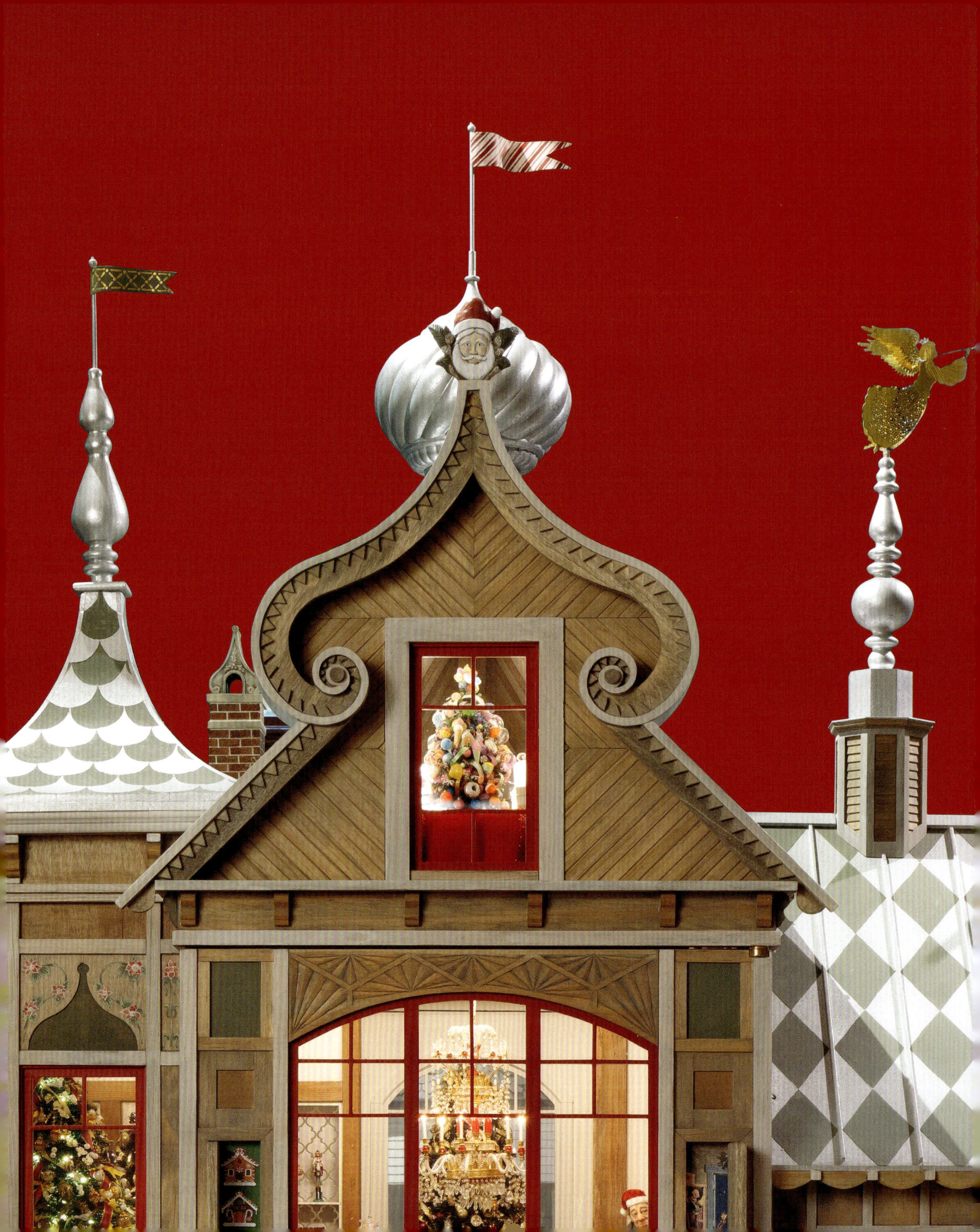

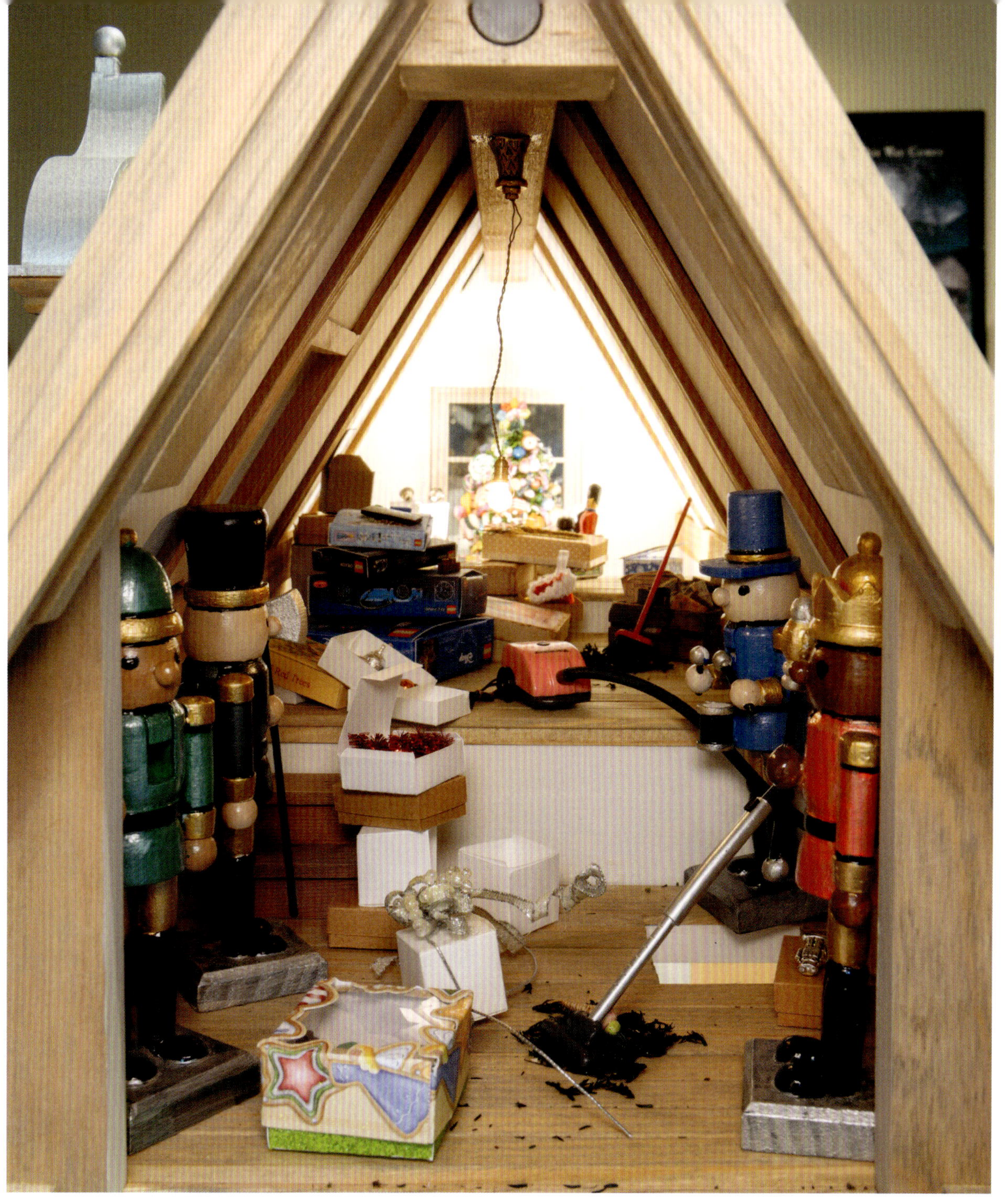

✳ Every proper home has an attic. And the Emporium is no exception. This attic stores tall nutcrackers, packages, and of course a vacuum to sweep up greeneries. The attic is the full width of the Emporium, so there is lots of room for storage and boxes of clutter.

Happy Christmas
to all, and to all a
good night!

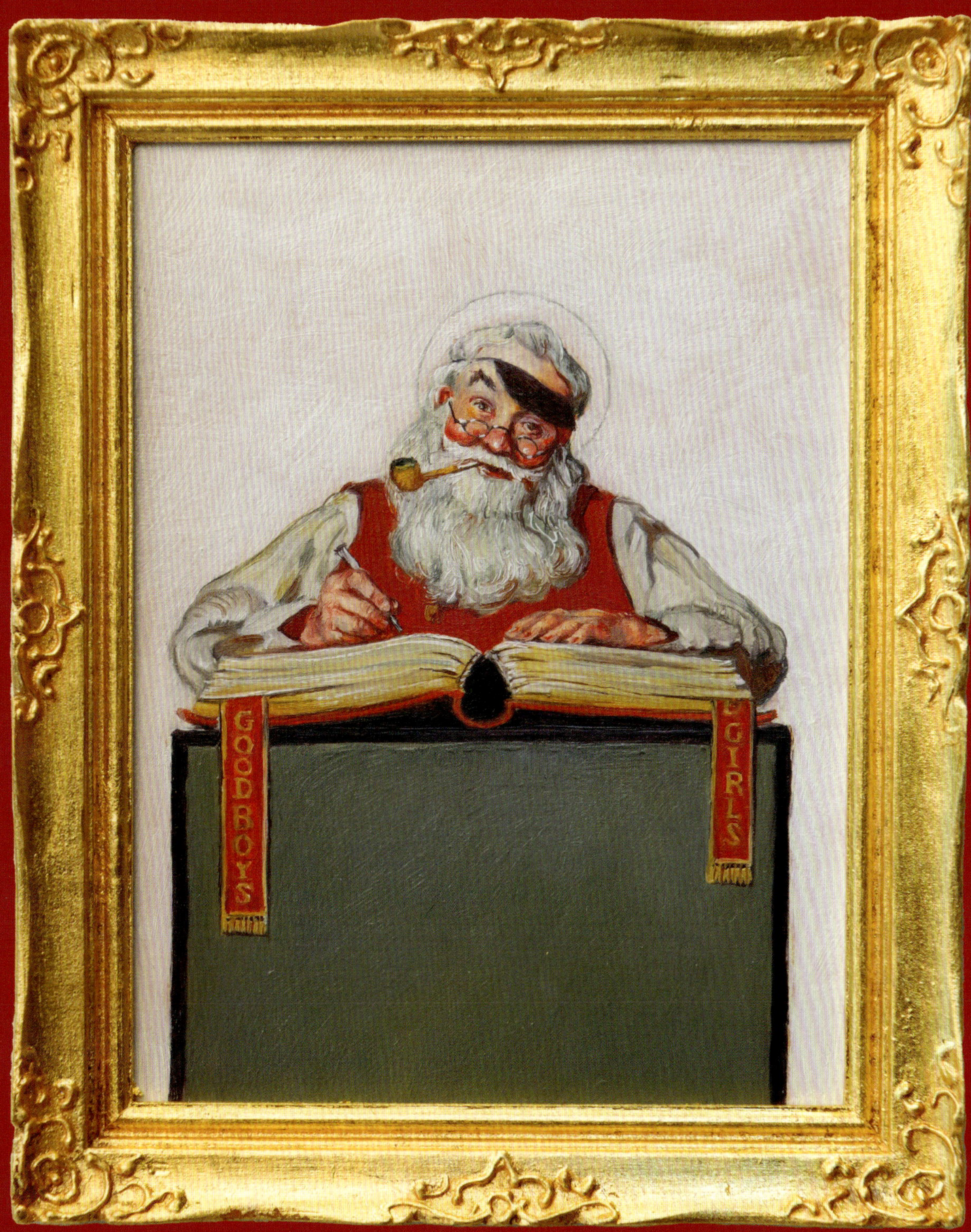

GOOD BOYS
GIRLS

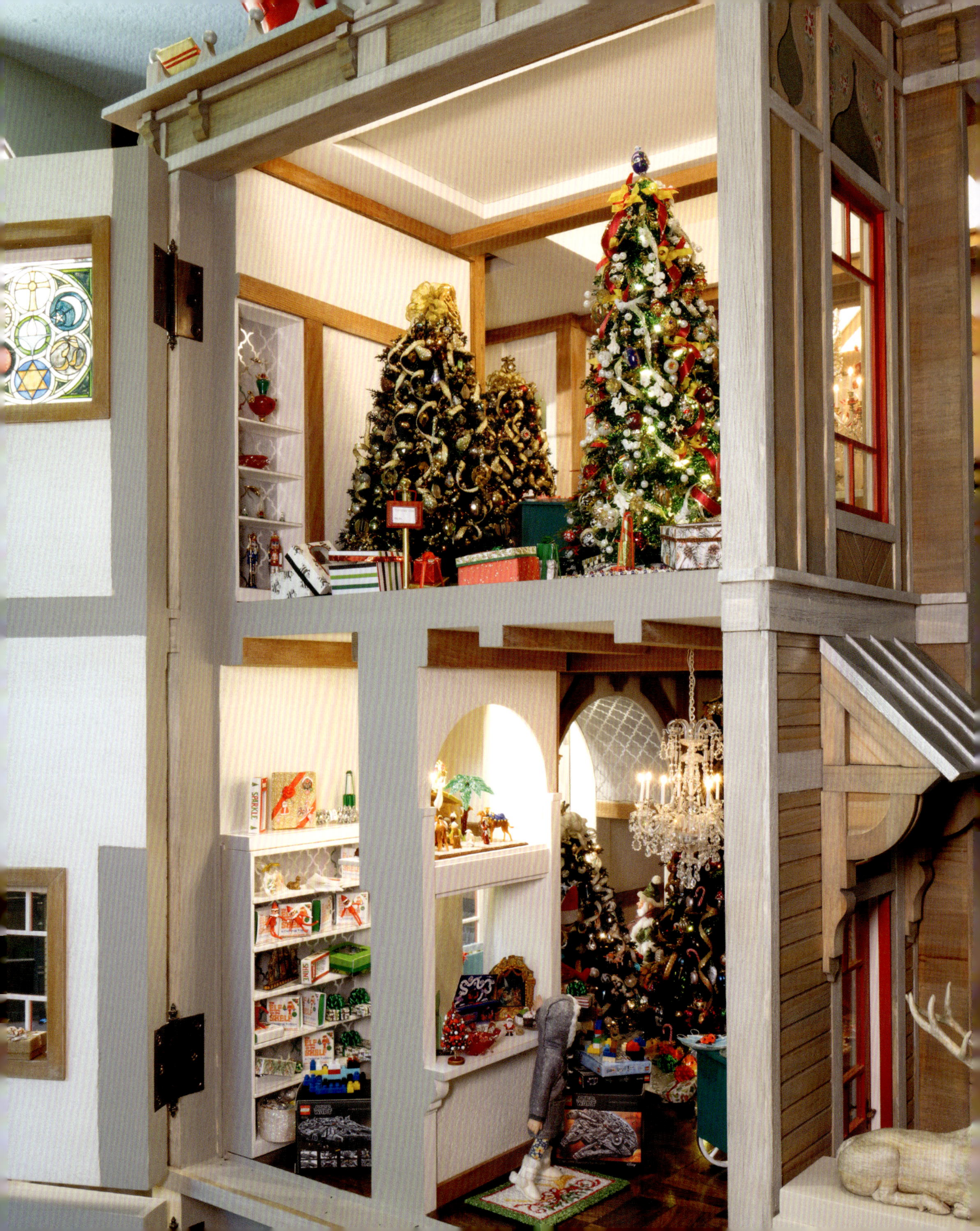

Appendix

Blueprints

These blueprints were created by Jon Fish
for the Christmas Emporium. This is a good
reference if one gets lost in all the details
offered within the photographs provided.

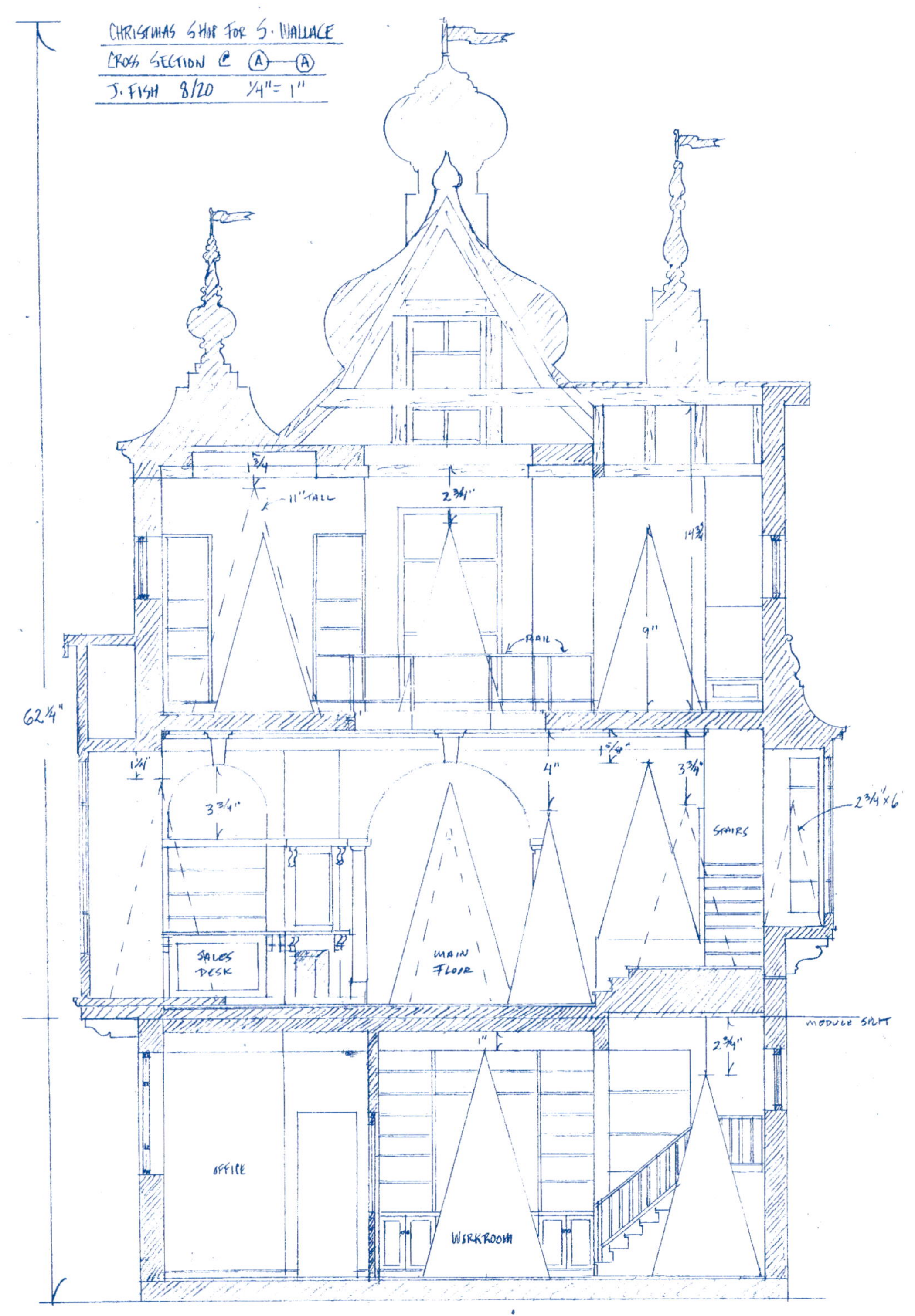

CHRISTMAS SHOP FOR S. WALLACE
CROSS SECTION @ A — A
J. FISH 8/20 1/4"= 1"
3/4
11" TALL
2 3/4"
14 3/4
9"
RAIL
62 1/4"
1 3/4
3 3/4"
4"
1 5/8"
3 3/4"
2 3/4" x 6
STAIRS
SALES DESK
MAIN FLOOR
MODULE SPLIT
1"
2 3/4"
OFFICE
WORKROOM

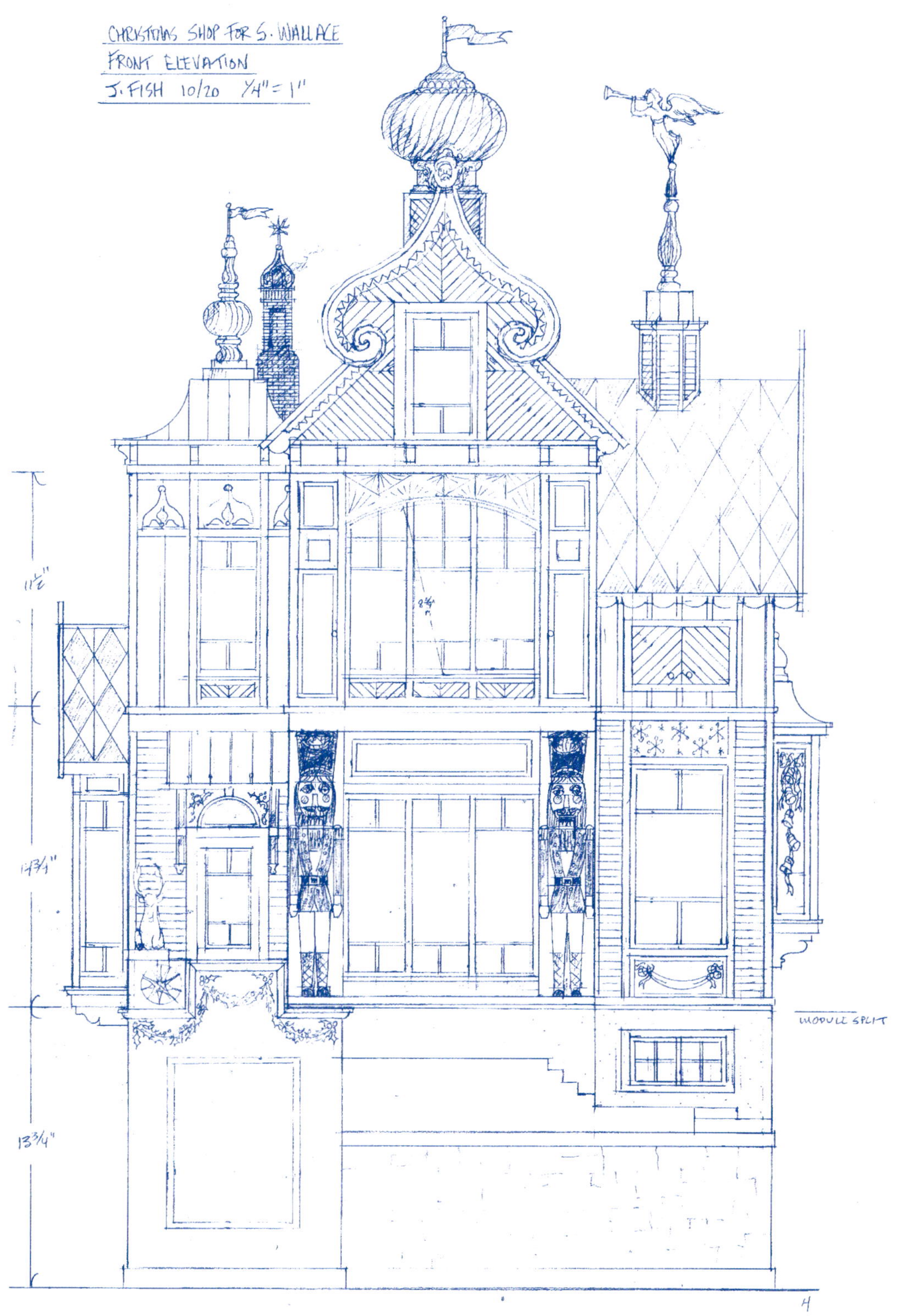

CHRISTMAS SHOP FOR S. WALLACE
FRONT ELEVATION
J. FISH   10/20   1/4" = 1"
MODULE SPLIT

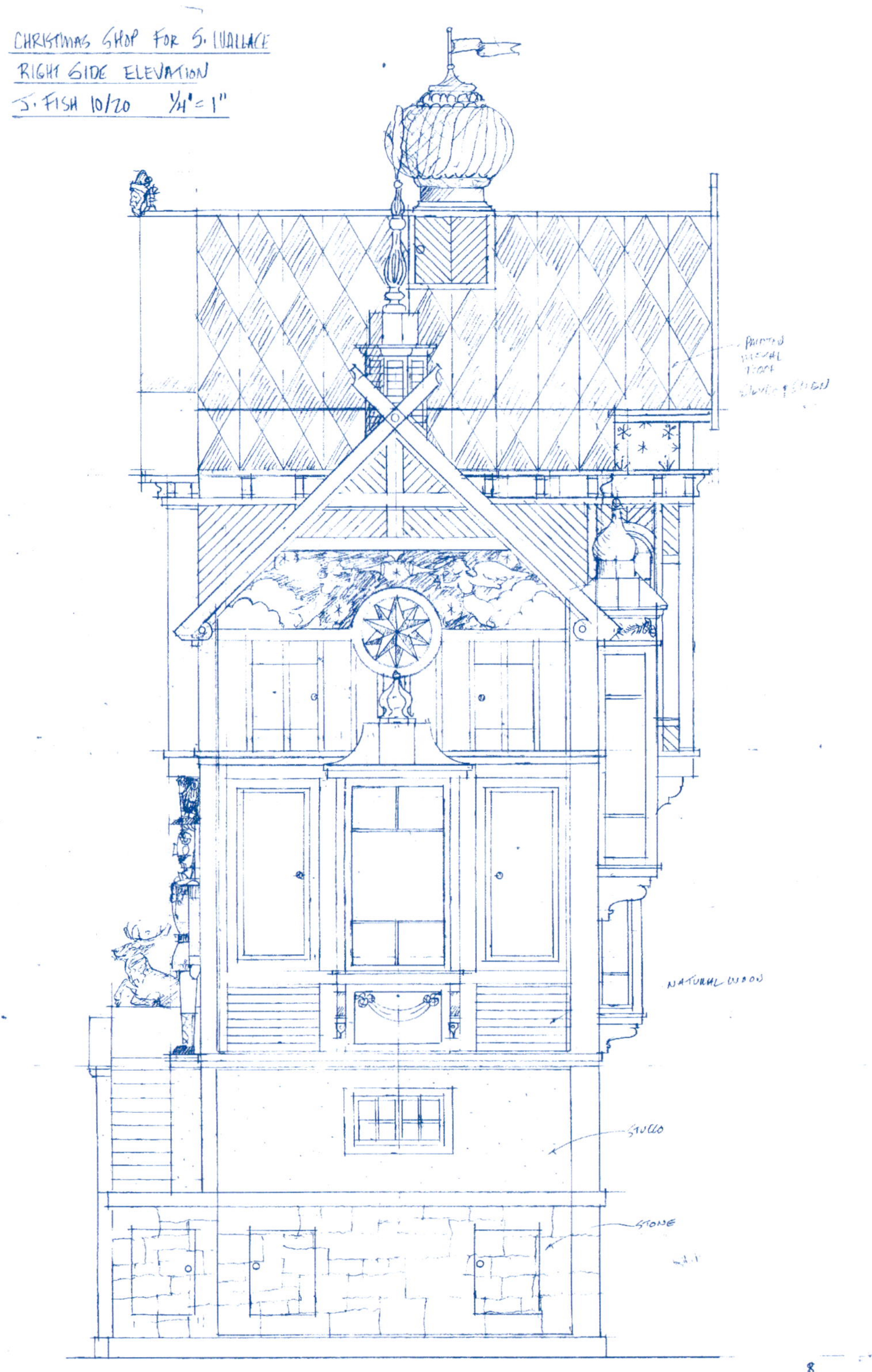

CHRISTMAS SHOP FOR S. WALLACE
RIGHT SIDE ELEVATION
J. FISH 10/20   1/4" = 1"
NATURAL WOON
STUCCO
STONE

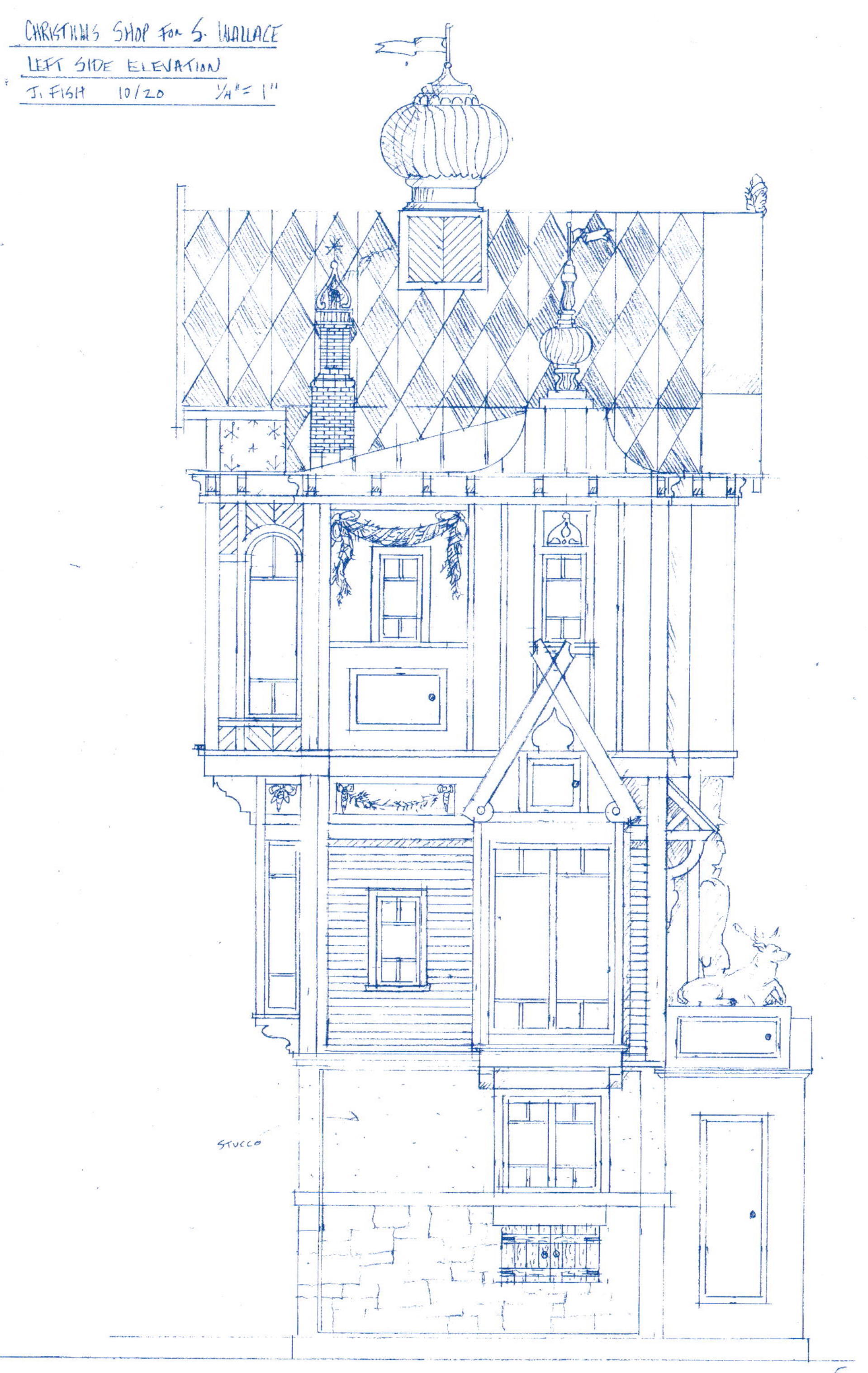

CHRISTMAS SHOP FOR S. WALLACE
LEFT SIDE ELEVATION
J. FISH   10/20   ¼"= 1"
STUCCO
5

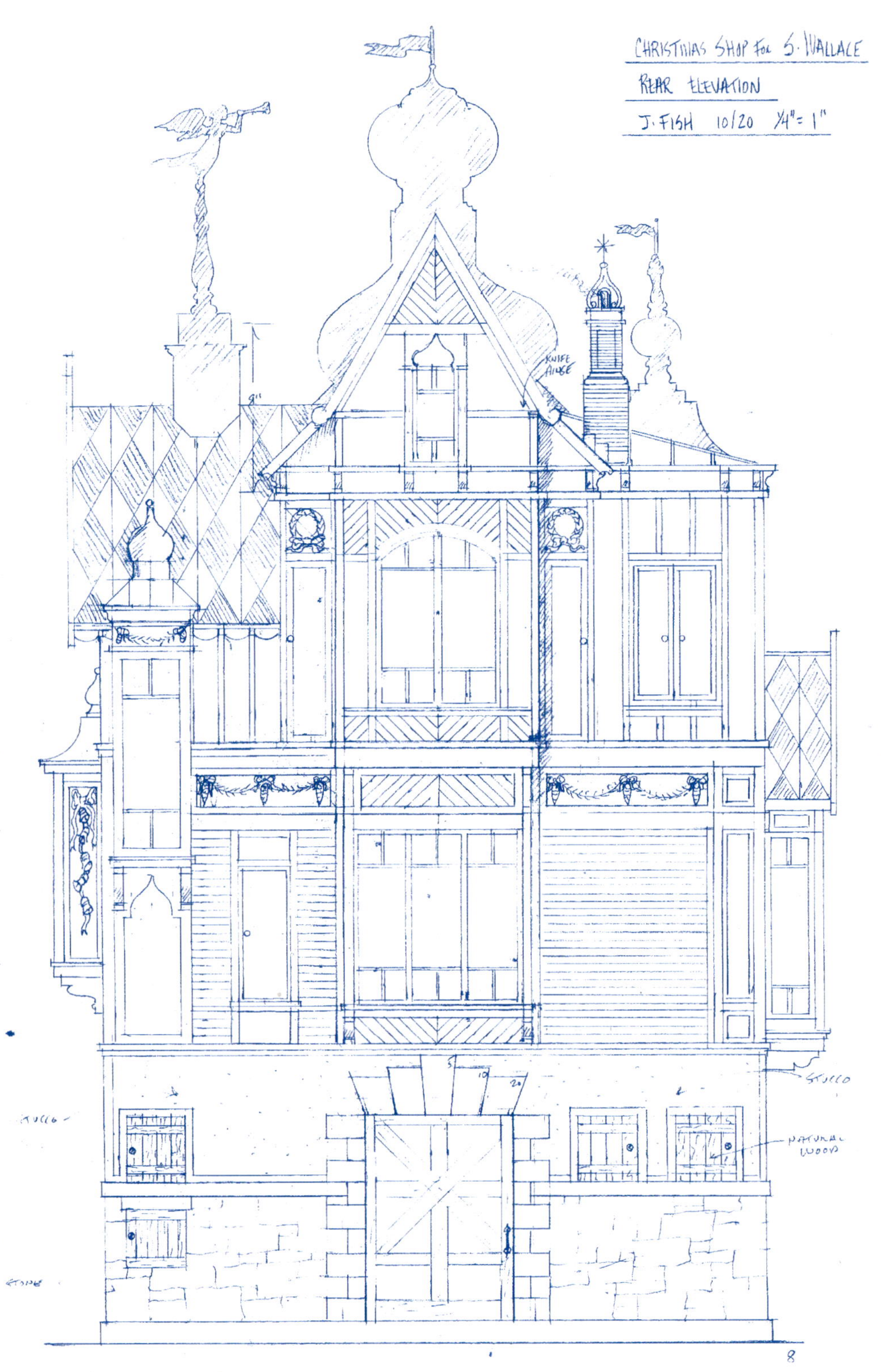

CHRISTMAS SHOP FOR S. WALLACE
REAR ELEVATION
J. FISH   10/20   1/4"=1"
KNIFE EDGE
STUCCO
NATURAL WOOD
STUCCO
STONE

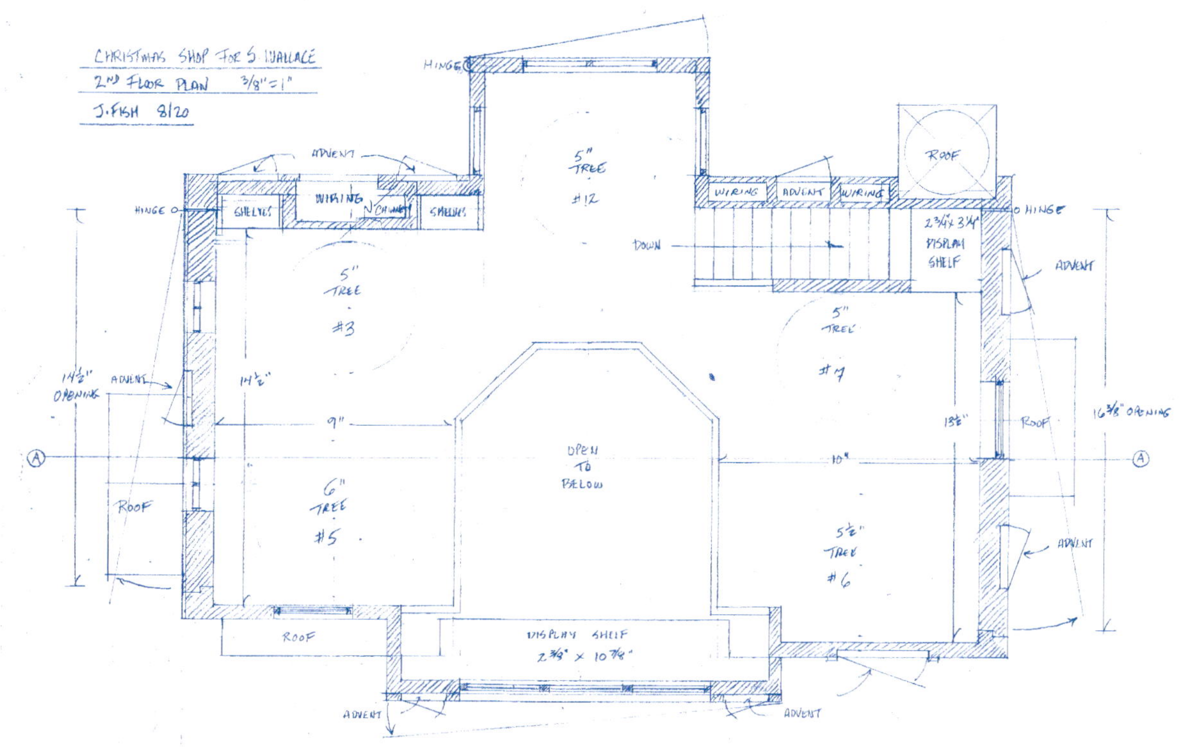

CHRISTMAS SHOP FOR S WALLACE
2ND FLOOR PLAN   3/8"=1"
J. FISH   8/20
HINGE
ADVENT
5" TREE #12
ROOF
WIRING
ADVENT
WIRING
DOWN
2 3/4" x 3 1/4" DISPLAY SHELF
HINGE O
SHELVES
WIRING
SHELVES
HINGE O
HINGE
ADVENT
ADVENT
5" TREE #3
14 1/2" OPENING
ADVENT
14 1/2"
9"
5" TREE #7
13 1/2"
ROOF
16 3/8" OPENING
A
OPEN TO BELOW
10"
A
ROOF
6" TREE #5
5 1/2" TREE #6
ADVENT
DISPLAY SHELF
2 3/8" x 10 7/8"
ADVENT
ADVENT

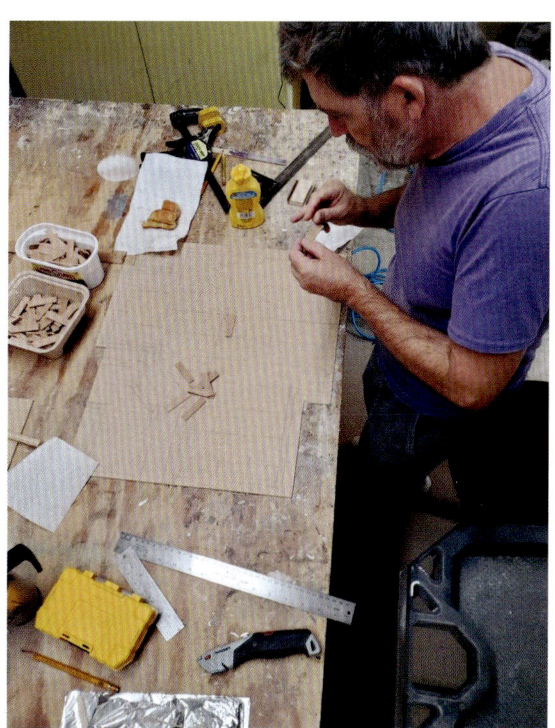

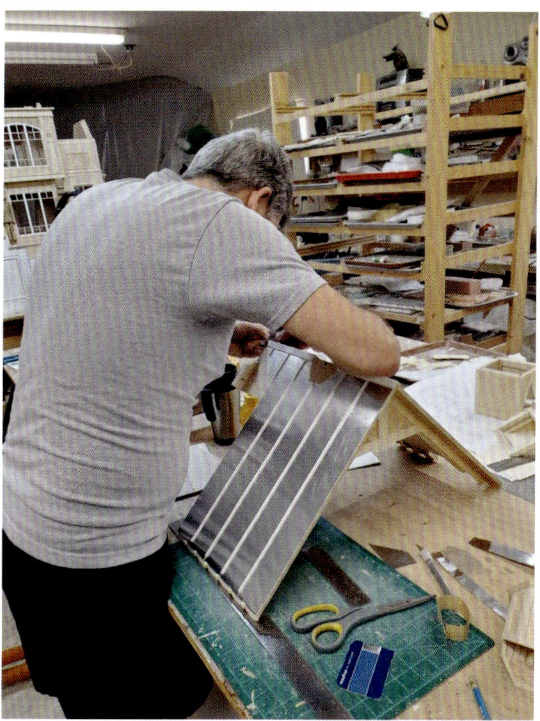

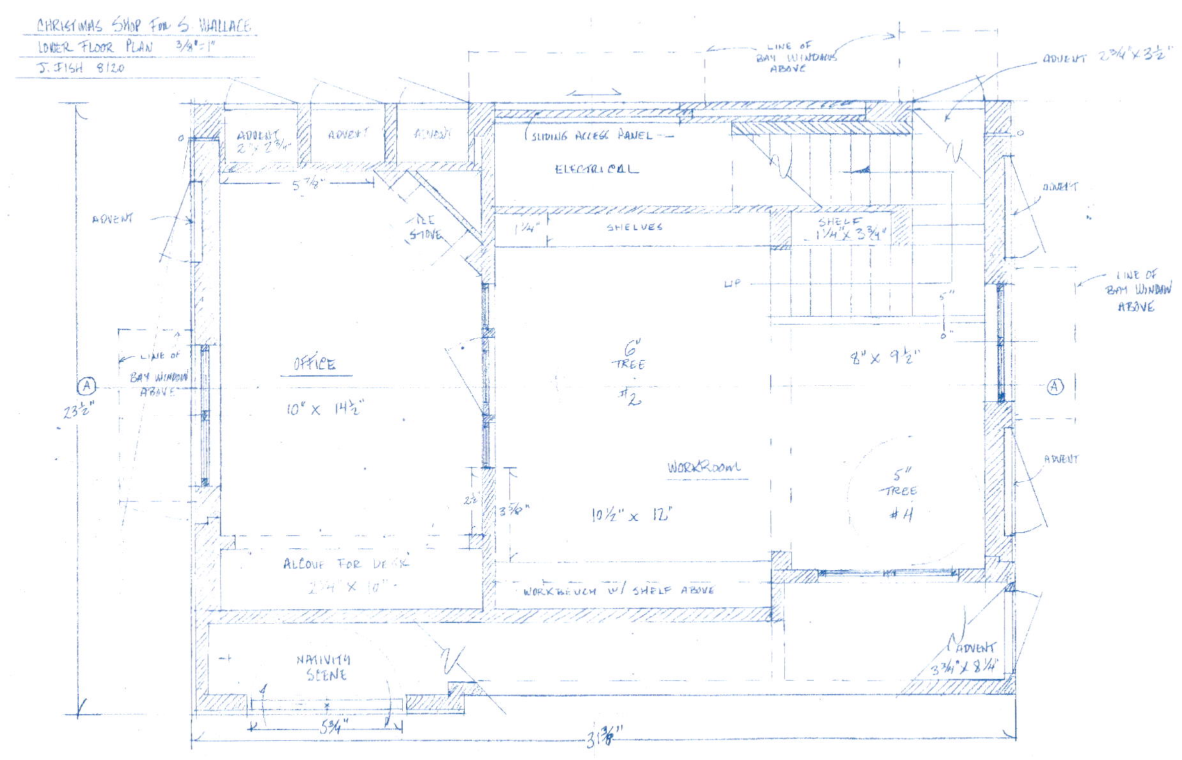

CHRISTMAS SHOP FOR S. WALLACE
LOWER FLOOR PLAN   3/8"=1'
J. FISH 8/20
LINE OF BAY WINDOWS ABOVE
ADVENT 2¾" X 3½"
ADVENT 2¾" X 2¾"
ADVENT
ADVENT
SLIDING ACCESS PANEL
ELECTRICAL
ADVENT
FIRE STONE
SHELVES
SHELF 1¼" X 3¾"
LINE OF BAY WINDOW ABOVE
ADVENT
LINE OF BAY WINDOW ABOVE
UP
OFFICE
10" X 14½"
6" TREE #2
8" X 9½"
WORKROOM
10½" X 12"
5" TREE #4
ADVENT
ALCOVE FOR DESK 2¾" X 10"
WORKBENCH W/ SHELF ABOVE
NATIVITY SCENE
ADVENT 3¾" X 8¼"
23½"
5¾"
31⅜"
5¾"

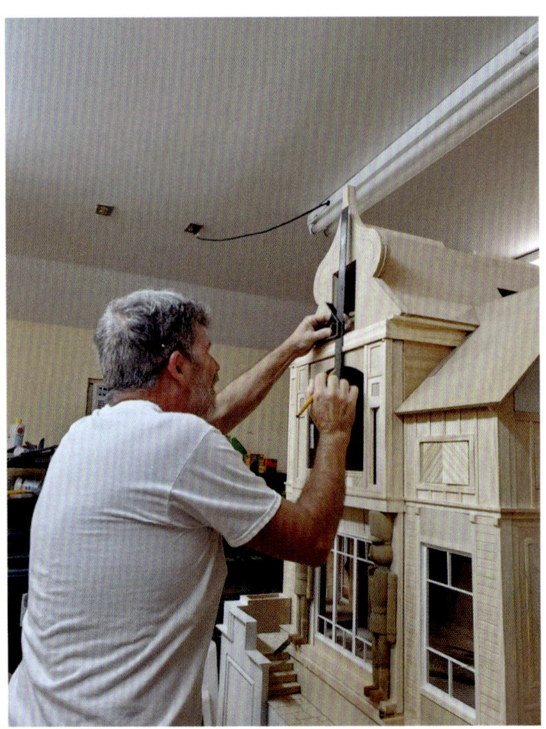

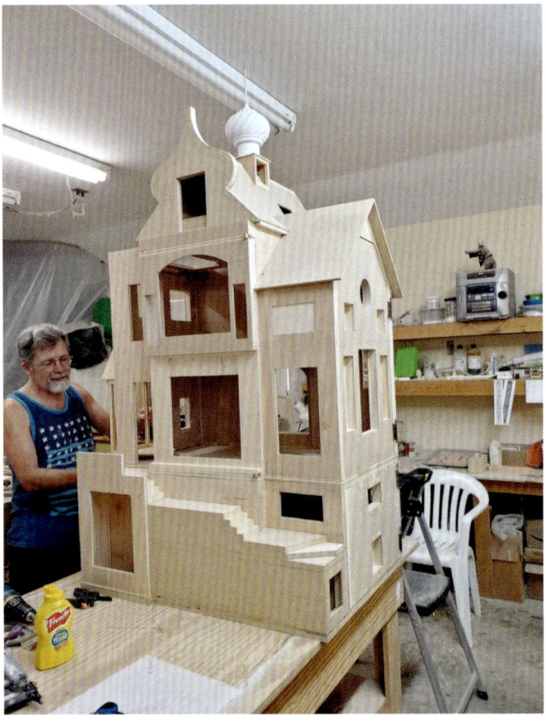

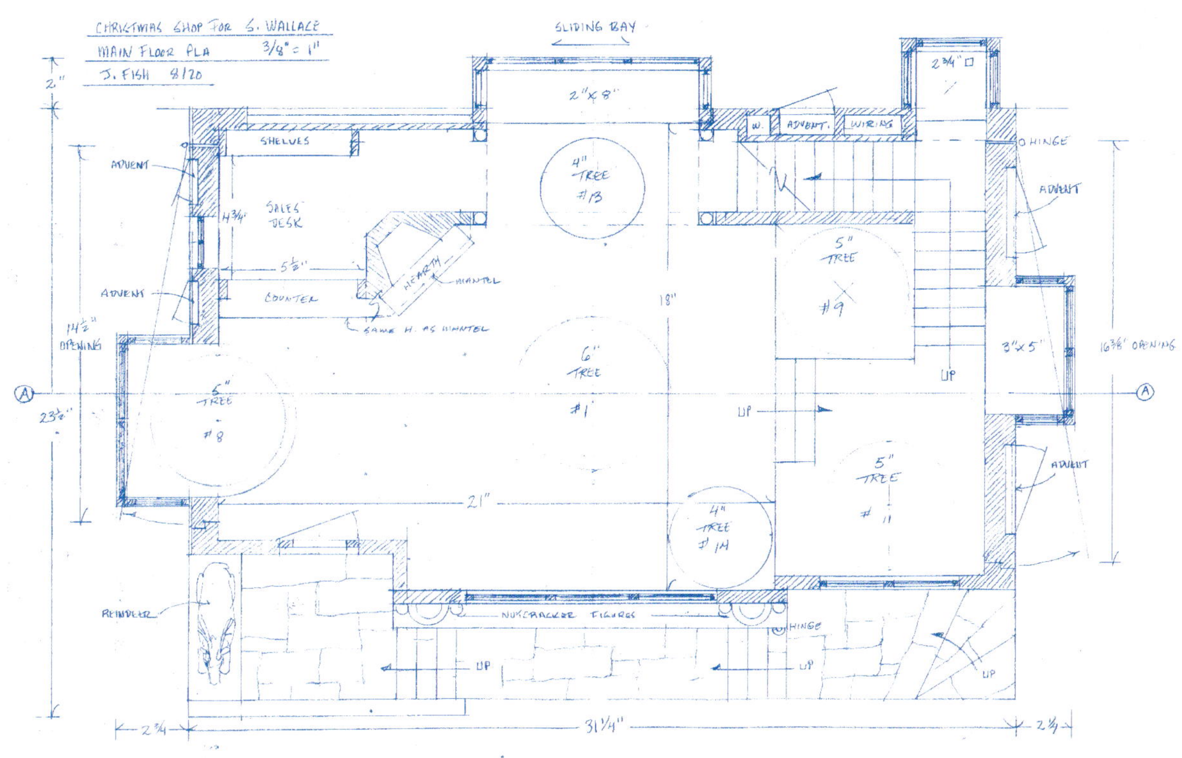

CHRISTMAS SHOP FOR S. WALLACE
MAIN FLOOR PLA   3/8" = 1"
J. FISH   8/20
SLIDING BAY
2"
2" X 8"
SHELVES
ADVENT
4" TREE #13
SALES DESK
4 3/4"
HEARTH
MANTEL
5 1/2"
ADVENT
COUNTER
SAME H. AS MANTEL
18"
5" TREE #9
2 3/4" □
W. ADVENT. WIRING
HINGE
ADVENT
3" X 5"
16 3/8" OPENING
14 1/2" OPENINGS
23 1/2"
5" TREE #8
6" TREE #1
UP
UP
5" TREE #11
ADVENT
4" TREE #14
21"
REINDEER
NUTCRACKER FIGURES
HINGE
UP
UP
UP
2 3/4"
31 1/4"
2 3/4"
A

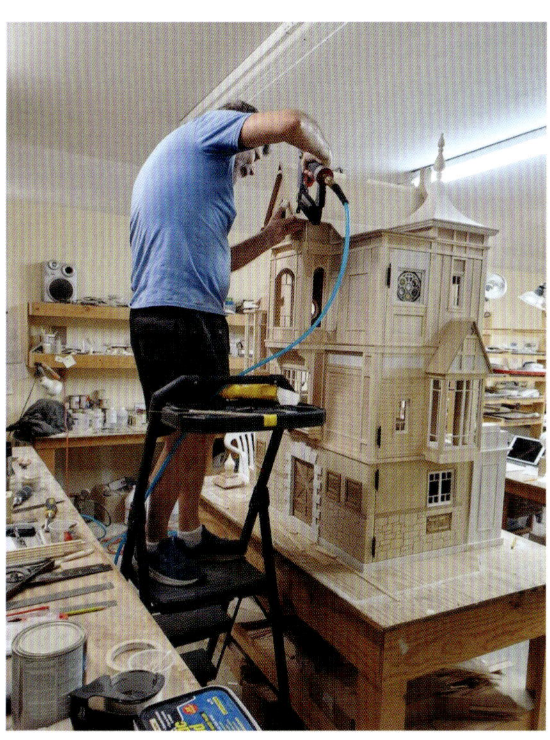

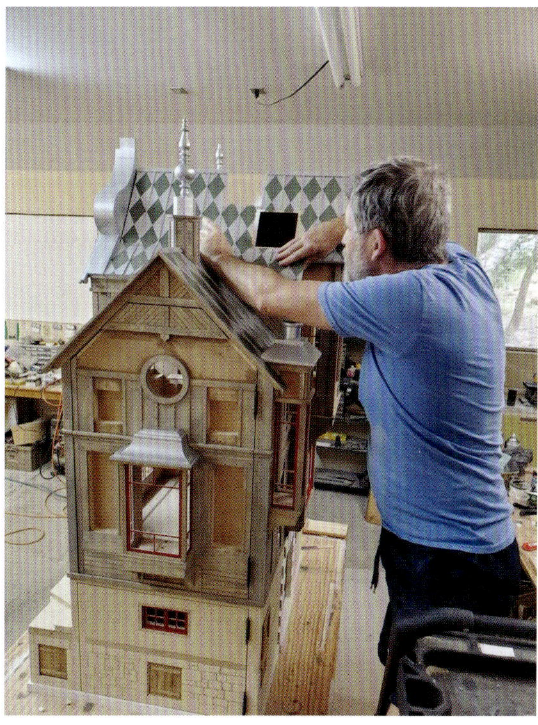

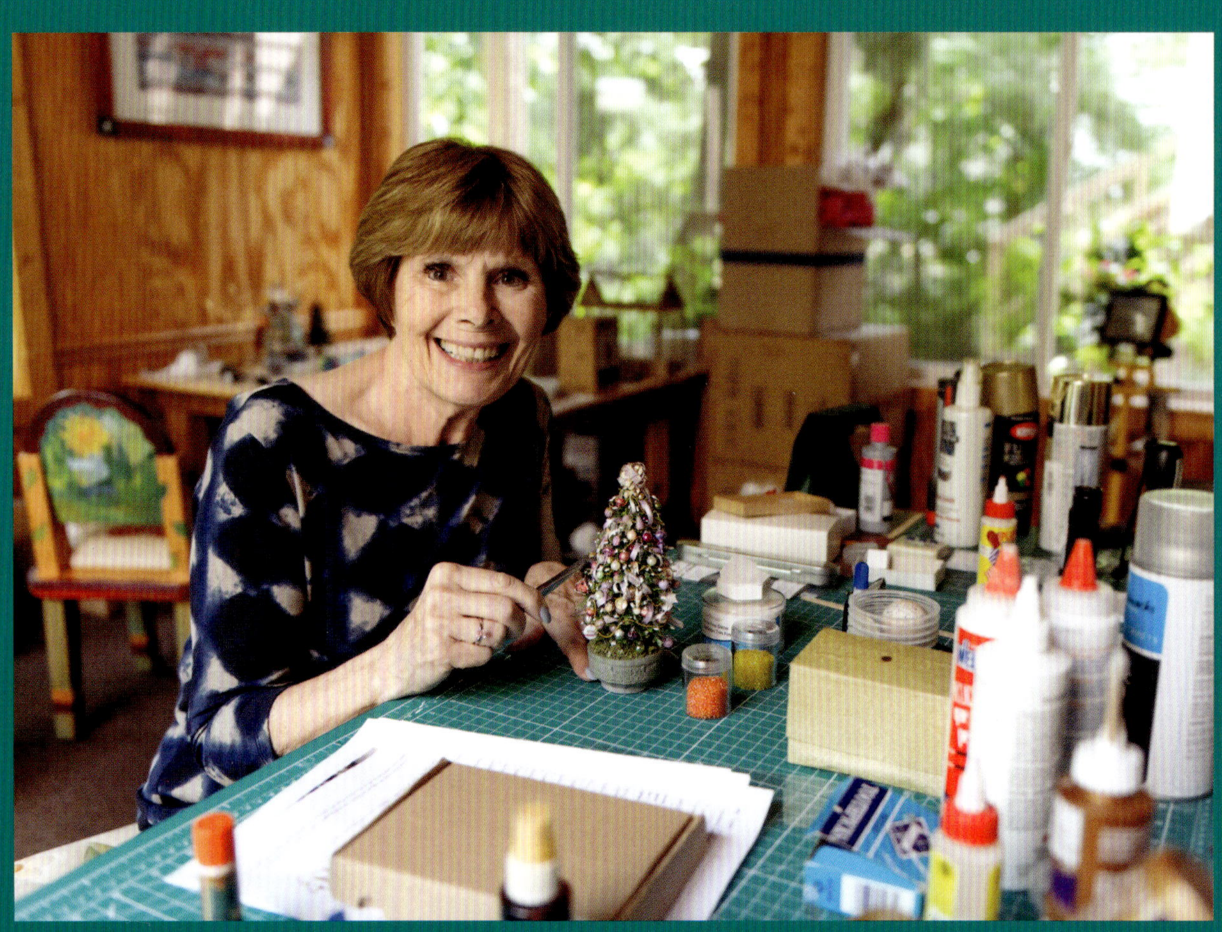

About the Artist

Sally Wallace has been creating miniatures for more than forty years and currently has more than twenty miniature structures in her home. For her, miniatures are magic. She is best-known for her Hogwarts creation, which is a miniature castle.

Christmas Emporium is her second book in her miniaturist series. *Russian Fantasy* was her first on the subject. In each book, she endeavors to "simply tell a story in pictures." In *Christmas Emporium,* she again describes a single miniature fantasy structure—a magical place to celebrate the Chrismas holiday. The work itself is a tribute to all of the artisans who contributed work to it and to all the miniaturists who enjoy the stories they tell in their "dollhouses."

The author's work has been published in every major magazine on the subject in the United States, England, and Spain, including *American Miniaturist, Dollhouse Miniatures*, *Dollhouse World*, and *Miniaturas*, among others, and her work has been featured in numerous books on the subject of miniatures.

Sally is a member of the International Guild of Miniature Artisans and actively partners in the international collaboration between miniaturists for every element that goes into making an authentic—albeit fantastical— environment, each created in the scale of $1/12$. She lives in Iowa with her husband and granddaughter.

For more information, visit her website: magicalminiatures.net.

About Terry E. Branstad

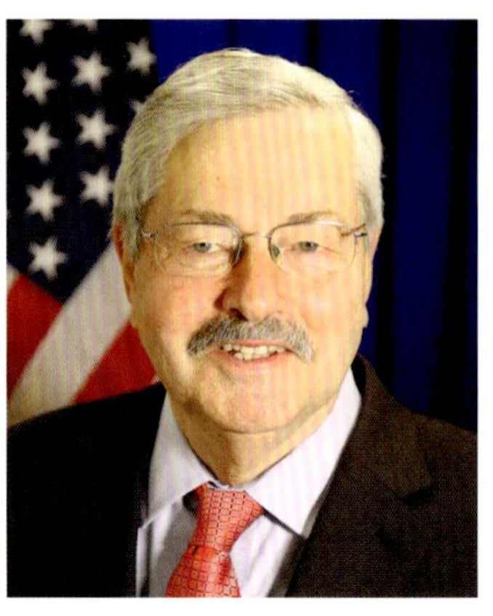

Terry Branstad was sworn in as governor of Iowa on January 14, 2011, and was sworn in for a second term on January 13, 2015.

Branstad is the longest-serving governor in US history, as well as Iowa's longest-serving governor, having previously served in office from 1983, at the age of 36, to 1999 and again from 2011 to 2017. He became Iowa's lieutenant governor in 1978 and was elected to the Iowa House of Representatives in 1972, 1974, and 1976.

Branstad received a bachelor's of arts in political science from the University of Iowa in 1969 and a Juris Doctor from Drake University Law School in 1974.

Branstad served as president of Des Moines University from 2003 to 2009. Under Branstad's leadership, the university became the first college in the United States to receive the "Platinum Level of Recognition" from the Wellness Council of America.

On May 24, 2017, Branstad was confirmed to serve as the US Ambassador to China. In May 2019, Branstad traveled to Tibet Autonomous Region amid heightening trade tensions between the United States and China. This diplomatic journey was designed to give the United States a better perception of Tibet and its people, cultural practices, and life. Branstad stepped down as US Ambassador to China in early October 2020.

He and his wife, Christine, live in Iowa and have three children and six grandchildren.

About Jon Fish

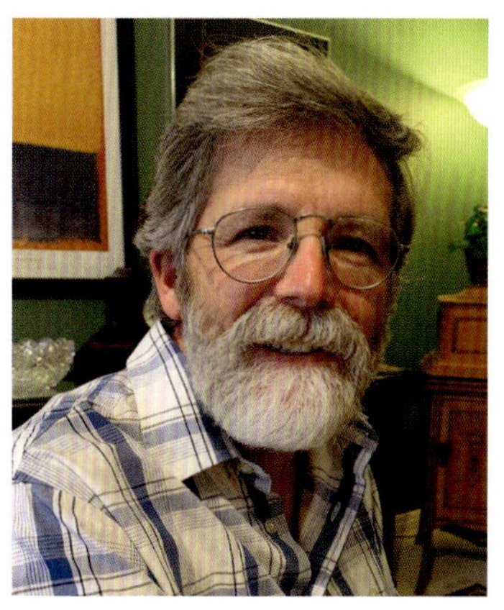

The Christmas Emporium building was crafted by miniaturist artist Jon Fish, who is known for his meticulous craftsmanship, many of his creations taking years to complete. Jon entered the world of miniatures forty years ago while working as a chef and living in Aspen, Colorado. At that time, crafting dollhouse miniatures was a widely popular hobby, and specialty shops dedicated to the craft were relatively common. By 1993, his skills had grown to the point that he was able to become a full-time miniatures artist, which he has been ever since. He is part of a global community of miniatures designers.

Jon has taught workshop classes, created unfinished kits so customers could create their own dollhouses, and has found a variety of other ways to branch out within the miniatures world. For the last twenty years, Jon has focused primarily on larger custom pieces, usually idealized or fanciful structures. While some of his clients like being heavily involved with the design process, others, such as his longtime, repeat clients, give him photos for inspiration and leave the design in his hands. "Some are more historical, others are more fantasy—it really varies from person to person, not unlike full-scale homebuilding," he said.

"People are always surprised that there's a whole world of miniatures out there—it's a little bit of an underground thing," he said. "But there are social media groups that are quite active, and there's quite a strong little industry on Etsy and Instagram. It's a whole little world."

His work has been widely featured in magazines world-wide, as well as included in books on the subject of important miniature design. He lives in New Braunfels, Texas.

About Rich Sanders

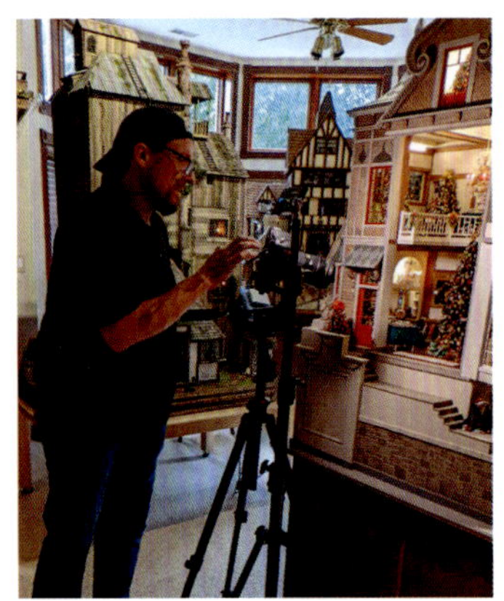

Des Moines, Iowa Photographer Rich Sanders has been providing his clients with rich images for more than two decades. A lifelong and second generation professional photographer, he fine-tuned his artistic eye while earning a BFA from the University of Northern Iowa, and worked in commercial photography studios in Minneapolis before launching his career as a professional photographer.

Rich brings to each of his clients' projects the professional, focused, and individual attention they deserve along with the creativity, skill and experience of a seasoned professional.

Acknowledgments

Special acknowledgments to the people who have become my friends and allow me the joy of working with them on my miniatures. Included in this list are Marcia McClain, David Iriarte, Philip Beglan, Jon Fish, Maria and Mario Ramos, Jack Cashmere, and Johannes Landman.

All of the contributors listed below helped my creations come to life. They have been patient with me and helped me make a vision into an actual miniature piece and I thank you for your incredible contributions, as below:

Jon Fish / Christmas Advent House
Ron Stetkewicz / Brass poles
Johannes Landman / Paintings
Marcia McClain / Rugs and skirts, chair
Jo Bevilacqua / Trees
Mable Malley / Trees
Wilson Santiago / Trees
Sally Wallace / Trees
Philip Beglan / Figures
Maryvonne Herholz / Ornaments
Natalie Frank / Stockings
Ulus Miniatures / Office supplies
Vitreus Ignis / Light fixtures and nativity set and
        glass Saint Basil's
Jack Cashmere / Nativity set
David Iriate / Desk and chair
Alison Davies / Tables
Erica Van Horn / Boxes
Barbara Sabia / Stained glass
Carl Sahlberg / Lighting
Orsolga Skulteti / Food and carts
Maritza Moran / Sleigh painting and chair
Jim Larson / Sleigh
Lighting Bug LTD / Light fixtures and nativity set
        wrapped packages
Ellen Betz / Ornaments

Jeanie Anderson / Food and carts
Frank Crescente / Chandelier
Aquisto Silver / Sleigh and reindeer
Hungarian Miniatures / Desk
Jack Cashmere / Nativity set
Maria Bevill / Fabergé egg tree
Silvia Leiner / Nutcrackers
Charlie Edwards / Wooden cabinet
Richard Sanders / Photos
St. Leger / Working toys
Victor Franco / Office supplies
MiniFanaberia / Vacuum
Sylvia Mobley / Nativity set

Credits for Quotations

All quotations of text and lyrics in this book are in the
public domain, and we thank these talented creators who
have become part of our holiday experiences worldwide:

Page 6: Shirley Sallay
Page 24: From *O Christmas Tree*
Page 28: From *Deck the Halls*
Page 88: Anonymous
Page 94: Anonymous
Pages 105–109: Clement Moore
Page 116: from *O Christmas Tree*
Page 119: from *Jolly Old St. Nicholas*
Page 146: from *Here We Come a-Caroling*
Page 150: Clement Moore
Page 158: Clement Moore